classic one-dish meals

editorial director
arthur hettich

special books editor
marie t. walsh

art director
joseph taveroni

associate editor
susan kiely tierney

art associate
walter schwartz

assistant editor
ceri e. hadda

editorial assistant
raeanne b. hytone

food consultant
grace manney

photographer
gordon e. smith

advertising manager
franklin d. clark

circulation coordinator
norm newmark

production manager
kathy maurer reilly

All recipes tested by Family Circle Great Ideas.

Created by Family Circle Magazine and published 1978 by Arno Press Inc., a subsidiary of The New York Times Company. Copyright © 1977 by The Family Circle, Inc. All rights reserved. Protected under Berne and other international copyright conventions. Title and Trademark FAMILY CIRCLE registered U.S. Patent and Trademark Office, Canada, Great Britain, Australia, New Zealand, Japan and other countries. Marca Registrada. This volume may not be reproduced in whole or in part in any form without written permission from the publisher. Printed in U.S.A. Library of Congress Catalog Card Number 78-59191. ISBN O-405-11409-5.

A New York Times Company Publication NYT

contents

IDAHO POTATO PUFF

Egg-rich potatoes top a tuna and green bean casserole.

Bake at 425° for 40 minutes.
Makes 6 servings.

- 4 mashed potatoes
- 4 eggs
- 1 teaspoon salt
- ½ teaspoon pepper
- 2 tablespoons chopped chives
- 2 tablespoons butter or margarine
- ½ pound fresh mushrooms, sliced
- 1 large onion, chopped (1 cup)
- 2 cans (7 ounces each) tuna in vegetable oil
- 1 package (10 ounces) frozen cut green beans

1. Combine mashed potatoes, 2 of the eggs, salt, pepper and 1 teaspoon of the chives in a large bowl; beat well.
2. Melt butter or margarine in a large skillet; add mushrooms and onion; sauté until soft.
3. Beat remaining 2 eggs in a medium-size bowl, add mushrooms and onion, tuna and green beans, mix well and turn into a buttered 8-cup shallow casserole. Top with mashed potatoes. Spread to cover surface; sprinkle with remaining chives.
4. Bake in hot oven (400°) 40 minutes, or until potatoes are brown.

FISH STEW CAJUN

Cajuns are descendants of the Acadians of Canada, who were deported to Louisiana in the mid-18th century.

Makes 6 servings.

- ½ cup chopped celery
- 1 medium-size onion, chopped (½ cup)
- 1 clove garlic, minced
- ¼ cup (½ stick) butter or margarine
- ⅓ cup all purpose flour
- ½ teaspoon salt
- ½ teaspoon leaf thyme, crushed
- ¼ teaspoon pepper
- 1 can (1 pound) tomatoes
- 1 can (13¾ ounces) chicken broth
- 1 can (8 ounces) minced clams
- ⅛ teaspoon bottled red pepper seasoning
- 1 can (about 1 pound) okra, drained
- 1 package (1 pound) frozen cod, haddock or turbot, cut into cubes
- 3 cups cooked rice

1. Sauté celery, onion and garlic in butter or margarine until soft in a kettle; stir in flour, salt, thyme and pepper. Cook, stirring constantly, until bubbly. Stir in tomatoes, chicken broth, clams and liquid and red pepper seasoning. Cook, stirring constantly, and stir until mixture thickens and bubbles 3 minutes.
2. Add okra and fish; bring to boiling; simmer 5 minutes.

3. Ladle into a shallow serving bowl; spoon rice around edge. Or, spoon rice in mounds in center of soup bowls; ladle fish stew around rice. Serve with a tossed green salad.

CHARLESTON CURRIED STEW

This exotic favorite has a distinctive Southern touch when sweet potato slices are added to the traditional curry.

Makes 6 servings.

- 2 pounds lamb shoulder cubed
- 2 tablespoon vegetable oil
- 1 large onion, chopped (1 cup)
- 2 cloves garlic, minced
- 1 tablespoon curry powder
- 1 tablespoon salt
- ¼ teaspoon pepper
- 1 can condensed chicken broth
- 1¼ cups water
- 3 large sweet potatoes, pared and sliced
- 1 pound green beans, cut into 1-inch pieces
- ¼ cup all purpose flour
- ½ cup water

1. Brown lamb, a few pieces at a time, in oil in a large kettle or Dutch oven; remove and reserve. Sauté onion and garlic in pan drippings. Stir in curry powder and cook 2 minutes; return lamb to kettle; stir in salt, pepper, chicken broth and the 1¼ cups water.
2. Bring to boil; lower heat; cover kettle; simmer 45 minutes, or until lamb is almost tender; add sweet potatoes and green beans; simmer 30 minutes, or until meat and vegetables are tender.
3. Combine flour and the ½ cup water in a cup; stir in bubbling liquid. Cook, stirring gently, until sauce thickens and bubbles 3 minutes.

BOSTON BAKED BEANS

Saturday night isn't official in Back Bay without a bubbling pot of beans.

Bake at 300° for 5 hours.
Makes 6 servings.

- 1 package (1 pound) dried navy or pea beans
- 1 medium-size onion, diced (½ cup)
- ½ cup dark molasses
- ½ teaspoon dry mustard
- ¼ cup firmly packed brown sugar
- 1 teaspoon salt
- ¼ pound lean salt pork, diced

1. Pick over beans and rinse. Place in a large bowl; add water to cover; let stand overnight; drain.
2. Combine beans and onion in a large saucepan; add water to cover; bring to boiling; cover saucepan. Simmer 1 hour, or until tender-firm. Drain cooking liquid into small bowl.
3. Measure 1 cup of the bean liquid, reserving the rest, and combine with

molasses, mustard, brown sugar and salt in a 4-cup measure.
4. Layer half of salt pork and all of beans in an 8-cup bean pot or deep casserole. Pour molasses mixture over top; add just enough more of reserved liquid to cover beans. Top with remaining salt pork, pressing down into liquid; cover.
5. Bake in slow oven (300°) 4 hours; uncover. Bake 1 hour longer or until as tender and dry as you like.
COOK'S TIP: After 2 hours baking, check beans; if dry, add more bean liquid to moisten. To prepare BOSTON BAKED BEANS in an electric slow cooker, follow above directions up to Step 4, placing beans mixture in cooker; cover. Cook on low (190° to 200°) 8 hours, or on high (290° to 300°) 4 hours, or until beans are tender. You can then lower slow cooker and hold beans for hours.

KANSAS CITY HAM STEAK

Men from the Midwest have always been known as great meat-and-gravy eaters.

Bake at 350° for 40 minutes.
Makes 4 servings.

- 1 ready-to-eat ham steak, cut 1-inch thick (about 1 pound)
- 1 small onion, chopped (¼ cup)
- 2 tablespoons butter or margerine
- 3 flat corn toaster cakes (from a 7-ounce package)
- 1 can (12 ounces) Mexican-style corn, drained
- 1 egg, slightly beaten
- 1 teaspoon dry mustard
  Dash pepper
- 2 envelopes (about 1 ounce each) mushroom gravy mix
  Water
- ¼ cup dry Sherry

1. Trim any excess fat from ham; score fat edge; place in a shallow 6-cup casserole.
2. Sauté onion in butter or margarine until soft in a large skillet; remove from heat. Crumble corn cakes into skillet; add corn, egg, mustard and pepper; toss lightly to mix. Spoon on top of ham; cover casserole with aluminum foil.
3. Bake in moderate oven (350°) 40 minutes.
4. While ham bakes, prepare gravy mix with water, following label directions; stir in Sherry
5. Lift ham with stuffing onto a heated large serving platter and carve into ½-inch thick slices, cutting through stuffing. Serve gravy separately to pour over.
COOK'S TIP: If you have a lot of leftover ham, you can prepare this dish, using slices of ham in the place of the ham steak, just line the casserole with aluminum foil to aid in removing stuffed ham from dish.

Southern Chicken Platter is a classic combo of chicken, okra, French fries and corn-on-the-cob chunks in a delectable Southern-style cream gravy.

Americans are great meat and potato fans and this sizzling steak platter is downright patriotic. Wreathed in lightly browned Duchesse Potatoes and Patio Peas with cherry tomatoes, it's a dish worthy of America's heartland.

ALL AMERICAN CLASSICS

COD MULLIGAN

Fish stews have been family favorites in South Boston for generations.

Makes 4 servings

- 1 package (1 pound) frozen cod fillets
- 2 slices bacon
- 2 medium-size onions, sliced
- 2 cups water
- 2 large potatoes, pared and cubed
- ½ cup diced green pepper
- 2 large carrots, pared and sliced
- 2 teaspoons salt
- ½ teaspoon celery seed

1. Remove cod from package and let stand at room temperature 15 minutes. Cut into 1-inch cubes.
2. Cook bacon until crisp in a large saucepan; drain on paper towels. Add onions and sauté until tender in pan drippings. Stir in water, potatoes, green pepper, carrots, salt and celery seed. Lower heat, simmer, covered, about 25 minutes.
3. Stir in cod cubes and simmer 10 minutes, or until fish flakes.

SOUTHERN CHICKEN PLATTER

Crisp, crunchy fried chicken with all the fixings. Shown on page 4.

Makes 4 servings.

- 1 broiler-fryer, cut up (about 3 pounds)
- ½ cup all purpose flour
- 1 teaspoon salt
- ¼ teaspoon pepper
  Lard or vegetable shortening
- 1 package (10 ounces) frozen okra
- 4 ears corn, shucked, cut into 1-inch pieces and cooked
  OR: 1 package (10 ounces) frozen whole-kernel corn
- 1 package (10 ounces) frozen French fried potatoes, cooked
  Cream Gravy (recipe follows)

1. Moisten chicken under running water; shake chicken pieces in flour, salt and pepper in a plastic bag to coat well. Allow coating to dry on chicken while heating fat.
2. Melt lard or shortening in a large skillet to a depth of 1 inch; heat until fat browns a cube of white bread in 60 seconds.
3. Add chicken, skin-side down; brown over moderate heat 10 minutes; turn, brown 10 minutes longer; drain off fat and reserve. Push chicken to one side of skillet.
4. Add okra and whole-kernel corn, if used, to skillet; pour ¼ cup water over vegetables; cover skillet; simmer 5 minutes, or until vegetables are crisply tender.
5. Remove chicken and vegetables to heated serving platter and keep warm. Make CREAM GRAVY in skillet. Add French fries and corn to platter;

spoon part of the gravy over and pass remaining in heated gravy boat.

CREAM GRAVY: Makes 2 cups. Return ¼ cup reserved fat to skillet with ¼ cup all purpose flour, 1 teaspoon salt and ¼ teaspoon pepper. Cook, stirring constantly, until mixture bubbles; stir in 1½ cups water. Cook, stirring constantly, until gravy thickens and bubbles 2 minutes; add ½ cup milk and heat slowly.

ALL-AMERICAN STEAK

Serving a steak on a sizzle platter with a ruffle of Duchesse Potatoes and a ring of colorful vegetables makes entertaining elegant, yet simple. Photo is on page 4.

Makes 6 servings

- 1 sirloin, chuck or round steak, 1½-inches thick (about 3 pounds)
  Unseasoned instant meat tenderizer
  Freshly ground pepper
  Duchesse Potatoes (recipe follows)
  Patio Peas (recipe follows)

1. Remove steak from refrigerator 1 hour before broiling. Sprinkle with meat tenderizer, following label directions; sprinkle with pepper. Place steak on a large sizzle platter or rack of broiler pan.
2. Broil, 4 inches from heat, 5 minutes for rare, 7 for medium and 10 minutes for well done.
3. Turn steak. (If not using a sizzle platter, place steak on a flameproof board or platter.) Fit a pastry tube with a large star tip. Fill with DUCHESSE POTATOES. Pipe potatoes in a pretty pattern around steak, leaving a well between them.
4. Broil, 4 inches from heat, 5 minutes for rare, 7 for medium and 10 minutes for well done. Spoon PATIO PEAS into well and serve with sautéed onion rings, if you wish.

DUCHESSE POTATOES

Makes 6 servings.

- 6 medium-size boiling potatoes
- 3 tablespoons butter or margarine
- 1 teaspoon salt
- ¼ teaspoon white pepper
- ¼ cup milk
- 2 eggs

1. Pare potatoes and quarter. Cook in boiling salted water in a large saucepan 15 minutes, or until soft, but still firm, when pierced with a two-tined fork; drain.
2. Return potatoes to saucepan over low heat. Toss potatoes in pan 3 minutes to fluff and dry them.
3. Add butter or margarine, salt, pepper and milk to saucepan; bring to

boiling; remove from heat. Mash potatoes with a potato masher; add eggs; beat with electric mixer at low speed until very smooth

PATIO PEAS

Makes 6 servings

- 1 pint cherry tomatoes, stemmed
- 2 tablespoons butter or margarine
- 1 bag (1 pound) frozen peas
- 1 teaspoon celery salt
- ¼ teaspoon lemon pepper
- ¼ cup water

1. Sauté cherry tomatoes in butter or margarine in a large saucepan 2 minutes; remove with a slotted spoon.
2. Toss peas in pan drippings; add celery salt, lemon pepper and water; bring to boiling; lower heat; cover.
3. Simmer 5 minutes, or until peas are tender; return tomatoes to saucepan and keep warm until serving time.

MARYLAND CRAB NEWBURG

Delmarva Shore cooks each have their favorite way of preparing crab. Here is an especially delicious one.

Bake at 350° for 1 hour.
Makes 8 servings.

- 2 cans (6¼ ounces each) crab meat
- 2 packages (10 ounces each) frozen peas
- 2 cans condensed cream of mushroom soup
- ¼ cup dry Sherry
- 1 can (6 ounces) sliced mushrooms, drained
- 1 can or jar (4 ounces) pimiento, drained and diced
- 3 slices white bread, cut in tiny cubes
- 3 tablespoons butter or margarine, melted

1. Drain crab meat; remove bony tissue, if any; break crab meat into bite-size chunks.
2. Cook peas, following label directions; drain.
3. Blend the mushroom soup and dry Sherry until smooth in a small bowl.
4. Layer half of the crab meat, peas, mushrooms and pimiento in a 10-cup casserole; repeat layers. Pour soup mixture over top.
5. Toss bread cubes with butter or margarine in a small bowl; sprinkle over mixture in casserole.
6. Bake in a moderate oven (350°) 1 hour, or until center bubbles and topping is toasted.
COOK'S TIP: If you wish to make this casserole ahead of time, do not top with bread. Cover and refrigerate it until about 1½ hours before serving; uncover. Sprinkle with buttered bread cubes and bake 1 hour, 20 minutes, or until center bubbles and topping is toasted.

JAMBALAYA CHOWDER

Make this the main dish. It's rich with meat, seafood and vegetables.

Makes 8 servings.

- 1 medium-size onion, chopped (½ cup)
- 1 small green pepper, halved, seeded and diced
- 1 clove garlic, crushed
- 2 tablespoons butter or margarine
- 2 cans condensed chicken and rice soup
- 2⅔ cups water
- 2 large tomatoes, peeled and diced
- 1 small bay leaf
- ½ teaspoon chili powder
- ¼ teaspoon leaf thyme, crumbled
- 1 package (about 8 ounces) frozen, shelled, deveined raw shrimp
- 1 can (5 ounces) chicken, diced
- 1 package (6 ounces) cooked ham, cubed

1. Sauté onion, green pepper and garlic in butter or margarine until soft in a large heavy saucepan or Dutch oven. Stir in soup, water, tomatoes, bay leaf, chili powder and thyme. Cover; simmer 10 minutes.
2. Stir in shrimp, chicken and ham; cover. Simmer 10 minutes longer, or until shrimp are tender. Ladle into soup bowls. Serve with hot buttered biscuits, if you wish.

HAM AND BROCCOLI DIVAN

Victorian restaurants in Chicago often featured this specialty.

Bake at 350° for 45 minutes.
Makes 8 servings.

- 1 cup regular rice
- 2 packages (10 ounces each) frozen broccoli spears
- ⅓ cup butter or margarine
- 2 cups soft bread crumbs (4 slices)
- 2 large onions, chopped (2 cups)
- 3 tablespoons all purpose flour
- 1 teaspoon salt
- ¼ teaspoon pepper
- 3 cups milk
- 4 cups cubed cooked ham
- 1 package (8 ounces) sliced swiss cheese, quartered

1. Cook rice, following label directions; spoon into a well-greased 13x9x2-inch casserole.
2. Cook broccoli, following label directions; drain well. Place in a single layer over rice in casserole.
3. Melt butter or margarine in a large skillet; measure out 2 tablespoons and sprinkle over bread crumbs in a small bowl; toss to coat and reserve.
4. Stir onions into remaining butter in skillet; sauté until soft. Stir in flour, salt and pepper. Cook, stirring constantly, until bubbly. Stir in milk; continue cooking and stirring until sauce thickens and bubbles 3 minutes.

Stir in ham; heat again just until bubbly; pour over layers in casserole.
5. Place cheese over sauce; sprinkle buttered bread crumbs over all.
6. Bake in moderate oven (350°) 45 minutes, or until bubbly and golden.
COOK'S TIP: This recipe is really a basic guide to a variety of dishes. Substitute cooked turkey, chicken, lamb, sliced hot dogs, or poached fish fillets for the ham in this recipe. Three cups cooked sliced potato or cooked macaroni, noodles or ziti can be substituted for the cooked rice in the recipe. Cooked whole green beans, cauliflowerets or sliced zucchini can be substituted for the broccoli. A ½ teaspoon crumbled basil, sage or mixed Italian herbs can be added to crumbs that top casserole.

MOCK POT ROAST

It's really zesty meatloaf, baked with a vegetable medley.

Bake at 375° for 1 hour, 15 minutes.
Makes 8 servings.

- 2 pounds meatloaf mixture (ground beef, pork and veal)
- ½ cup quick-cooking rolled oats
- 2 eggs
- ½ tablespoon prepared horseradish
- 1 teaspoon dry mustard
- 3 teaspoons salt
- ¼ teaspoon pepper
- 1 teaspoon bottled gravy coloring
- 8 small carrots, pared
- 8 small potatoes, pared
- 16 small white onions, peeled
- 1 package (10 ounces) frozen peas

1. Mix meatloaf mixture lightly with rolled oats, eggs, catsup, horseradish, mustard, 2 teaspoons of the salt and pepper until well blended. Mound into a loaf-shape in a shallow baking pan; brush with gravy coloring.
2. Halve carrots, lengthwise; arrange with potatoes and onions around meat; sprinkle with the remaining 1 teaspoon salt. Cover pan with aluminum foil.
3. Bake in moderate oven (375°) 40 minutes; uncover; add peas. Cover again; bake 30 minutes. Uncover; baste meat and vegetables with pan juices; bake 5 minutes longer, or until vegetables are tender.

SANTA FE BARBECUE

The closer you live to the Mexican border, the more chili powder you'll want to use.

Makes 4 servings.

- 1 tablespoon butter or margarine
- 1 large onion, chopped (1 cup)
- 1 clove garlic, minced
- 2 to 4 teaspoons chili powder
- 1 can (1 pound) tomatoes

- 1 tablespoon brown sugar
- 1 teaspoon dry mustard
- 1 teaspoon salt
- ⅛ teaspoon pepper
- 2 teaspoons cider vinegar
- 2 whole cloves
- 1 bay leaf
- 1½ cups cubed cooked beef or lamb
- 1 package (8 ounces) noodles
- 2 tablespoons chopped parsley
- 1 package (10 ounces) frozen zucchini, cooked

1. Melt butter or margarine in large skillet; add onion and garlic; sauté over low heat about 5 minutes, or until onion is tender. Stir in chili powder; cook 2 minutes.
2. Stir in tomatoes, brown sugar, dry mustard, salt, pepper, vinegar, whole cloves and bay leaf; bring to boiling; reduce heat; simmer 45 minutes.
3. Add meat cubes; simmer 15 minutes longer to blend flavors.
4. While barbecue mixture simmers, cook noodles, following label directions; drain; stir in chopped parsley.
5. Arrange parsleyed noodles on platter; spoon the barbecued meat over. Arrange zucchini around edge.

CARIBBEAN FISH DINNER

From Puerto Rico comes a fabulous way with fish and tropical fruits.

Makes 4 servings.

- ¼ cup olive or vegetable oil
- 4 cloves garlic, chopped
- 1 bunch green onions, sliced
- 1 sweet red pepper, halved, seeded and chopped
- 1½ cups converted rice
- ¼ teaspoon leaf thyme, crumbled
- Juice of 1 lime
- 4 cups chicken broth
- 1 teaspoon salt
- 1½ pounds red snapper, haddock or cod
- OR: 2 packages (12 ounces each) frozen cod or haddock
- 1 banana, cut into ½-inch-thick slices
- 1 orange, peeled and cut into sections

1. Heat oil and sauté garlic, green onions and pepper until golden in a nonstick oval fish skillet (see Cook's Guide). Stir in rice, thyme and lime juice. Stir in chicken broth and salt; cover.
2. Simmer 20 minutes, or until liquid is almost absorbed and rice is tender. Add fish pieces, pushing them down into rice.
3. Simmer 10 minutes; turn fish carefully and simmer another 10 minutes. Place fish on serving platter.
4. Stir banana and orange sections into skillet, spooning rice over fruit. Heat 1 to 2 minutes. Spoon rice around fish pieces. Serve sprinkled with sliced green onions, if you wish.

MANHATTAN CLAM CHOWDER

Clam chowder made the way New Yorkers like it—with tomatoes and thyme.

Makes 6 servings.

    1 large onion, chopped (1 cup)
    ⅔ cup finely minced celery
    2 teaspoons finely minced green
       pepper
    1 clove garlic, minced
    2 tablespoons butter or margarine
    1 large potato, pared and diced
    3 cups hot water
    3 fresh tomatoes, peeled, seeded
       and diced
       OR: 1 can (1 pound) tomatoes,
       chopped
    1 pint freshly opened clams, minced
       OR: 2 cans (8 ounces each) minced
       clams
    2 teaspoons salt
    ¼ teaspoon pepper
    ½ teaspoon leaf thyme, crumbled
       Dash cayenne
    1 teaspoon minced parsley
    3 to 4 soda crackers, coarsely
       crumbled

1. Simmer onion, celery, green pepper and garlic in butter or margarine in a kettle 20 minutes.
2. Add potato and water. Cook until potato is tender, about 15 minutes.
3. Add tomatoes, clams and their juice, salt, pepper, thyme and cayenne. Bring to boiling; stir in minced parsley and pour soup into a tureen over crushed crackers.

CALIFORNIA PORK SCALLOP

Cooking pork chops with an orange flavor goes back to Gold Rush days in California.

Bake at 350° for 1 hour.
Makes 4 servings.

    1 large onion, chopped (1 cup)
    ¼ cup (½ stick) butter or margarine
    1½ cups water
    1 can (6 ounces) frozen
       concentrate for orange juice
    1 package (8 ounces) bread
       stuffing mix
    ¼ teaspoon ground sage
    8 thin pork chops
    ¼ cup firmly packed brown sugar
    ½ teaspoon dry mustard
    1 teaspoon Worcestershire sauce
    2 acorn squash
    2 tablespoons butter or margarine,
       melted
       Salt and pepper
    1 can (11 ounces) chicken gravy

1. Sauté onion in butter or margarine until soft in a medium-size skillet; stir in water and ¼ cup of the orange juice concentrate.
2. Bring to boiling; pour over bread stuffing and sage in a medium-size bowl; stir to moisten well.
3. Alternate 3 layers of stuffing and 2 layers of pork chops, beginning and ending with stuffing, in a greased 8-cup shallow casserole.

4. Combine remaining ½ cup orange juice concentrate, brown sugar, mustard and Worcestershire sauce in a cup; drizzle over top.
5. Quarter squash and remove seeds; arrange around edge of casserole; brush with melted butter or margarine and sprinkle with salt and pepper; cover casserole with aluminum foil.
6. Bake in moderate oven (350°) 45 minutes; remove foil; bake 15 minutes longer, or until top is crusty brown.
7. Heat chicken gravy in a small saucepan; serve separately in a heated gravy boat.

BRIDIE'S BAKED CHICKEN

Bridie McAndrews oven-bakes her chicken for a succulent treat.

Bake at 375° for 1 hour.
Makes 4 servings.

    1 broiler-fryer, cut up (about 3
       pounds)
    1 can condensed golden mushroom
       soup
    1 leek, thinly sliced (1 cup)
       OR: 1 large onion, chopped (1 cup)
    1 can (3 or 4 ounces) chopped
       mushrooms
    ¼ cup dry white wine
    2 tablespoons lemon juice
       Hot cooked rice or hot buttered
       noodles

1. Arrange chicken pieces in a single layer in a 13x9x2-inch baking dish.
2. Combine soup, leek or onion, mushrooms and liquid, wine and lemon juice in a medium-size bowl; spoon sauce over chicken.
3. Bake in moderate oven (375°) 1 hour, or until chicken is tender and richly browned. Serve with rice or noodles and broccoli, if you wish.

PENNSYLVANIA HOT POT

Hearty lean chuck, half-moons of golden acorn squash, potatoes and onions bake in a tomato broth.

Bake at 350° for 3 hours.
Makes 6 servings.

    2 pounds lean boneless chuck, cut
       into 1-inch cubes
    ¼ cup all purpose flour
    2 cups tomato juice
    2 beef bouillon cubes
    1 tablespoon sugar
    ¼ cup finely chopped parsley
    2 cloves garlic, minced
    1 tablespoon salt
    ¼ teaspoon pepper
    4 medium-size potatoes, pared and
       thinly sliced (4 cups)
    8 small onions, quartered
    1 acorn squash, halved and seeded
    2 tablespoons butter or margarine

1. Trim all fat from beef. Shake cubes, a few at a time, with flour in a plastic bag to coat well.

2. Combine tomato juice, bouillon cubes and sugar in a small saucepan; bring just to boiling, crushing cubes to dissolve.
3. Combine parsley, garlic, salt and pepper in a cup.
4. Layer vegetables and meat into a 12-cup deep casserole: Put in half of each of potatoes, onions and beef, sprinkling each layer lightly with seasoning mixture; repeat with remaining potatoes, onions, beef and seasoning mixture.
5. Cut each squash half into 6 slices; pare; arrange on top. Pour hot tomato juice mixture over; dot with butter or margarine; cover.
6. Bake in moderate oven (350°) 3 hours, or until beef is tender.

IOWA PORK DINNER

Brown sugar-glazed pork shoulder is served with vegetables for a stick-to-the-ribs farm style meal. Shown on page 9.

Bake at 400° for 10 minutes.
Makes 6 servings.

    1 smoked pork shoulder roll (about
       3 pounds)
    1 tablespoon mixed pickling spices
    1 medium-size onion, sliced
    1 small yellow turnip, sliced and
       pared
    6 medium-size potatoes, pared
    6 ears corn, halved
       OR: 1 package (10 ounces) whole
       kernel corn
    ¼ cup firmly packed brown sugar
    1 tablespoon prepared mustard

1. Place pork roll in a large kettle; tie pickling spice in cheesecloth; add to kettle with onion; cover with water. Bring to boiling; lower heat; cover kettle; simmer 1 hour, 15 minutes.
2. Add turnip slices and simmer 15 minutes; add potatoes and simmer 20 minutes; add corn and simmer 10 minutes, or until meat and vegetables are tender when pierced with a two-tined fork.
3. Remove casing from pork roll; place roll in a shallow baking pan; combine brown sugar and mustard in a cup; spread over pork.
4. Bake in hot oven (400°) 10 minutes, or until well glazed. Place on a heated platter and surround with piles of turnip slices, potatoes and corn. Serve with additional prepared mustard, if you wish.

☞

Iowa Pork Dinner combines a brown sugar-glazed pork shoulder with hearty vegetables. The result is a delicious yet economical meal. Recipe is on this page.

WISCONSIN STRATA

That old standby—ham and cheese—becomes a main dish when baked in an egg and milk custard. Photograph is on page 10.

Bake at 350° for 40 minutes.
Makes 4 servings.

- **8 slices white toaster bread (see Cook's Guide)**
- **¼ cup (½ stick) butter or margarine, melted**
- **1 tablespoon prepared mustard**
- **8 slices cooked ham**
- **8 slices Swiss or Jarlsberg cheese**
- **3 eggs**
- **2 cups milk**

1. Spread bread with a mixture of butter or margarine and prepared mustard; put together with slices of ham and cheese; cut each sandwich, crosswise, into 4 triangles.
2. Line up sandwiches, pointed-side up, in an 8-cup shallow casserole. Beat eggs with wire whip in a medium-size bowl until well blended; beat in milk until smooth; pour over sandwiches, coating bread evenly. Cover dish with plastic wrap and refrigerate at least 2 hours, or overnight. Remove plastic wrap.
3. Bake in moderate oven (350°) 40 minutes, or until puffed and golden.
COOK'S TIP: Sliced chicken or turkey or tuna salad can be substituted for the ham; American, Cheddar or Muenster can be substituted for the Swiss or Jarlsberg cheese used in this recipe.

SWEET POTATO CASSEROLE

Southern favorites—pork and sweet potatoes—bake with an aromatic flavor.

Bake at 400° for 30 minutes.
Makes 6 servings.

- **2 pounds ground pork**
- **1 small onion, chopped (¼ cup)**
- **2 teaspoons salt**
- **½ teaspoon pepper**
- **½ teaspoon poultry seasoning, crumbled**
- **2 eggs**
- **½ cup dry bread crumbs**
- **¼ cup vegetable shortening**
- **2 packages (12 ounces each) frozen candied sweet potatoes**
- **1 tablespoon aromatic bitters**
- **1 can (1 pound, 4 ounces) pineapple chunks in juice**

1. Combine pork, onion, salt, pepper,

Wisconsin Strata is the perfect make-ahead supper. Ham and Swiss cheese are layered between bread slices and baked until golden in an egg custard. Recipe on this page.

poultry seasoning, eggs and crumbs in a large bowl. Blend well and shape into 1-inch balls.
2. Heat shortening in a large skillet; brown balls on all sides. Cook slowly until pork is cooked through, about 30 minutes. Drain on paper towels.
3. Remove frozen sweet potatoes from packages and place in an 8-cup shallow casserole. Mix bitters and pineapple with juice and pour over sweet potatoes. Place meatballs over top of casserole.
4. Bake in hot oven (400°) 30 minutes, or until potatoes are tender.

INDIAN HARVEST BAKE

Farm fresh vegetables and tuna are layered to bake with a rich cheese topping.

Bake at 350° for 1 hour.
Makes 6 servings.

- **2 cans (6½ ounces each) tuna in vegetable oil**
- **½ cup frozen chopped onion**
- **1 teaspoon chili powder**
- **1 teaspoon leaf oregano, crumbled**
- **½ teaspoon salt**
- **¼ teaspoon cumin seed, crushed**
- **2 medium-size zucchini, sliced**
- **1 green pepper, halved, seeded and cut into strips**
- **2 large tomatoes, sliced**
- **1 package (10 ounces) frozen whole kernel corn, thawed**
- **2 cups grated longhorn or mild Cheddar cheese (8 ounces)**

1. Drain 1 tablespoon oil from tuna into an 8-cup flameproof casserole; add onion and sauté until golden. Mix together chili powder, oregano, salt and cumin seed in a cup.
2. Layer ⅓ each of vegetables, ⅓ tuna and ⅓ cup cheese over onion in casserole. Repeat layers, sprinkling each layer with a small amount of seasoning mixture; cover casserole.
3. Bake in moderate oven (350°) 1 hour, or until vegetables are tender.

FLORIDA FISH ROLLS

Bananas and fish fillets are glazed with a lime and mustard sauce.

Bake at 350° for 30 minutes.
Makes 6 servings.

- **2 cups soft bread crumbs (4 slices)**
- **⅓ cup diced pared cucumber**
- **¼ cup finely chopped green pepper**
- **2 tablespoons grated onion**
- **2 tablespoons chopped parsley**
- **1 teaspoon leaf thyme, crumbled**
- **1 teaspoon salt**
- **⅛ teaspoon pepper**
- **½ teaspoon grated lime rind**
- **¼ cup (½ stick) butter or margarine, melted**
- **3 tablespoons water**
- **7 firm bananas**
- **6 fillets of sole, flounder or haddock**

- **6 teaspoons lime juice**
- **1 tablespoon prepared mustard**
- **1 tablespoon Worcestershire sauce**
- **2 tablespoons chili sauce**

1. Combine the bread crumbs, cucumber, green pepper, onion, parsley, thyme, ½ teaspoon of the salt, pepper, lime rind, 3 tablespoons of the melted butter or margarine and water in a large bowl; mix well. Peel and dice 1 of the bananas; add to stuffing mixture.
2. Sprinkle fish fillets with remaining ¼ teaspoon salt and 1 teaspoon of the lime juice. Place ⅓ cup stuffing mixture in center of each fillet and roll fish around stuffing; secure with wooden food picks. Place, seam-side down, in a 12-cup shallow casserole. Mix mustard, Worcestershire sauce, chili sauce and remaining 5 teaspoons lime juice in small bowl. Brush fish rolls with part of mustard-lime sauce.
3. Bake in moderate oven (350°) 20 minutes. Peel remaining 6 bananas and place in casserole; brush with remaining mustard-lime sauce. Bake 10 minutes longer, or until fish flakes when tested with a fork.

BOSTON CLAM CHOWDER

New England cooks keep the family going through rough winters with this heart-warming, yet simple to make soup.

Makes 6 servings.

- **3 slices bacon, chopped**
- **1 large onion, chopped (1 cup)**
- **4 medium-size potatoes, pared and diced (3 cups)**
- **3 cups water**
- **1 teaspoon salt**
- **¼ teaspoon pepper**
- **2 cans (8 ounces each) minced clams**
- **1 bottle (8 ounces) clam juice**
- **3 tablespoons all purpose flour**
- **4 cups milk**
- **2 tablespoons minced parsley**

1. Cook bacon until crisp in a large heavy saucepan or Dutch oven. Remove bacon with a slotted spoon; drain on paper towels; reserve. Add onion to bacon drippings in saucepan; sauté until soft.
2. Add potatoes, 2 cups of the water, salt and pepper; cover. Simmer 15 minutes, or until potatoes are tender. Remove from heat.
3. Drain liquid from clams into a 4-cup measure; reserve clams. Add bottled clam juice and remaining cup of water. Blend in flour.
4. Add clam liquid and milk to potato mixture in saucepan. Cook over medium heat, stirring constantly, until chowder bubbles 3 minutes.
5. Add clams; heat just until piping hot. Ladle into soup bowls. Sprinkle with parsley and reserved bacon. Serve with pilot crackers, if you wish.

IOWA CORN CHOWDER

Just the right combination of bacon, onion, potatoes and corn.

Makes 4 servings.

- 4 slices bacon, chopped
- 1 large onion, chopped (1 cup)
- 3 medium-size potatoes, pared and diced (2 cups)
- 2½ cups water
- 1 teaspoon salt
- ¼ teaspoon pepper
- 2 cans (about 1 pound each) whole kernel corn
- 1 tall can evaporated milk (1⅔ cups)
- ¼ cup all purpose flour
  Paprika

1. Cook bacon until crisp in a large heavy saucepan or Dutch oven. Add onion; sauté until soft.
2. Add potatoes, 2 cups of the water, salt and pepper; cover. Simmer 15 minutes, or until potatoes are tender.
3. Stir in corn with liquid and evaporated milk; heat to bubbling. Blend flour with remaining ½ cup water; stir into chowder.
4. Cook over medium heat, stirring constantly, until mixture thickens and bubbles 3 minutes. Ladle into soup bowls; sprinkle each with paprika.

CAPE COD CLAM PIE

Clams and crackers bake in a custard under a flaky pastry.

Bake at 450° for 15 minutes,
then at 350° for 30 minutes.
Makes one 9-inch pie.

- 1 package piecrust mix
- 2 eggs
- 2 cans (8 ounces each) minced clams
- ¼ cup milk
- ½ cup coarse unsalted, soda cracker crumbs
- 1 teaspoon salt
- ¼ teaspoon pepper
- 2 tablespoons butter or margarine

1. Prepare piecrust mix, following label directions, or make pastry from your own favorite two-crust recipe. Roll out half to a 12-inch round on a lightly floured pastry cloth or board; fit into a 9-inch pie plate.
2. Beat eggs with wire whip in a medium-size bowl; measure 1 tablespoon into a cup and reserve.
3. Drain liquid from clams; measure ¾ cup and stir into beaten eggs with the clams, milk, cracker crumbs, salt and pepper. Spoon into prepared pastry shell; dot the filling evenly with the butter or margarine.
4. Roll out the remaining pastry to an 11-inch round; cut several slits near center to let steam escape; cover pie. Trim overhang to ½ inch; fold edges under, flush with rim; flute all around.

Stir 1 teaspoon cold water into beaten egg in cup; brush over pastry.
5. Bake in very hot oven (450°) 15 minutes; lower oven temperature to moderate (350°). Bake 30 minutes longer, or until golden. Cool for 15 minutes on a wire rack.

SCALLOPED OYSTERS

Always a favorite, and traditional at Thanksgiving in New England.

Bake at 350° for 30 minutes.
Makes 6 servings.

- 4 cans (8 ounces each) oysters OR: 2 pints fresh oysters
- 1 cup light cream
- ¼ cup (½ stick) butter or margarine
- 1 package (5 ounces) oyster crackers, crushed
- ¼ cup chopped parsley
- ½ teaspoon salt
- 1 teaspoon Worcestershire sauce
  Dash bottled red pepper seasoning
- 1 package (10 ounces) frozen peas, cooked and drained
  Paprika

1. Drain liquid from oysters; measure ½ cup. Combine with the light cream in a 2-cup measure.
2. Melt butter or margarine in a medium-size saucepan; stir in crushed oyster crackers, parsley and salt; mix.
3. Spread half the buttered crackers in a 6-cup shallow casserole; spoon drained oysters over; cover with remaining buttered crackers.
4. Stir Worcestershire sauce and red pepper seasoning into cream mixture; pour over crackers.
5. Bake in moderate oven (350°) 30 minutes, or until top is golden; spoon peas around edge; sprinkle with paprika before serving.

WESTERN FRANKFURTER PIE

Crisp lettuce layers with barbecued franks in this California favorite.

Bake at 350° for 15 minutes,
then broil for 3 minutes.
Makes 6 servings.

- 1 head iceberg lettuce
- 2 cups cold water
- 1 teaspoon salt
- 1 cup cornmeal
- 1 egg, slightly beaten
- 1 cup shredded Cheddar cheese (4 ounces)
- 1 tablespoon butter or margarine
- ½ cup chopped celery
- 1 medium-size onion, chopped (½ cup)
- 1 package (1 pound) frankfurters
- 1 can (8 ounces) tomato sauce
- ½ teaspoon leaf oregano, crumbled

1. Core, rinse and drain lettuce completely; shred; refrigerate in a plastic bag or plastic crisper.

2. Combine water and salt in a large saucepan; place over heat. Gradually stir in cornmeal. Cook, stirring until thickened, about 5 minutes. Remove from heat. Stir a little hot mixture into egg in a small bowl; blend into saucepan. Add ½ cup cheese; stir until cheese melts.
3. Press mixture against sides and bottom of a 6-cup flameproof shallow casserole.
4. Bake in moderate oven (350°) 15 minutes.
5. Melt butter or margarine in a large saucepan. Add celery and onion; sauté until soft. Cut frankfurters into 1-inch pieces; add with tomato sauce and oregano. Bring to boiling.
6. Remove casserole with cornmeal from oven; place half the shredded lettuce in shell. Top with frankfurter mixture, then with remaining lettuce. Sprinkle with remaining ½ cup cheese.
7. Broil, 4 inches from heat, 3 minutes, or until cheese melts.

BEEF AND POTATO BOATS

Edible containers hold beef in sour cream sauce and fluffy mashed potatoes—all topped with cheese.

Bake at 400° for 1 hour,
then at 400° for 20 minutes.
Makes 4 servings.

- 4 large baking potatoes
- 4 slices bacon
- ¾ pound ground beef
- 3 green onions, trimmed and sliced
- 1½ teaspoons salt
- ½ cup dairy sour cream (from an 8-ounce container)
- 2 tablespoons butter or margarine
  Milk
- ¼ cup grated process American cheese

1. Bake potatoes in hot oven (400°) 1 hour, or until tender.
2. Sauté bacon until crisp; drain on paper towels, then crumble. Pour off all drippings from pan.
3. Mix ground beef lightly with green onions; shape into a large patty in same pan; brown 5 minutes on each side, then break up into small chunks. Stir in ½ teaspoon of the salt, sour cream and crumbled bacon; remove from heat.
4. Split baked potatoes in half; scoop out centers, being careful not to break shells. Place shells in a shallow baking pan. Mash potatoes; beat in remaining 1 teaspoon salt, butter or margarine and just enough milk to make them creamy but still stiff.
5. Spoon beef mixture into shells, dividing evenly; top with mashed potatoes; sprinkle with cheese.
6. Bake in hot oven (400°) 20 minutes, or until cheese is bubbly hot.

HAM MADEIRA

Madeira wine flavors ham steak to perfection for a fast supper dish.

Makes 6 servings.

- 1 ham steak (about 1½ pounds)
- ¾ cup Madeira wine
- 1 envelope (cup-size) instant cream of mushroom soup
- 2 tablespoons prepared horseradish mustard
- 1 package (9 ounces) frozen whole green beans

1. Trim excess fat from ham; score remaining fat at 2-inch intervals around side of ham.
2. Fry fat trimmings in an electric frypan set at 350° until you have 2 tablespoons of melted fat. Remove remaining pieces with slotted spoon.
3. Brown ham steak 3 minutes on each side; stir in Madeira and bring to bubbling; stir in instant mushroom soup and horseradish mustard until sauce is very smooth; cover frypan.
4. Lower temperature to 200°; simmer 10 minutes; place frozen green beans in skillet; cover frypan; simmer 10 minutes longer, or until green beans are tender. Serve with buttered acorn squash slices, if you wish.

BURGUNDY BEEF BALLS

A cost-cutting classic.

Makes 6 servings.

- 1½ pounds ground round or chuck
- 1 egg
- ½ cup soft bread crumbs (1 sice)
- ½ cup milk
- 1½ teaspoons salt
- ½ teaspoon garlic salt
- 3 tablespoons butter or margarine
- 1 pound small white onions, peeled
- 1 pound small mushrooms, trimmed
- 1 teaspoon sugar
- ⅓ cup all purpose flour
- 1 can condensed beef broth
- 1 cup dry red wine
- 1 medium-size carrot, pared and sliced
- 1 bay leaf

1. Combine ground beef, egg, bread crumbs, milk, 1 teaspoon of the salt and garlic salt in a large bowl; mix lightly until well blended. Shape into 24 balls.
2. Melt butter or margarine in a kettle or Dutch oven; add onions and mushrooms; sprinkle with sugar. Brown quickly; remove with a slotted spoon to a shallow pan.
3. Add meatballs to drippings in kettle; brown. Remove meatballs; combine with onions and mushrooms.
4. Blend flour and remaining ½ teaspoon salt into drippings in kettle; stir in beef broth until smooth, then add wine and carrot. Bring to boiling, stirring constantly. Return meatballs, onions and mushrooms; add bay leaf; cover. Simmer 35 minutes; remove bay leaf.
5. Spoon mixture into a heated serving dish; sprinkle with chopped parsley, if you wish.

COOK'S TIP: This too is a good basic recipe that can be made with many flavorful variations. Ground meatloaf mixture (beef, veal and pork), ground lamb or ground veal can be substituted for the ground beef in this recipe. A bunch of leeks, trimmed cut into 2-inch pieces and well washed can be substituted for the whole white onions. The carrots can be changed into diced turnip or acorn squash, or you can add 1 package (10 ounces) frozen peas, to the basic recipe for the last 10 minutes of cooking.

VEAL PAPRIKAS

Hungarian-Americans really know how to make veal delicious, with paprika.

Bake at 350° for 30 minutes.
Makes 2 servings.

- ¾ pound veal shoulder, cut into 1-inch pieces
- 3 tablespoons all purpose flour
- 3 teaspoons paprika
- ½ teaspoon salt
- 2 tablespoons butter or margarine
- ¼ cup frozen chopped onion
- 1 medium-size carrot, pared and sliced
- ⅓ cup chopped celery
- ½ cup water
- ½ cup dairy sour cream (from an 8-ounce container)

1. Shake veal cubes in mixture of flour, 1 teaspoon of the paprika and salt in a plastic bag to coat evenly.
2. Brown meat in butter or margarine in a large skillet; push to one side. Stir in onion, carrot, celery and remaining 2 teaspoons paprika; saute lightly, then mix with meat.
3. Stir in water and sour cream. Spoon into a small shallow baking dish that fits into toaster oven.
4. Bake in toaster oven set at moderate (350°) 30 minutes, or until veal is tender. Serve with buttered noodles, if you wish.

COQ AU VIN, NEW ORLEANS

Long, slow cooking gives this aristocrat its mellow flavor.

Bake at 350° for 2 hours, 15 minutes.
Makes 6 servings.

- 1 stewing chicken, cut up (about 4 pounds)
- ⅓ cup all purpose flour
- 1½ teaspoons salt
- 3 tablespoons butter or margarine
- ½ cup diced cooked ham
- 12 small white onions, peeled
- 3 cups dry red wine
- 1 can (3 or 4 ounces) mushroom caps
- 1 clove garlic, minced
- 6 peppercorns
- 6 whole cloves
- 1 bay leaf
  Hot cooked rice

1. Shake chicken pieces with flour and salt in a plastic bag to coat well.
2. Brown pieces, a few at a time, in butter or margarine in a large skillet; place in a 12-cup casserole; sprinkle with ham and top with onions.
3. Stir red wine, mushrooms and liquid and garlic into drippings in the pan; bring to boiling, scraping brown bits from bottom of pan. Pour over chicken mixture.
4. Tie peppercorns, whole cloves and bay leaf in cheesecloth; add to casserole; cover.
5. Bake in moderate oven (350°) 2 hours, 15 minutes, or until chicken is very tender.
6. Uncover; remove spice bag and let chicken stand 5 to 10 minutes, or until fat rises to top; skim off. Serve with hot cooked rice and garnish with parsley, if you wish.

CHICKEN PARMESAN

An easy and pleasing variation of a classic Italian-American veal dish.

Bake at 425° for 45 minutes.
Makes 2 servings.

- 2 tablespoons olive or vegetable oil
- 1 whole chicken breast (about 12 ounces)
- ½ teaspoon leaf oregano, crumbled
- ¼ teaspoon salt
  Paprika
- 1 large tomato, halved
- 1 can (3 or 4 ounces) sliced mushrooms
  Grated Parmesan cheese

1. Pour oil into a small shallow baking pan; place in a toaster oven set at hot (425°) to heat, about 5 minutes. Remove pan from oven.
2. Halve chicken breast and place, skin-side down, in hot oil. Sprinkle with half the oregano and salt. Sprinkle lightly with paprika.
3. Bake in toaster oven 20 minutes. Turn chicken pieces; add tomato halves to baking pan; sprinkle with remaining oregano and salt and a little paprika. Bake 15 minutes longer, or until tender.
4. Spoon drippings in pan over chicken. Pour mushrooms and their liquid over chicken; sprinkle with Parmesan cheese. Bake 5 minutes, or until mushrooms are heated.

CALIFORNIA CHICKEN CURRY

Nectarines make a delightful fruit in curry.

Makes 4 servings.

- **1 broiler-fryer, quartered (2 ½ pounds)**
- **1 teaspoon salt**
- **¼ teaspoon pepper**
- **2 tablespoons vegetable oil**
- **1 to 3 teaspoons curry powder**
- **3 nectarines**
- **½ cup flaked coconut**
- **2 green onions, sliced**

1. Season chicken with salt and pepper. Heat oil and curry powder in a large skillet.
2. Brown chicken slowly on all sides; cover and cook 30 minutes, or until tender when pierced with a fork. Remove chicken to a heated platter and keep warm.
3. Slice nectarines into drippings in pan. Sprinkle with coconut and onions. Cook 5 minutes, or until lightly browned. Spoon sauce over chicken. Serve at once with rice and chopped peanuts, if you wish.

NEW ORLEANS JAMBALAYA

Creole cooks love to entertain in quantity. Here's their chicken, ham and shrimp combo —plenty for a gang. Shown on page 14.

Makes 12 servings.

- **2 broiler-fryers, cut up (about 3 pounds each)**
- **¼ cup vegetable oil**
- **3 cups diced cooked ham**
- **2 cloves garlic, minced**
- **3 large onions, chopped (3 cups)**
- **3 cans (1 pound each) stewed tomatoes**
- **2 teaspoons salt**
- **¼ teaspoon bottled red pepper seasoning**
- **1 large bay leaf**
- **3 cups sliced celery**
- **1 package (1 pound) frozen deveined shelled raw shrimp**
- **2 cups uncooked regular rice**
- **¼ cup chopped parsley**

1. Brown chicken, a few pieces at a time, in oil in a large kettle; remove and reserve.
2. Brown ham lightly in kettle. Stir in garlic and onions; sauté 5 minutes, or until soft; return chicken with tongs to kettle.
3. Stir in tomatoes, salt, red pepper seasoning and bay leaf.

☞

New Orleans Jambalaya is generously laden with seafood, meat and vegetables. It's a festive dish made famous by Creole cooks. Recipe is on this page.

4. Bring to boiling; lower heat; cover. Simmer 30 minutes. Stir in celery, shrimp and rice, making sure all rice is covered with liquid; cover kettle.
5. Simmer 30 minutes longer, or until chicken and rice are tender; remove bay leaf. Stir in parsley. Serve in heated soup tureen with hot buttered corn bread and frosty mugs of beer, if you wish.

MRS. OAKIE'S LAMB STEW

Marjoram for lamb is this Denver, Colorado cook's flavor secret.

Makes 6 servings.

- **2 tablespoons vegetable oil**
- **2 pounds boneless stewing lamb, cubed**
- **4 cups water**
- **1 medium-size onion, sliced**
- **2 envelopes or teaspoons instant beef broth**
- **1 teaspoon salt**
- **⅛ teaspoon pepper**
- **¾ teaspoon celery salt**
- **¾ teaspoon leaf marjoram, crumbled**
- **6 small potatoes, pared and quartered**
- **1 package (10 ounces) frozen peas and carrots**
- **2 tablespoons cornstarch**

1. Heat oil in a Dutch oven or heavy kettle; brown lamb; drain off drippings. Add water, onion, instant beef broth, salt, pepper, celery salt and marjoram.
2. Cover and simmer 1 ½ hours. Remove from heat; let stand about 10 minutes; skim off fat.
3. Add potatoes and cook 15 minutes; add peas and carrots and cook 15 minutes longer, or until vegetables are tender.
4. Blend ¼ cup water into cornstarch in a cup. Stir into bubbling stew. Cook, stirring constantly, until liquid thickens and bubbles 3 minutes. Sprinkle with chopped parsley.

SHORT-RIB CHILI

Chili puts punch in this thrifty, rib-sticking beef and bean stew.

Makes 8 servings

- **4 pounds short ribs**
- **1 large onion, chopped (1 cup)**
- **1 green pepper, halved, seeded and diced**
- **2 cloves garlic, chopped**
- **2 tablespoons chili powder**
- **1 can (1 pound) tomatoes**
- **1 can (4 ounces) green chili peppers, drained and chopped**
- **1 envelope or teaspoon instant beef broth**
- **1 cup boiling water**
- **1 teaspoon salt**
- **2 tablespoons all purpose flour**
- **¼ cup water**
- **2 cans (1 pound each) kidney beans,**

drained
- **1 can (12 or 16 ounces) whole kernel corn, drained**

1. Trim away as much fat as possible from short ribs. Heat heavy kettle or Dutch oven; melt enough fat to make 2 tablespoons drippings. Brown ribs well on all sides; remove. Drain off all but 2 tablespoons fat.
2. Sauté onion, green pepper and garlic in same kettle. Stir in chili powder; cook, stirring constantly, about 2 minutes. Add tomatoes and green chili peppers. Dissolve instant beef broth in boiling water; stir into tomato mixture; add salt. Return ribs to kettle. Bring to boiling; lower heat; cover. Simmer 2 hours, or until meat is tender and falls from bones.
3. Remove meat to serving bowl; keep warm. Carefully remove the bones and skim fat from sauce in kettle. Blend flour and water in a cup; mix well. Stir into the sauce. Cook, stirring constantly, until the sauce thickens and bubbles 3 minutes. Add kidney beans and corn; heat about 5 minutes. Spoon over short ribs.

PASTA DEL SOL

Lasagna—Florida style—with orange juice in the sauce.

Bake at 350° for 30 minutes.
Makes 6 servings.

- **1 pound ground pork**
- **1 medium-size onion, chopped (½ cup)**
- **1 clove garlic, minced**
- **3 tablespoons all purpose flour**
- **1½ cups Florida orange juice**
- **1 teaspoon salt**
- **¼ teaspoon pepper**
- **¼ teaspoon leaf sage, crumbled**
- **¼ teaspoon ground cinnamon**
- **1 container (1 pound) creamed cottage cheese**
- **1 egg**
- **¼ cup chopped parsley**
- **½ teaspoon grated orange rind**
- **6 lasagna noodles, cooked**

1. Shape pork into a large patty in a large skillet. Brown over medium heat 5 minutes; turn and brown 5 minutes longer; break up with a fork; push to one side. Add onion and garlic; sauté until soft.
2. Blend in flour. Stir in orange juice, salt, pepper, sage and cinnamon. Cook until mixture thickens and bubbles 3 minutes.
3. Mix cottage cheese, egg, parsley and orange rind in a medium-size bowl. Layer 3 lasagna noodles on bottom of an 11x7-inch casserole. Spoon half of cheese mixture and pork mixture over noodles; repeat for a second layer.
4. Bake in moderate oven (350°) 30 minutes, or until bubbly hot. Garnish with orange slices, if you wish.

15

IOWA BEAN BAKE

Meaty dried beans from the heartland of America bake into a tangy treat.

Bake at 325° for 2 hours, 30 minutes.
Makes 8 servings.

    1 package (1 pound) dried lima,
      navy or Great Northern beans
    6 cups water
 2½ teaspoons salt
    1 pound ground chuck or round
    1 egg
  ¼ cup seasoned dry bread crumbs
    2 tablespoons vegetable oil
    1 large onion, chopped (1 cup)
  ½ cup light molasses
  ½ cup chili sauce
  ¼ cup prepared mustard

1. Pick over beans and rinse under running water. Combine beans and water in a large kettle. Bring to boiling; cover kettle; boil 2 minutes; remove from heat; let stand 1 hour. Return kettle to heat; bring to boiling; add 2 teaspoons of the salt; lower heat; simmer 1 hour, or until beans are firm but tender.
2. Combine ground beef, egg, bread crumbs and remaining ½ teaspoon salt in a medium-size bowl; shape into small meatballs.
3. Brown meatballs in vegetable oil in a 12-cup flameproof casserole or a large skillet; remove with slotted spoon. Sauté onion in pan drippings; stir in molasses, chili sauce and mustard; bring to boiling.
4. Drain beans, reserving liquid. Combine beans, meatballs and onion mixture in casserole; add enough reserved liquid to cover beans; cover.
5. Bake in slow oven (325°) 2 hours, adding more reserved liquid, if needed, to prevent beans from drying out. Remove cover; bake 30 minutes longer, or until beans are very tender.

TAMALE BAKE

The Mexican influence is evident in Southern Californian cooking.

Bake at 400° for 1 hour.
Makes 6 servings.

    1 cup corn meal
    1 pound ground beef
    1 medium-size onion, chopped
      (½ cup)
  ½ cup chopped green pepper
    1 envelope (1½ ounces) spaghetti
      sauce mix
    1 tablespoon chili powder
    1 can (about 1 pound) tomatoes
    1 can (7 ounces) pitted ripe olives,
      halved
    1 cup grated Cheddar cheese
      (4 ounces)

1. Cook cornmeal, following label directions for cornmeal mush. Pour about half into an 8-cup shallow casserole, spreading evenly; pour remainder into a greased 9x5x3-inch loaf pan; chill.
2. Press ground beef into a large patty in a large skillet; brown 5 minutes on each side; break up into chunks; push to one side.
3. Add onion and green pepper; sauté just until soft. Stir in spaghetti sauce mix, chili powder and tomatoes.
4. Bring to boiling, stirring constantly; remove from heat. Stir in olives and ¾ cup of the grated cheese. Pour over cornmeal mush in casserole. (This much can be done ahead; chill. Take from refrigerator 30 minutes before baking.)
5. Remove cornmeal mush from loaf pan by inserting onto a cutting board. Divide in half, lengthwise, then cut each half into thirds; cut each piece diagonally, to make 12 wedges. Arrange around edge of baking dish; sprinkle remaining cheese on top.
6. Bake in hot oven (400°) 1 hour, or until bubbly hot.

SEAFOOD GUMBO

Gumbo is the culinary pride of New Orleans and its greatest gift to American cuisine.

Makes 8 servings.

  ¼ cup (½ stick) butter or margarine
    3 tablespoons all purpose flour
    2 large onions, chopped (2 cups)
    1 clove garlic, minced
    1 can (1 pound, 12 ounces)
      tomatoes
    1 can condensed chicken broth
    2 cups water
    1 teaspoon salt
    1 tablespoon Worcestershire sauce
  ¼ teaspoon bottled red pepper
      seasoning
    1 pound crab meat
      OR: 2 cans (6¼ ounces each)
      crab meat
    1 pint oysters
      OR: 2 cans (8 ounces each)
      oysters
    2 tablespoons filé powder
    8 cups hot cooked rice

1. Make a roux (the flavor base for so many Creole dishes) by melting butter or margarine in a heavy kettle; stir in flour. Cook over low heat, stirring constantly, until flour turns a rich brown, about 15 minutes.
2. Stir in onion and garlic. Cook, stirring often, until soft, about 10 minutes. Add tomatoes, chicken broth, water, salt, Worcestershire sauce and red pepper seasoning; cover.
3. Simmer 15 minutes to develop flavors. Add crab meat and oysters with their liquid. Continue cooking just until oysters curl, about 5 minutes.
4. Sprinkle filé powder into gumbo and stir in to thicken broth. Serve in deep bowls over hot cooked rice.
COOK'S TIP: Reheating filé powder makes the gumbo stringy, so always add it at the last minute.

RIO GRANDE TURKEY SALAD

In Texas, where winter is short, main-dish salads are often the perfect answer to, "What's for dinner?"

Makes 4 servings.

    1 head iceberg lettuce
    2 cups diced cooked turkey
    1 medium-size avocado, halved,
      pitted, peeled and cut into
      crescents
    2 cups corn chips or miniature tacos
  ½ cup pitted ripe olives
      Tomato Dressing (recipe follows)

1. Core, rinse and drain lettuce completely. Refrigerate in plastic bag or plastic crisper until serving time.
2. Remove a few outer leaves of lettuce and line a chilled salad platter or bowl. Shred remaining lettuce coarsely and sprinkle onto platter.
3. Arrange turkey, avocado, corn chips and ripe olives on lettuce. Serve with TOMATO DRESSING.

TOMATO DRESSING: Makes 1½ cups. Combine 1 can (8 ounces) tomato sauce with tomato bits, ¼ cup wine vinegar, ¼ cup vegetable oil, 1 small onion, chopped (¼ cup), 2 tablespoons chopped parsley, 1 teaspoon salt, 1 teaspoon chili powder, 1 clove garlic, minced, ⅛ teaspoon pepper and 3 drops liquid red pepper seasoning in a jar with a screw top. Cover and shake thoroughly to blend. Shake again just before using.

CHEESE STRATA

Homemakers of the Finger Lake District of New York serve Cheddar cheese this delicious way.

Bake at 350° for 1 hour.
Makes 4 servings.

    6 slices day-old bread
    3 tablespoons butter or margarine,
      softened
    1 cup shredded Cheddar cheese
      (4 ounces)
    6 eggs, slightly beaten
 1½ cups milk
    1 teaspoon dry mustard
  ½ teaspoon salt
  ⅛ teaspoon pepper

1. Butter bread on a wooden board; cut into small cubes. Alternate layers of bread cubes and Cheddar cheese in a buttered 8-cup casserole.
2. Blend eggs, milk, dry mustard, salt and pepper in a medium-size bowl; pour over bread-cheese mixture.
3. Cover with plastic wrap; refrigerate overnight.
4. Bake in moderate oven (350°) 1 hour, or until puffed and golden. Garnish with watercress, bacon curls and crushed potato chips, if you wish.

(Recipes continued on page 104.)

CHILI HEROES

Zippy meatballs are served on toasted frankfurter rolls—so good, yet simple.

Makes 8 servings.

- 2 pounds ground beef
- 1 to 3 teaspoons chili powder
- 1 teaspoon salt
- ⅛ teaspoon pepper
- 2 tablespoons butter or margarine
- 1 medium-size onion, chopped (½ cup)
- 1 clove garlic, minced
- 2 cans (11 ounces each) beef gravy
- ¼ cup catsup
- 8 split frankfurter rolls, toasted
  Corn chips
  Sweet or sour pickles

1. Combine ground beef with half of the chili powder, salt and pepper in a medium-size bowl, mixing lightly, just until well blended. Shape into 32 balls.
2. Melt butter or margarine in a large heavy skillet; add meatballs and brown, turning after about 5 minutes, stir in beef gravy, catsup, and remaining chili powder. Bring to boiling; lower heat; cover skillet; simmer 15 minutes to blend flavors.
3. Spoon 4 meatballs and gravy into each buttered frankfurter roll and serve with corn chips and assorted sweet or sour pickles and a tall glass of lemonade.

SANDWICH BURGERS

Not every burger has to be round. Shape these to fit your favorite sandwich bread.

Makes 6 servings.

- 2 pounds ground beef
- 2 eggs
- 1 medium-size onion, chopped (½ cup)
- 1 cup finely chopped raw spinach
- 1 cup grated Cheddar cheese (4 ounces)
- 2 teaspoons salt
- ½ teaspoon celery salt
- ¼ teaspoon pepper
- 6 slices sandwich bread

1. Preheat broiler, following manufacturer's directions.
2. Combine ground beef with eggs, onion, spinach, cheese, salt, celery salt and pepper in a medium-size bowl; mix lightly until well blended; divide into 6 portions.
3. Press each into a square, the same size as bread slice, on a square of wax paper.
4. Grill, 4 inches from heat, 4 to 8 minutes on each side, or until beef is done as you like. Serve on sandwich bread with catsup and canned French fried onion rings. Serve with a large fruit salad/dessert made of pears, nectarines and cherries and topped with dairy sour cream.

BARBECUED KNACKWURST

Fat franks simmer in a zippy sauce that you can use with other sausages, too.

Makes 8 servings.

- 1 medium-size onion, chopped (½ cup)
- 2 tablespoons vegetable oil
- 2 cans (8 ounces each) tomato sauce
- 3 tablespoons molasses
- 3 tablespoons cider vinegar
- 3 tablespoons prepared mustard
- ½ teaspoon salt
- ½ teaspoon leaf basil, crumbled
- 2 packages (1 pound each) knackwurst
- 8 split frankfurter rolls

1. Sauté onion in oil, in a large heavy skillet over medium heat, just until soft. Stir in tomato sauce, molasses, vinegar, mustard, salt and basil; simmer, uncovered, stirring several times, 5 minutes.
2. Score knackwurst lightly across top to a depth of 1-inch.
3. Arrange knackwurst in sauce; cover; simmer 15 minutes or until puffed and bubbly-hot.
4. Place rolls under broiler to toast. Place knackwurst and sauce on rolls. Serve with potato salad and coleslaw.
COOK'S TIP: Hot dogs can also be prepared the same way, except score only to a depth of ½-inch.

FIESTA CHEESEBURGERS

Cheese-toasted buns are a delicious addition to barbecued burgers.

Makes 6 servings.

- 2 pounds ground beef
- 1 cup soft bread crumbs (2 slices)
- ½ cup milk
- 2 teaspoons salt
- ¼ teaspoon pepper
- 6 split hamburger buns
  Butter or margarine
  Prepared mustard
- 1 jar (5 ounces) process cheese spread

1. Mix ground beef lightly with bread crumbs, milk, salt and pepper in a medium-size bowl; shape into 6 patties about 1-inch thick.
2. Preheat broiler, following manufacturer's directions.
3. Grill, 4 inches from heat, 4 to 8 minutes on each side, or until beef is done as you like.
4. While meat cooks, spread bottom halves of buns with butter or margarine and mustard; spread top halves with cheese.
5. Toast buns along with meat patties, 2 to 3 minutes, or just until toppings bubble up. Put together with meat patties and serve with tall glasses of chilled tomato juice and a hearty salad of marinated red kidney beans and iceburg lettuce and dressing.

PEPPERS AND SAUSAGES

Choose sweet or hot Italian sausages or a combination of both to cook with red and green peppers, seasoned with Italian herbs.

Makes 8 servings.

- 2 pounds sweet or hot Italian sausages
- ¼ cup olive oil
- 3 large green peppers, halved, seeded and diced
- 2 large red peppers, halved, seeded and quartered
- 1 teaspoon salt
- 1 teaspoon mixed Italian herbs, crumbled
- ¼ teaspoon freshly ground pepper
- 8 hero rolls

1. Preheat broiler, following manufacturer's directions.
2. Grill Italian sausages on broiler pan, 6 inches from heat, turning often, 30 minutes, or until done as you like.
3. While sausages cook, brush peppers with oil on same broiler pan; broil, turning and brushing often, until soft; season with salt, Italian herbs and pepper; put to side of pan to keep warm. Toast hero rolls on side of broiler.
4. Split hero rolls and spoon on pepper mixture; top with grilled sausages. Serve with an antipasto salad and dry red Italian wine.
COOK'S TIP: Brown-n-serve sausages or regular breakfast sausages can be substituted for the Italian sausages.

PIZZAIOLA SAUSAGES

Onions, tomatoes and basil give sausages an Italian street fair flavor.

Makes 8 servings.

- 2 pounds sweet or hot Italian sausages
- ¼ cup olive or vegetable oil
- 2 large onions, thinly sliced
- 1 clove garlic, minced
- 4 large tomatoes, chopped
- 2 teaspoons salt
- 2 teaspoons leaf basil, crumbled
- ¼ teaspoon freshly ground pepper
- 8 hero or club rolls

1. Preheat broiler, following manufacturer's directions.
2. Grill Italian sausages, 6 inches from heat, turning often, 30 minutes, or until done as you like.
3. While sausages cook, heat oil in a large heavy skillet; sauté onions and garlic until soft. Stir in tomatoes, salt, basil and pepper; simmer 20 minutes. Add sausages; simmer 10 minutes.
4. Split hero or club rolls and toast on side of grill; spoon sausages and sauce onto rolls; serve with ripe olives and pickled hot peppers.

(Recipes continued on page 21.)

ALL AMERICAN CLASSICS

17

There's nothing that can compare to the delight of tasting home-baked bread, still warm from the oven and dripping with butter. And whether you're serving a hearty soup or haute cuisine, a flavorful loaf of bread is sure to complement the meal. Presented here is an international array of breads, each one more tempting than the next! Recipes and bread names, turn page.

Shown from the top on page 18: Yankee Anadama Bread, Italian Sourdough Bread, English Cheese Bread. Shown from left to right on page 19: Russian Pumpernickel, French Whole Wheat Bread, German Two-Tone Rye. Recipes start on this page.

YANKEE ANADAMA BREAD

Cornmeal and molasses are added to yeast dough for a traditional New England bread. Shown on page 18.

Bake at 375° for 35 minutes.
Makes 2 loaves.

    1½ cups water
    ½ cup cornmeal
    2 teaspoons salt
    ¼ cup vegetable shortening
    ½ cup light molasses
    2 envelopes active dry yeast
    ½ cup very warm water
    6 cups all purpose flour
       Melted butter or margarine

1. Combine 1½ cups water, cornmeal, salt, shortening and molasses in a medium-size saucepan. Heat, stirring constantly, until mixture thickens and bubbles; pour into a large bowl and cool until lukewarm.
2. Sprinkle yeast and 1 teaspoon sugar into the ½ cup very warm water in a small bowl. ("Very warm water" should feel comfortably warm when dropped on wrist.) Stir until well blended and allow to stand 10 minutes, or until mixture begins to bubble. Stir into cornmeal mixture.
3. Beat in 2 cups flour until smooth; add 3 more cups flour, one at a time, until mixture forms a soft dough.
4. Turn dough out onto a lightly floured pastry cloth or board. Knead until smooth and elastic, about 8 minutes, using only as much additional flour as needed to keep dough from sticking.
5. Place dough in a greased large bowl; turn to cover with shortening; cover with a clean towel. Let rise in a warm place, away from draft, 45 minutes, or until double in bulk.
6. Punch dough down; knead a few times. Divide dough in half, then divide one half into 14 even-sized balls, rolling each ball between palms of floured hands until surface is smooth. Arrange 14 balls in a greased 9-inch layer-cake pan. Repeat with remaining half of dough in a second layer-cake pan.
7. Brush tops of loaves with melted butter or margarine and sprinkle lightly with cornmeal. Let rise in a warm place, away from draft, 30 minutes, or until double in bulk.

8. Bake in moderate oven (375°) 35 minutes, or until loaves give a hollow sound when tapped. Remove from pans to wire racks; cool completely. Loaves will break into separate rolls for serving.

RUSSIAN PUMPERNICKEL

Hearty and crusty, just waiting to be sliced and coated with butter. Photo, page 19.

Bake at 350° for 50 minutes.
Makes 2 loaves.

    4½ cups all purpose flour
    1½ cups whole rye flour
    1 envelope active dry yeast
    ½ cup whole bran cereal
    ½ cup cornmeal
    1 tablespoon salt
    1¾ cups water
    2 tablespoons dark molasses
    1 square unsweetened chocolate
    1 tablespoon butter or margarine
    1 cup prepared mashed potatoes, cooled
    1 teaspoon caraway seeds
       Cornmeal

1. Combine all purpose flour and rye flour in a medium-size bowl.
2. Measure 2 cups flour mixture into a large bowl; add yeast, bran cereal, cornmeal and salt.
3. Combine water, molasses, chocolate and butter or margarine in a small saucepan; heat slowly until chocolate and butter or margarine melt. (Do not allow mixture to get too hot—if it does, cool before adding to yeast mixture.)
4. Add to yeast mixture; beat at medium speed of electric mixer 2 minutes, scraping down side of bowl often with rubber scraper. Add mashed potatoes and 1 cup of flour mixture.
5. Beat at high speed 2 minutes, scraping down side of bowl often. Stir in caraway seeds and enough remaining flour mixture to make a soft dough.
6. Turn dough out onto a lightly floured pastry cloth or board; knead 10 minutes, or until smooth and elastic, adding only as much additional flour as needed to keep dough from sticking.
7. Place dough in a greased large bowl; turn to cover with shortening. Let rise in a warm place, away from draft, 45 minutes, or until double in bulk.
8. Punch dough down; turn out onto pastry cloth or board; knead 1 minute. Divide in half; roll out half to a 15x10-inch rectangle. Roll up tightly from long side, jelly-roll fashion; pinch long seam tightly to seal. Turn ends under loaf for rounded ends.
9. Place loaf, seam-side down, on a greased large cookie sheet sprinkled with cornmeal. Repeat shaping with second half of dough. Cover loaves; let rise in a warm place 45 minutes, or until double in bulk.
10. Bake in moderate oven (350°) 50 minutes, or until loaves give a hollow sound when tapped. Cool completely on wire racks.
BAKER'S TIP: Canadian cooks, please dissolve yeast in ½ cup very warm water and 1 teaspoon sugar in a 1-cup measure, *before* adding to 2 cups flour. Reduce water in Step 3 to 1¼ cups.

(Recipes continued on page 124.)

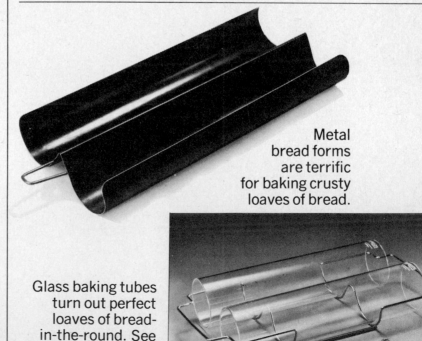

Metal bread forms are terrific for baking crusty loaves of bread.

Glass baking tubes turn out perfect loaves of bread-in-the-round. See Buyer's Guide, page 125, for both items.

HOT TUNA HEROES

Hero sandwiches are one-dish meals—you eat the dish!

Bake at 350° for 15 minutes.
Makes 6 servings.

- 3 cans (6½ ounces each) tuna
- 1 cup frozen chopped onion
- 3 tablespoons wine vinegar
- ½ cup catsup
- ½ teaspoon salt
- ½ teaspoon leaf oregano, crumbled
- ¼ teaspoon pepper
- ¼ cup chopped parsley
- 6 hero rolls

1. Drain oil from tuna; flake tuna and combine with onion, vinegar and catsup in a medium-size bowl. Add salt, oregano, pepper and parsley; toss to blend.
2. Hollow out hero rolls (reserve crumbs for casserole topping). Divide tuna mixture among hero rolls.
3. Bake in toaster oven set on moderate (350°) 15 minutes, or until filling is heated through.

SHRIMP EGG FU YUNG

Tiny shrimp and vegetable pancakes are fried golden brown and served with piquant, soy-flavored sauce.

Makes 4 servings.

- 2 teaspoons cornstarch
- ¾ cup water
- 1 envelope or teaspoon instant chicken broth
- 2 teaspoons soy sauce
- 1 teaspoon cider vinegar
- 1 teaspoon sugar
- 6 eggs
- 1 package (8 ounces) frozen raw shelled deveined shrimp, cooked and diced (1 cup)
- 1 can (1 pound) bean sprouts, drained
- ½ cup chopped green onion
- ½ teaspoon salt
- 1 tablespoon vegetable or peanut oil

1. Blend cornstarch with water until smooth in a small saucepan; stir in instant chicken broth, soy sauce, vinegar and sugar. Cook, stirring constantly, until the sauce thickens and bubbles 3 minutes; remove from heat; keep warm.
2. Beat the eggs in a medium-size bowl, then stir in the shrimp, bean sprouts, green onion and salt.
3. Heat a large heavy skillet slowly over low heat. Test temperature by sprinkling in a few drops of water. When drops bounce about, temperature is right. Lightly grease the skillet with some of the oil.
4. Measure a scant ¼ cup egg mixture for each pancake into pan. (Wait until one has set before pouring in the next one.) Bake until set and under-

side is golden; turn; brown the other side. Repeat with the rest of the mixture, lightly greasing skillet when needed.
5. As pancakes are finished, stack on a heated serving plate and keep warm. Serve warm with sauce.

POLYNESIAN PORK

The sweet-sour combination of tropical fruits goes so well with pork.

Makes 6 servings.

- 2 pounds pork shoulder, cubed
- 2 tablespoons vegetable oil
- 1 large onion, chopped (1 cup)
- 1 can condensed chicken broth
- 1¼ cups water
- 2 teaspoons salt
- 2 acorn squash, cut into ½-inch slices, pared and seeded
- 1 package (9 ounces) frozen artichoke hearts
- 1 teaspoon grated lime or lemon rind
- 1 tablespoon lime or lemon juice
- 1 can (13¼ ounces) pineapple chunks
- 3 tablespoons cornstarch
- ¼ cup firmly packed brown sugar

1. Brown pork cubes, a few at a time, in oil in a large kettle or Dutch oven; remove; reserve. Sauté onion in pan drippings until soft; return browned pork to kettle; add chicken broth, water and salt; bring slowly to boiling; lower heat; cover kettle.
2. Simmer 1 hour, or until pork is almost tender; add acorn squash slices and cook 15 minutes; add artichoke hearts and cook 15 minutes longer, or until meat and vegetables are tender; stir in lime or lemon rind and juice.
3. Drain liquid from pineapple into a cup; blend in cornstarch and sugar. Add pineapple chunks to kettle.
4. Stir cornstarch mixture into bubbling liquid in kettle; cook, stirring gently, until sauce thickens and bubbles, 3 minutes. Garnish with lime or lemon slices, if you wish.

CHICKEN BANGKOK

Hot and spicy chicken with peppers and almonds makes a quick and exotic meal.

Makes 6 servings.

- 3 whole chicken breasts
- ¼ cup peanut or vegetable oil
- 1½ teaspoons salt
- 1 medium-size onion, chopped (½ cup)
- 1 cup diagonally sliced celery
- 1 green pepper, halved, seeded and cut into strips
- 1 can (1 pound, 4½ ounces) pineapple chunks in juice
- ¾ cup pineapple juice
- 2 tablespoons soy sauce
- ¼ teaspoon bottled red pepper seasoning

- 1 bay leaf
- 2 tablespoons cornstarch
- ¼ cup cold water
- ½ cup toasted slivered almonds
  Hot cooked rice

1. Bone chicken breasts with a sharp knife; remove skin. Cut each breast half into thin strips.
2. Heat oil in a wok or a large skillet over high heat. Add strips of chicken; sprinkle with salt. Cook, stirring constantly, 3 minutes. Add onion, celery and green pepper; stir-fry 2 minutes. Add pineapple with juice, pineapple juice, soy sauce, red pepper seasoning and bay leaf.
3. Stir-fry and bring to boiling; reduce heat to medium; cover and cook 4 minutes.
4. Blend together cornstarch and cold water in a cup; stir into hot liquid. Cook, stirring constantly, until sauce thickens and bubbles 3 minutes. Sprinkle with almonds. Serve with hot cooked rice.

LOTUS CHOW MEIN PIE

A pastry crust and Chinese vegetables turn pork leftovers into something special.

Bake at 375° for 40 minutes.
Makes 4 servings.

- 1 tablespoon vegetable or peanut oil
- 2 cups diced cooked pork
- 4 green onions, chopped
- 2 stalks celery, sliced
- 1 can (1 pound) Chinese vegetables, drained
- 1 can (13¾ ounces) chicken broth
- ½ teaspoon ground ginger
- 2 tablespoons cornstarch
- 2 tablespoons dry Sherry
- 1 tablespoon soy sauce
- ⅓ cup cold water
- 2 cups buttermilk biscuit mix

1. Heat oil in a large skillet; add pork, green onions and celery; sauté 5 minutes, or until celery is tender and pork is lightly browned. Stir in Chinese vegetables, chicken broth and ginger. Bring to boiling.
2. Mix cornstarch, Sherry and soy sauce in a small bowl; add to skillet. Bring to boiling, stirring constantly; cook just until thickened, about 1 minute. Turn into a 9-inch pie plate.
3. Add water to biscuit mix in large bowl; stir with a fork just until mixture is moist.
4. Turn dough out onto lightly floured pastry board and knead it 8 or 10 times. Roll out ¼-inch thick. Cut out a 9-inch circle to fit pie plate. Make several cuts in center for steam to escape. Fit pastry on top of pork filling, pressing dough to edge of plate.
5. Bake in moderate oven (375°) 40 minutes, or until pastry is brown.

(Recipes continued on page 104.)

In these energy-conscious days of high fuel costs, it's easier than you think to turn out economical and appetizing meals. Your electric appliances are the key ingredients. No mere "frills," they help make cooking quicker and more efficient.

FAST FOOD, AMERICAN-STYLE

In this chapter you'll find fabulous recipes for your pressure cooker, toaster oven, electric wok, slow cooker, electric fry pan and microwave oven. Descriptions of recipes shown, page 33.

FISH CHOWDER TIVOLI

Northern California has had communities of Danes for generations. This chowder is a favorite among them.

Makes 6 servings.

1 package (1 pound) frozen cod fillets
1 package (1 pound) frozen flounder fillets
4 cups water
1 large onion, chopped (1 cup)
1 cup sliced carrots
½ cup diced celery
2 teaspoons salt
¼ teaspoon white pepper
2 tablespoons all purpose flour
1 tablespoon cornstarch
1 cup milk
1 tablespoon lemon juice
1 tablespoon parsley, chopped
1 tablespoon chopped fresh dill
  Sour cream

1. Allow frozen cod and flounder to stand at room temperature 20 minutes; cut into 1-inch cubes.
2. Combine water, onion, carrots, celery, salt and pepper in a large saucepan; cook 2 minutes. Add cod and flounder; simmer 5 minutes. Combine flour and cornstarch in a 2-cup measure; stir milk into mixture and pour into boiling soup gradually, stirring constantly; simmer 5 minutes.
3. Remove saucepan from heat; add lemon juice, stirring gently. Sprinkle with chopped parsley and dill and serve in hot soup bowls, topping each serving with sour cream.

CHICKEN FLORIDA

Chicken and peas in a spicy orange sauce. Delicious with rice or fresh biscuits.

Makes 4 servings

1 cup orange juice
2 tablespoons brown sugar
20 tablespoons cider vinegar
1 teaspoon ground nutmeg
1 teaspoon leaf basil, crumbled
1 clove garlic, minced
½ cup all purpose flour
1 teaspoon salt
⅛ teaspoon pepper
1 broiler-fryer, cut up (2½ pounds)
2 tablespoons vegetable oil
1½ cups orange sections.
1 package (10 ounces) frozen peas

1. Combine orange juice, brown sugar, vinegar, nutmeg, basil and garlic in a medium-size saucepan. Simmer over low heat 10 minutes.
2. Combine flour, salt and pepper in a plastic bag; shake chicken, a few pieces at a time, to coat.
3. Heat oil in a large skillet; add chicken, a few pieces at a time, and brown on all sides. Add orange sauce. Cover and simmer 30 minutes. Add orange sections and peas; simmer 5 minutes, or until chicken is tender.

CROQUE MONSIEUR

These French fried sandwiches make ham and cheese a whole meal.

Makes 4 servings.

8 slices white bread
¼ cup (½ stick) butter or margarine, softened
4 slices cooked ham
1 package (6 ounces) process Gruyere cheese slices
  OR: 4 slices Muenster cheese
2 eggs
¼ cup milk
1 tablespoon Dijon or sharp mustard

1. Spread bread slices with part of the butter or margarine; sandwich ham and cheese slices between buttered bread slices.
2. Beat eggs with milk and mustard with a fork in a pie plate; dip sandwiches, one at a time, into egg mixture, turning with pancake turner to coat second side.
3. Heat part of remaining butter in a large skillet; add sandwiches; cook 5 minutes, or until bread is golden; turn sandwiches; add remaining butter to skillet; cook 5 minutes longer, or until bread is golden.

RICOTTA REGAL

This super sandwich won a prize at the 1977 National Sandwich Contest.

Bake at 325° for 1 hour.
Makes 6 servings.

18 slices white sandwich bread
½ cup (1 stick) butter or margarine, melted
1 pound sweet Italian sausage, cut into ½-inch slices
6 eggs
1 container (1 pound) ricotta cheese
½ cup chopped fresh mushrooms
2 tablespoons shredded Swiss cheese
2 tablespoons grated Romano cheese
2 tablespoons chopped pimiento

1. Trim crusts from bread. Roll slices thin with a rolling pin. Butter sides and bottom of an 11½x7½x2-inch glass baking dish and line with 12 slices of bread. Brush bread with melted butter or margarine.
2. Brown sausage in a skillet over medium heat; drain on paper towels.
3. Combine eggs and ricotta cheese in a large bowl. Beat with wire whip until smooth. Stir in sausage, mushrooms, cheese and pimiento. Pour into bread-lined baking dish. Cover with remaining bread slices. Brush top with melted butter.
4. Bake in slow oven (325°) 1 hour, or until a knife inserted in center comes out clean. Cut into 6 sandwiches. Garnish with melon balls.

VEGETABLE SOUP KELLY

A hearty lunch soup with chick peas, salami and celery.

Makes 4 servings.

1 cup sliced celery
1½ cups water
½ pound salami, diced
1 can condensed green pea soup
1 can (about 1 pound) chick peas
¼ cup chili sauce
1 tablespoon grated onion
¼ teaspoon mixed Italian herbs, crumbled
1 beef bouillon cube
  Sliced salami (optional)
  Watercress (optional)

1. Simmer celery in water in a medium-size saucepan 10 minutes, or just until crisply tender.
2. Stir in salami, green pea soup, chick peas, chili sauce, onion, Italian herbs and beef bouillon cube, crushing bouillon cube with a spoon. Bring to boiling, then simmer 5 minutes to blend flavors.
3. Ladle into heated soup bowls or cups. Top with sliced salami and watercress, if you wish.

TACO CHEESE PIE

Quiche goes Tex-Mex when beef is baked with chilies and taco seasoning in a pie.

Bake at 425° for 25 minutes.
Makes 6 servings.

1 pound ground beef
1 package (1¼ ounces) taco seasoning mix
¾ cup water
1 package piecrust mix
1 cup shredded Monterey Jack or sharp Cheddar cheese (4 ounces)
1 can (4 ounces) green chilies, seeded and diced

1. Brown beef in a medium-size saucepan; drain off fat. Stir in taco seasoning mix and water; cover. Simmer, following label directions; cool 10 minutes.
2. Prepare piecrust mix, following label directions, or make pastry from your favorite two-crust recipe, adding ½ cup of the shredded cheese to pastry. Roll out half of pastry to an 11-inch round on a lightly floured pastry cloth or board; fit into an 8-inch pie plate. Trim pastry overhang to ½ inch.
3. Add remaining ½ cup cheese and green chilies to meat mixture; spoon into prepared pastry shell.
4. Roll out remaining pastry to a 10-inch round; cover pie. Trim overhang to ½ inch; turn edge under, flush with rim; flute edge. Cut slits near center to let steam escape.
5. Bake in hot oven (425°) 25 minutes, or until pastry is golden.

Remove from oven; let pie stand 5 minutes before serving.

CALICO FRANKS

Frozen mixed vegetables with an onion sauce speed up preparation of this light main dish.

Bake at 375° for 30 minutes.
Makes 4 servings.

- 2 packages (8 ounces each) frozen mixed vegetables with onion sauce (see Cook's Guide)
- 1½ cups milk
- 1 pound frankfurters, sliced
- 1 cup soft bread crumbs (2 slices)
- 1 package (4 ounces) shredded Cheddar cheese

1. Combine frozen vegetables with milk in a large saucepan; heat, following label directions. Stir in frankfurters; spoon into a 6-cup casserole.
2. Mix bread crumbs and cheese in a small bowl; sprinkle over casserole.
3. Bake in moderate oven (375°) 30 minutes, or until casserole is bubbly and crumb topping is golden.

MILE HIGH DINNER PIE

Try this special trick for a super-crisp crust —bake the top separately.

Bake at 400° for 15 minutes.
Makes 4 servings.

- 3 frozen patty shells (from a 10-ounce package)
- ¼ cup frozen chopped onions
- 1 tablespoon butter or margarine
- 1 tablespoon all purpose flour
- 1 cup milk
- 1 package (10 ounces) frozen green peas with sliced mushrooms
- 1 can condensed cream of chicken soup
- 1 tablespoon lemon juice
- ¼ teaspoon dillweed
- 1½ cups cubed cooked chicken
- 1 cup cubed cooked ham

1. Thaw patty shells 20 minutes; overlap in a circle. Roll to an 8-inch circle, turning over frequently, on a lightly floured cookie sheet to keep edges even while rolling. Chill 20 minutes in freezer.
2. Bake in hot oven (400°) 15 minutes, or until brown and puffed.
3. Sauté onion in butter or margarine until soft in a large saucepan; stir in flour. Blend in milk and cook, stirring, until mixture bubbles and thickens slightly. Add peas with mushrooms. Return to boil; cover; reduce heat and simmer 8 minutes. Stir in soup, lemon juice and dillweed, mixing until smooth. Add chicken and ham and heat thoroughly.
4. Turn into a heated 6-cup shallow casserole. Top with the baked pastry and serve at once.

BURGUNDY BEEF

Sliced beef and gravy in a boilable cooking bag means a hearty meat and potato casserole in minutes.

Bake at 400° for 15 minutes.
Makes 2 servings.

- 2 packages (5 ounces each) frozen gravy with sliced beef in a cooking bag (see Cook's Guide)
- 1 cup cooked green beans
- 1 tablespoon dry red wine
- 2 cups prepared instant mashed potatoes
- ¼ teaspoon garlic powder

1. Cook gravy with sliced beef in a cooking bag, following label directions. Open pouch and pour into mixing bowl; stir in green beans and wine.
2. Combine mashed potatoes and garlic powder; line a 4-cup shallow casserole with potatoes; spoon beef mixture into center of potatoes.
3. Bake in hot oven (400°) 15 minutes, or until potatoes are golden. Serve with a crisp green salad tossed with blue cheese dressing, if you wish.

VEAL GENOA

Two Italian favorites team in this quick one-dish dinner, thanks to frozen foods, which trim preparation time to minutes.

Bake at 375° for 15 minutes.
Makes 6 servings.

- 1 package (8 ounces) green noodles
- 1 can condensed cream of mushroom soup
- ½ cup dairy sour cream (from an 8-ounce container)
- 1 container (8 ounces) whipped cream cheese
- ½ cup grated Parmesan cheese
- 2 tablespoons milk
- 1 can (3 or 4 ounces) sliced mushrooms
- 6 frozen breaded veal patties (about 1¼ pounds)
- 3 tablespoons butter or margarine
- 2 pimientos, diced
- 1 package (8 ounces) mozzarella cheese
- ½ cup meatless spaghetti sauce (from a 15-ounce jar)

1. Cook noodles, following label directions; drain and keep warm.
2. Blend soup with sour cream, cream cheese, Parmesan cheese and milk in a bowl; stir in mushrooms and liquid.
3. Brown veal patties on both sides in butter or margarine in a large skillet. Drain on paper towels.
4. Combine drained noodles, soup mixture and pimentos in a 12-cup shallow casserole. Arrange veal patties on top. Cut mozzarella into slices; arrange on top of casserole. Spoon spaghetti sauce in center.
5. Bake in a moderate oven (375°) 15

minutes, or until cheese melts. Garnish with parsley, if you wish.

COUNTRY CHICKEN CHOWDER

A wholesome meal-in-a-bowl you make in minutes from kitchen staples.

Makes 6 servings.

- ½ cup chopped frozen onion
- 2 tablespoons butter or margarine
- 2 cans condensed chicken noodle soup
- 1 soup can water
- 1 cup cubed cooked chicken
- 1 can (1 pound) cream-style corn
- 1 small can evaporated milk
- ¼ teaspoon white pepper
- 2 tablespoons chopped parsley

1. Sauté onion in butter or margarine just until soft in a medium-size saucepan.
2. Stir in soup, water, chicken, corn, evaporated milk and pepper. Heat just to boiling.
3. Pour into heated soup bowls; sprinkle with parsley, if you wish.

SPINACH CHOWDER

A variation of the classic Vichyssoise— flavored with spinach and served hot.

Makes 4 servings.

- 1 package (10 ounces) frozen chopped spinach
- 2 cans condensed cream of potato soup
- 2 cups milk
- 2 envelopes or teaspoons instant chicken broth
- 1 tablespoon instant minced onion
- 4 hard-cooked eggs, shelled and sliced

1. Combine frozen spinach, cream of potato soup, milk, instant broth and onion in a large, heavy saucepan.
2. Heat slowly, stirring occasionally, 20 minutes, or until spinach is thawed; cover. Simmer 5 minutes.
3. Ladle into soup bowls; garnish each serving with hard-cooked egg.

SHORT ORDER TIPS

- Freeze individual portions of ground beef, chicken and fish, for quick and easy thawing.
- Prepare individual meat loaves and shape into patties, logs or in muffin pan cups; wrap, label and freeze.
- When making meatloaf or roasting meat or poultry, line pan with aluminum foil for easier clean up.
- Slice mushrooms on an egg slicer.
- Small appliances can speed up cooking time. An electric toaster-broiler oven heats up more quickly than a conventional one. A wok or large skillet can be used for quick stirfrying of meat, fish and vegetables.

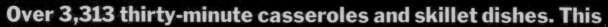

Over 3,313 thirty-minute casseroles and skillet dishes. This

Create a uniquely delicious main dish using our chart and your imagination. There's almost no end to the economical and nutritious combinations you can zap up in just thirty minutes. Great for busy families on the go or when unexpected guests drop in.

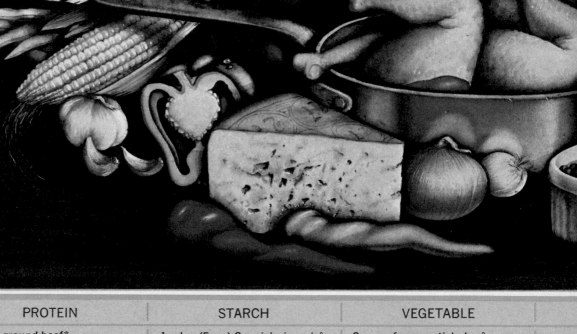

PROTEIN	STARCH	VEGETABLE	
1 lb. ground beef* 4 thin pork chops* 4 chicken fillets* 1 lb. shrimp or fillet of sole 4 thin beef steaks* 1 lb. sliced bacon*	1 pkg. (5 oz.) Spanish rice mix° 1 can (1 lb.) cannellini beans 2 cups sliced cooked potatoes 1 pkg. (10 oz.) frozen French fried potatoes 3 cups cooked egg noodles 2 cups cooked brown rice	2 cups frozen artichokes° 2 cups cubed eggplant 2 cups frozen green beans 2 cups cooked cauliflowerets 2 cups cooked peas 1 pkg. (10 oz.) frozen asparagus° 1 can (1 lb.) whole white onions	
8 slices cooked beef 2 cups cooked cubed pork 1 lb. frankfurters, scored* 8 slices cooked turkey 12 thick slices salami 2 cups cubed cooked lamb 8 slices boiled ham	1 pkg. (7¼ oz.) chicken-flavor rice and vermicelli mix+ ° 2 cans (1 lb.) pork and beans 1 can (1 lb.) sweet potatoes 3 cups cooked kasha 2 cups packaged precooked rice+ 2 cups cooked ziti	2 cups frozen mixed vegetables 2 cups chopped cooked broccoli 1 pkg. (10 oz.) fresh spinach 2 cups cooked sliced carrots 2 large zucchini, thinly sliced 1 can (1 lb.) whole kernel corn 2 sweet red peppers, diced	

2 cans (6½ oz.) tuna
1 can (1 lb.) salmon
2 cans (6¾ oz.) ham+
2 cans (5 oz.) chicken
1 can (12 oz.) luncheon meat+
2 cans (6½ oz.) crab meat
1 can (12 oz.) corned beef
	2 cups cooked bulgar wheat
	1 can (1 lb.) whole potatoes
	2 cans (1 lb.) red kidney beans
	1 pkg. (1 lb.) frozen hash brown
	    potatoes°
	2 cups elbow macaroni
	1 pkg. (5 oz.) curry rice mix°
		2 cups frozen wax beans
		2 cups cooked yellow squash
		1 bag (1 lb.) frozen green
		    beans, broccoli, onions and
		    mushrooms+
		1 can (1 lb.) Italian tomatoes
		1 pkg. (1 oz.) frozen succotash
		2 large tomatoes, diced	

*Brown quickly in skillet.	+See Cook's Guide.	°Cook, following pkg. directions.	

is menu planning at its best—quick, easy and appetizing!

Just choose one ingredient from each of the first 4 columns and bring to bubbling in a large skillet or flameproof casserole. Then follow the cooking and topping directions from columns 5 or 6. It's that simple! Makes 4 servings.

SAUCES AND HERBS	SKILLET DISHES	CASSEROLES
2 env. (1 oz.) white sauce mix° 1 can golden mushroom soup 1 pkg. (10 oz.) Italian-style vegetables with seasonings+° 1 tsp. leaf tarragon 1 can (11 oz.) chicken gravy 1 tsp. mixed Italian herbs	Crushed potato chips‡ Dry bread crumbs tossed with crumbled blue cheese Buttered popcorn and garlic salt‡ Toasted slivered almonds Halved cherry tomatoes Parsley Dumplings (page 97)	2 cups prepared mashed potatoes‡ Sliced American cheese‡ Sesame Seed Twists (page 97)‡ 1 container sour cream and 1 Tbs. flour & sesame seeds‡ Sliced scored cucumber Herb Drop Biscuits (page 97)‡
2 env. (4 to a pkg.) instant cream of chicken soup+° 2 cans (8 oz.) tomato sauce 1 tsp. leaf basil 2 Tbs. chopped parsley 1 pkg. (10 oz.) Hawaiian-style vegetables with seasonings+°	Red onion rings French fried potato sticks+ Seeded and sliced hot peppers Shredded Swiss cheese Herb-flavored croutons Chopped peanuts and raisins Sliced Muenster cheese	Onion Biscuits (page 97)‡ Crushed corn chips Shredded mozzarella cheese‡ Chopped green olives, parsley and garlic Refrigerated buttermilk biscuits‡ Cornbread stuffing mix
1½ cups barbecue sauce plus ¼ cup red cooking wine+ 1 pkg. (8 oz.) frozen peas with cream sauce+° 1 tsp. leaf marjoram 1 can cream of mushroom soup 1 cup sour cream & ½ cup milk	Sliced green onions & lemon rind Hungarian Dumplings (page 97) Red apple slices Sliced ripe olives Grated Parmesan cheese Orange sections Crushed whole-wheat flakes+	Buttered sliced French bread Parsley topped tomato slices Golden Glow Pastry (page 97)‡ Canned pears and chutney Sliced hard-cooked egg‡ Chinese noodles Wheatgerm and cashews
‡Add for last 15 minutes.	Simmer 15 to 30 minutes.	Bake at 400° 20 to 30 minutes.

KETTLE BEEF SOUP

A meal-in-one supper soup that you can almost cut with a knife.

Makes 8 servings.

- 1 pound ground round or chuck
- 3 cups frozen chopped onion
- 1 clove garlic, minced
- 2 envelopes or teaspoons instant beef broth
- 3 cups boiling water
- 2 cans (1 pound, 12 ounces each) Italian tomatoes
- 1 cup dry red wine
- ½ teaspoon mixed Italian herbs, crumbled
- ½ teaspoon salt
- ¼ teaspoon lemon-pepper seasoning
- 1 package (8 ounces) beef-flavored rice and vermicelli mix (see Cook's Guide)
- 1 bag (1 pound) frozen mixed vegetables

1. Brown ground beef in a large kettle or Dutch oven, breaking meat up with a wooden spoon as it cooks.
2. Add onion and garlic. Cook, stirring occasionally, until soft.
3. Stir in instant beef broth, water, tomatoes, wine, Italian herbs, salt and lemon-pepper seasoning. Bring to boiling; lower heat; simmer 30 minutes.
4. Add rice mix and vegetables; simmer 20 minutes longer.
5. Serve in heated soup bowls with toasted buttered crackers, if you wish.

CALIFORNIA POT PIE

Hardly the usual tuna casserole, this biscuit-crowned dish is ready to bake in 15 minutes.

Bake at 375° for 25 minutes.
Makes 6 servings.

- 1 cup frozen chopped onion
- ¾ cup diced celery
- 3 tablespoons butter or margarine
- 3 tablespoons all purpose flour
- ½ teaspoon leaf tarragon, crumbled
- ¼ teaspoon leaf thyme, crumbled
- 1 can (3 ounces) sliced mushrooms
- ¾ cup light cream
- ½ cup mayonnaise or salad dressing
- 1 tablespoon lemon juice
- ½ teaspoon salt
- ⅛ teaspoon pepper
- 2 cans (7 ounces each) tuna, drained and flaked
- 1 can (14 ounces) artichoke hearts, drained
- 1 package (8 ounces) refrigerated buttermilk biscuits

1. Sauté onion and celery in butter or margarine in a medium-size saucepan 3 minutes, or until soft; blend in flour, tarragon and thyme. Drain mushroom liquid into saucepan; add cream. Cook, stirring constantly, until sauce thickens and bubbles 1 minute. Blend in mayonnaise or salad

dressing, lemon juice, salt and pepper.
2. Stir in mushrooms, tuna and artichoke hearts; heat to bubbling; pour into an 8-cup shallow casserole. Arrange refrigerated biscuits on top of casserole, not quite touching.
3. Bake in moderate oven (375°) 25 minutes, or until biscuits are brown and mixture is bubbly.

DILLED TUNA BAKE

Delicate dill adds a special touch to tuna.

Bake at 400° for 20 minutes.
Makes 4 servings.

- 3 tablespoons butter or margarine
- ½ cup frozen chopped onion
- 1 cup sliced celery
- 3 tablespoons all purpose flour
- 1 teaspoon dillweed
- ½ teaspoon salt
  Dash pepper
- 2 cups milk
- 1 can (6½ ounces) tuna, drained
- 1 can (8 ounces) peas, drained
- 1 package (8 ounces) refrigerator biscuits

1. Melt butter or margarine in a medium-size saucepan; add onion and celery; sauté 5 minutes.
2. Blend in flour, dillweed, salt and pepper; cook, stirring constantly, until mixture bubbles; slowly stir in milk.
3. Cook, stirring constantly, until sauce thickens and bubbles 3 minutes.
4. Flake tuna; stir in with peas; bring to boiling, stirring often.
5. Pour into a 6-cup shallow casserole; arrange biscuits on top.
6. Bake in hot oven (400°) 20 minutes, or until biscuits are golden.

CURRIED CHICKEN BAKE

Start with chicken chow mein in a cooking bag and quickly have a delicious casserole.

Bake at 375° for 15 minutes.
Makes 2 servings.

- 2 packages (5 ounces each) frozen chicken chow mein in a boilable cooking bag (see Cook's Guide)
- 1 teaspoon curry powder
- 2 cups cooked rice
- 1 cup cooked peas
  Chopped peanuts

1. Cook chicken chow mein in boilable cooking bag, following label directions. Open cooking bag and pour contents into a mixing bowl; stir in curry powder.
2. Line a 4-cup shallow casserole with cooked rice; spoon curried chicken down center of rice; arrange peas in a ribbon around chicken; sprinkle with chopped nuts.
3. Bake in moderate oven (375°) 15 minutes, or until bubbly hot. Serve with an avocado and pineapple salad, if you wish.

PORK CHOPS ASCAN

Inspired by a French recipe; pork is seasoned with allspice and poached in red wine.

Makes 6 servings.

- 6 pork chops (about 2 pounds)
- 2 tablespoons vegetable oil
- 4 leeks, cut into ¾-inch slices
  OR: 1 large onion, chopped (1 cup)
- 1 teaspoon salt
- ¼ teaspoon pepper
- 12 prunes
- ¾ cup dry red wine
- ¼ cup chicken broth
  Pinch ground allspice
- 1 package (9 ounces) frozen whole green beans
- 1 package (10 ounces) frozen French fried potatoes
- 1 tablespoon all purpose flour

1. Remove fat from edges of chops. Heat oil in a large skillet; brown chops on both sides; remove and reserve.
2. Sauté leek or onion in pan drippings until golden. Return chops to skillet; sprinkle with salt and pepper. Add prunes, red wine, chicken broth and allspice. Cover; cook 30 minutes, or until chops are almost tender.
3. Pile chops in one side of skillet; add green beans and potatoes; cover. Cook 5 minutes.
4. Stir flour into 2 tablespoons cold water in a cup; stir into bubbling liquid in pan; cook, stirring constantly, until sauce bubbles 1 minute.

FISH GUMBO

Hot with cayenne and cool with bananas, this is a Creole fish stew worth making.

Makes 6 servings.

- 2 tablespoons butter or margarine
- 1 medium-size onion, chopped (½ cup)
- ¼ cup finely chopped green pepper
- 1 clove garlic, minced
- 1 tablespoon all purpose flour
- 1 can (13¾ ounces) chicken broth
- 1 can (1 pound) tomatoes
- ⅓ cup chopped parsley
- 1 small bay leaf
- ¼ teaspoon leaf thyme, crumbled
- 1 teaspoon salt
- ⅛ teaspoon pepper
- 2 pounds frozen cod fillets, thawed and cut into 2-inch chunks
- 1 package (10 ounces) frozen okra, thinly sliced
- 1 teaspoon lemon juice
- 1 teaspoon Worcestershire sauce
- ⅛ teaspoon cayenne pepper
- 4 bananas, cut into 1½-inch slices
- 3 cups hot cooked rice

1. Melt butter or margarine in a large kettle. Add onion, green pepper and garlic. Sauté 5 minutes, or until soft. Add flour; cook 3 minutes, stirring well. Pour in chicken broth; stir well.
2. Add tomatoes, parsley, bay leaf,

thyme, salt and pepper. Bring to boiling; reduce heat; simmer, covered, 20 minutes.

3. Add fish and okra; simmer 10 minutes. Discard bay leaf. Stir in lemon juice, Worcestershire sauce, cayenne and bananas. Serve over hot cooked rice in deep soup bowls.

SPINACH FRITTATA

Frittata is an omelet with a generous touch of Spanish flavor.

Makes 4 servings.

- 1 package (10 ounces) frozen chopped spinach
- ½ pound fresh mushrooms, sliced OR: 1 can (4 ounces) sliced mushrooms
- ¼ cup finely chopped onion
- 3 tablespoons butter or margarine
- 8 eggs
- ½ teaspoon seasoned salt Dash pepper
- ⅓ cup grated Parmesan cheese

1. Cook spinach, following package directions. Drain well, pressing out excess water.
2. Cook mushrooms and onion in butter or margarine until tender in a large skillet with a flameproof handle.
3. Beat eggs, salt and pepper in a large bowl; stir in drained spinach. Pour over mushrooms and onions.
4. Cook over low heat until eggs are set, about 7 minutes. Sprinkle with Parmesan cheese.
5. Broil, 6 inches from heat, 3 minutes. Cut in wedges to serve. Garnish with peppers, if you wish.

DEVILED EGG BAKE

Supper's speedy, if you keep some hard-cooks in the 'frig.

Bake at 350° for 15 minutes.
Makes 4 servings.

- 6 hard-cooked eggs, shelled
- ¼ cup mayonnaise or salad dressing
- 2 tablespoons prepared mustard
- ¼ teaspoon salt
- 1 can (6½ ounces) tuna, drained and flaked
- 1 can condensed cream of shrimp soup
- ½ cup milk
- 4 cups hot cooked rice

1. Halve eggs crosswise; remove yolks and mash in a small bowl. Blend in mayonnaise or dressing, mustard and salt, then pile back into whites.
2. Combine tuna with soup and milk in a medium-size saucepan. Heat, stirring often, just until bubbly.
3. Line a 6-cup shallow casserole with rice; arrange filled eggs in rice; spoon tuna sauce over.
4. Bake in moderate oven (350°) 15 minutes, or until bubbly hot.

CHUCK WAGON CASSEROLE

Beans and beef have been favorites in the Southwest and on the plains—now they're combined in a hearty stew.

Bake at 350° for 30 minutes.
Makes 6 servings.

- 2 cups cubed cooked beef
- 3 tablespoons all purpose flour
- ½ pound bacon, cut in 1-inch pieces
- 1 can condensed beef broth
- 1 teaspoon paprika
- 1 teaspoon leaf tarragon, crumbled
- 1 can (1 pound) red kidney beans, drained
- 1 can (1 pound) chick peas, drained
- 1 can (12 or 16 ounces) whole kernel corn, drained
- 1 cup chopped celery

1. Shake beef cubes with flour in a plastic bag to coat evenly.
2. Cook bacon until crisp in large skillet; remove; drain on paper towels. Pour off all but 2 tablespoons fat.
3. Add beef cubes and brown; remove. Stir any remaining flour into drippings in pan, then stir in beef broth, paprika and tarragon. Cook, stirring constantly, until mixture thickens and bubbles 3 minutes.
4. Combine kidney beans, chick peas, corn and celery in an 8-cup shallow casserole; top with beef cubes and bacon; pour sauce over.
5. Bake in moderate oven (350°) 30 minutes, or until bubbly.

SICILIAN BEEF

Rolled beef is smothered with tomatoes and wreathed with pasta wheels.

Makes 8 servings.

- 1 rump or round roast (about 3 pounds)
- 2 tablespoons olive or vegetable oil
- 1 large onion, chopped (1 cup)
- 2 cloves garlic, minced
- 1 tablespoon chopped parsley
- 1½ teaspoons leaf oregano, crumbled
- 1 teaspoon leaf basil, crumbled
- 1 teaspoon salt
- ¼ teaspoon seasoned pepper
- 1 can (2 pounds, 3 ounces) Italian tomatoes
- 2 tablespoons all purpose flour
- ½ cup water
- 1 package (8 ounces) shell macaroni, cooked and drained
- 1 package (9 ounces) Italian green beans, cooked

1. Brown roast slowly in oil in a large kettle or Dutch oven; remove and reserve. Sauté onion and garlic in drippings until soft; stir in parsley, oregano, basil, salt, pepper and tomatoes. Return meat to kettle; cover. Bring to boiling; lower heat.
2. Simmer, turning meat several times, 2 hours, 30 minutes, or until tender. Remove from kettle and keep warm.

3. Blend flour with water until smooth in a cup; stir into liquid in kettle. Cook, stirring constantly, until sauce thickens and bubbles 3 minutes. Taste and season with salt, if needed.
4. Slice meat. Spoon macaroni shells into a heated deep casserole; arrange meat slices on top. Spoon sauce over meat and pasta. Edge casserole with Italian beans.

QUICK VEAL PARMIGIANA

Easy to make, yet so flavorful.

Broil for 5 minutes.
Makes 6 servings.

- 6 frozen veal patties
- 2 tablespoons all purpose flour
- ½ teaspoon salt
- ¼ teaspoon pepper
- 2 tablespoons olive or vegetable oil
- 1 jar (about 10 ounces) meatless spaghetti sauce
- ½ cup water
- 1 envelope or teaspoon instant beef broth
- 1 package (8 ounces) noodles
- 1 package (8 ounces) sliced mozzarella cheese
- ¼ cup grated Parmesan cheese

1. Shake veal pieces in a mixture of flour, salt and pepper in a plastic bag to coat both sides; brown in hot oil in a large skillet.
2. Stir in spaghetti sauce, water and instant beef broth to blend sauce; cover; simmer about 15 minutes, or until veal is tender.
3. Cook noodles, following label directions; drain; place in a 6-cup flameproof baking dish that will take broiler heat. Spoon hot veal and sauce over, stirring with fork to coat noodles; top with sliced mozzarella cheese, then with grated Parmesan cheese.
4. Broil, 4 inches from heat, 5 minutes, or until cheese melts.

SHORT ORDER TIPS

• Combine leftover vegetables to make new and appetizing side dishes. Try peas and carrots; broccoli, mushrooms and water chestnuts; stewed tomatoes with corn in basil butter; lima beans and corn with bacon bits. Add fruits, too, such as carrot slices with golden raisins in honey-butter sauce; pineapple pieces with sweet potatoes in lemon juice-maple syrup sauce.

• Combine canned soup and vegetables to create a new dish: Tomato soup with corn and bacon bits; chicken noodle soup with mixed vegetables and pimiento pieces; beef noodle soup with carrots.

JIFFY CASSOULET

Continental classics are possible in minutes with modern American convenience foods.

Bake at 350° for 1 hour.
Makes 8 servings.

- **6 slices bacon**
- **2 pounds ground meat loaf mixture**
- **1 can (about 1 pound) red kidney beans, drained**
- **1 can (about 1 pound) white kidney beans, drained**
- **1 can (about 1 pound) sliced carrots, drained**
- **1 can (about 1 pound) stewed tomatoes**
- **1 tablespoon dried parsley flakes**
- **2 teaspoons salt**
- **1 teaspoon leaf thyme, crumbled**
- **¼ teaspoon pepper**

1. Sauté bacon just until fat starts to cook out in a large skillet with a heatproof handle; remove and drain on paper towels; reserve.
2. Shape meatloaf mixture into a large patty in same pan; brown 5 minutes on each side. Pour off all drippings; break meat into chunks.
3. Stir in drained beans and carrots, tomatoes, parsley, salt, thyme and pepper; bring to boiling; top with bacon.
4. Bake in moderate oven (350°) 1 hour, or until bubbly hot.
COOK'S TIP: Wrap the handle of a conventional skillet with aluminum foil and the pan becomes heatproof.

CHEESE AND VEGETABLE PIE

Zucchini and tomato sauce bake in a pastry made from refrigerated crescent rolls.

Bake at 375° for 45 minutes.
Makes 6 servings.

- **3 tablespoons vegetable or olive oil**
- **2 medium-size zucchini, thinly sliced**
- **2 medium-size onions, thinly sliced**
- **2½ teaspoons salt**
- **1 clove garlic, minced**
- **3 tablespoons chopped parsley**
- **1 can (8 ounces) tomato sauce**
- **½ teaspoon leaf oregano, crumbled**
  Dash pepper
- **1 container (15 ounces) ricotta cheese**
  OR: 1 container (1 pound) cream-style cottage cheese
- **4 eggs**
- **1½ cups milk**
- **1 package (8 ounces) refrigerated crescent rolls**
- **1 package (8 ounces) mozzarella cheese, sliced**

1. Heat oil in a large skillet; add zucchini and onions; sauté, stirring often, until tender. Stir in 2 teaspoons of the salt; push to one side.
2. Sauté garlic and parsley, stirring constantly, 1 minute; add tomato sauce, oregano and pepper. Cook, stirring occasionally, 15 minutes.
3. Beat ricotta or cottage cheese, eggs and remaining ½ teaspoon salt in a large bowl; gradually beat in milk.
4. Line a fluted 10-inch quiche dish or 10-inch pie plate with unrolled and separated crescent rolls, overlapping slightly and pressing edges of dough triangles together. Spoon tomato-zucchini mixture into bottom of shell, spreading evenly. Set dish on oven shelf, then pour in cheese mixture.
5. Bake in moderate oven (375°) 40 minutes, or just until set in center. Arrange cheese slices on top of pie. Bake 5 minutes longer, or until cheese melts. Garnish with parsley.

WEST COAST TUNA BAKE

Chunks of cream cheese make such a quick, rich sauce.

Bakes at 350° for 30 minutes.
Makes 4 servings.

- **1 package (8 ounces) elbow macaroni, cooked and drained**
- **1 can (6½ ounces) tuna, drained and flaked**
- **1 package (10 ounces) frozen peas, cooked and drained**
- **¼ cup sliced stuffed olives**
- **¼ cup frozen chopped onion**
- **½ teaspoon salt**
- **¼ teaspoon seasoned pepper**
- **1 can condensed cream of mushroom soup**
- **1 package (3 or 4 ounces) cream cheese, cubed**

1. Combine macaroni, tuna, peas, olives and onion in an 8-cup casserole; toss lightly; sprinkle with salt and seasoned pepper; toss again. Stir in soup until well blended; fold in cream cheese; cover.
2. Bake in moderate oven (350°) 30 minutes, or until bubbly hot.

LIMAS ITALIAN STYLE

Continental dishes don't have to take time —try this dish and see!

Makes 4 servings.

- **2 packages (10 ounces each) frozen Fordhook lima beans**
- **1 medium-size onion, chopped (½ cup)**
- **½ pound ground lean beef**
- **¼ pound chicken livers, chopped**
- **1 clove garlic, minced**
- **1 tablespoon vegetable oil**
- **1 can (8 ounces) tomato sauce**
- **1 can (6 ounces) tomato paste**
- **1 teaspoon salt**
- **1 teaspoon sugar**
- **½ teaspoon mixed Italian herbs, crumbled**
  Grated Parmesan cheese

1. Cook lima beans, following label directions, in a large saucepan.
2. Brown onion, beef, chicken livers and garlic in oil in a large saucepan. Add tomato sauce, tomato paste, salt, sugar and Italian herbs; simmer 5 minutes.
3. Drain limas; add to saucepan. Simmer 5 minutes. Serve with grated Parmesan cheese.

LAMB CHOPS PROVENÇAL

Basil is characteristic of the more pungent cooking of Southern France.

Makes 6 servings.

- **6 shoulder lamb chops (3 pounds)**
- **2 tablespoons olive or vegetable oil**
- **2 large onions, sliced**
- **2 cloves garlic, minced**
- **2 teaspoons salt**
- **¼ teaspoon pepper**
- **1½ teaspoons leaf basil, crumbled**
- **3 small zucchini, trimmed and sliced**

1. Trim fat from chops. Heat oil in a large skillet; brown chops on both sides over high heat; remove and reserve.
2. Add onions to skillet; sauté just until soft. Return chops to pan; add garlic, salt, pepper and basil. Cover skillet. Lower heat to medium; cook 10 minutes.
3. Add zucchini slices to skillet; sauté 2 minutes to coat slices; cover skillet. Cook 5 minutes, or until lamb chops and zucchini are tender.

UPSIDE DOWN DINNER

Ham cubes bubble with pineapple in a skillet supper topped with a cornbread crust.

Bake at 400° for 25 minutes.
Makes 4 servings.

- **⅓ cup butter or margarine**
- **⅓ cup firmly packed light brown sugar**
- **1 package (10 ounces) frozen Fordhook lima beans**
- **1 cup cubed cooked ham**
- **1 can (8¼ ounces) crushed pineapple in juice**
- **1 tablespoon prepared mustard**
- **1 tablespoon catsup**
- **¼ teaspoon ground cloves**
- **1 package (15 or 16 ounces) cornbread mix**

1. Melt butter or margarine in a 10-inch skillet with an oven-proof handle. Add sugar and stir until dissolved. Stir in limas, ham, pineapple and juice, mustard, catsup and cloves. Simmer 5 minutes.
2. Prepare cornbread, following package directions. Pour batter over lima-ham mixture in skillet, being sure to coat mixture completely.
3. Bake in hot oven (400°) 25

minutes, or until a toothpick inserted into the center of the cornbread comes out clean. Let rest 10 minutes. Invert on serving dish. Cut into wedges.

RUSSIAN TUNA ROLL

A modern version of the classic Coulibiac, with tuna and rice as the filling.

Bake at 400° for 30 minutes.
Makes 6 servings.

- 1 **package (6 ounces) chicken flavored rice mix**
- 2 **cans (6½ ounces each) tuna**
- 1 **can condensed cream of celery soup**
- 1 **package piecrust mix**
- ½ **cup dairy sour cream (from an 8-ounce container)**

1. Prepare rice mix, following label directions; cool slightly.
2. Break tuna into large chunks; add to rice. Stir in ⅓ cup of the soup.
3. Prepare piecrust mix, following label directions. Roll out on a lightly floured pastry cloth or board to a 14x11-inch rectangle. Spoon tuna mixture down center third of pastry, bring sides up and over filling to meet. Press long edges together and pinch seam tightly with fingers. Pinch each end of roll tightly together and fold under roll so all the filling is completely enclosed. Ease roll carefully onto a cookie sheet.
4. Bake in hot oven (400°) 30 minutes, or until golden brown. Slide pastry roll from cookie sheet onto a cutting board or platter.
5. Bring remaining soup to boiling in a small saucepan. Just before serving, remove pan from heat and stir in sour cream; serve with roll.

LAMB AND RAISIN PILAF

When you brown the chops in the broiler instead of a skillet, you save both cooking and clean-up time.

Bake at 375° for 50 minutes.
Makes 4 servings.

- 4 **shoulder lamb chops**
- 1 **teaspoon salt**
- 1 **teaspoon leaf rosemary, crumbled**
- ⅛ **teaspoon pepper**
- 1 **cup frozen chopped onion**
- ¼ **cup (½ stick) butter or margarine**
- ½ **cup golden raisins**
- ⅔ **cup toasted slivered almonds**
- 2¼ **cups water**
- 2 **envelopes or teaspoons instant chicken broth**
- 1 **tablespoon dried mint flakes, crushed**
- ¼ **teaspoon lemon-flavored salt**
- 1 **cup uncooked converted rice**
- 1 **package (10 ounces) frozen peas and carrots**
- ¼ **cup orange marmalade**

1. Sprinkle lamb chops lightly with salt, rosemary and pepper; arrange on broiler pan.
2. Broil, 5 inches from heat, 4 minutes, or until brown.
3. Sauté onion in butter or margarine in a large heatproof skillet 3 minutes, or until soft. Add raisins, almonds, water, broth, mint and lemon-flavored salt. Simmer 2 to 3 minutes. Stir in rice; bring to boiling. Cover with foil.
4. Bake in moderate oven (375°) 20 minutes, or until rice is almost tender and most of the liquid absorbed. Add peas and carrots, tossing lightly to mix; arrange chops, browned sides up, around edge of pan; recover.
5. Bake 20 minutes; uncover, brush chops with orange marmalade; bake 10 minutes longer, or until chops are well glazed, liquid is absorbed and rice is tender. Fluff up rice with a fork. Serve with a romaine salad, if you wish.

BEEF AND MACARONI INGRAM

A jiffy to make—you don't have to precook the macaroni.

Makes 6 servings.

- 1 **pound ground beef**
- 1 **medium-size green pepper, halved, seeded and chopped**
- 1 **medium-size onion, chopped (½ cup)**
- 1 **clove garlic, minced**
- 1 **can (24 ounces) mixed vegetable juice (see Cook's Guide)**
- 1 **cup uncooked elbow macaroni**
- 2 **tablespoons Dijon mustard**
- 1 **tablespoon Worcestershire sauce**
- 1 **tablespoon vinegar**
- 1 **teaspoon seasoned salt**
- ¼ **teaspoon seasoned pepper Few drops bottled red pepper seasoning**
- 1 **package (8 ounces) sliced Cheddar cheese**

1. Brown beef, pepper, onion and garlic in a large skillet; drain off fat.
2. Stir in mixed vegetable juice, uncooked macaroni, mustard, Worcestershire sauce, vinegar, seasoned salt and pepper and red pepper seasoning; bring to boiling; reduce heat and cover skillet.
3. Simmer 20 minutes, stirring occasionally, or until macaroni is tender. Top beef and macaroni with cheese slices; cover skillet; simmer 3 minutes, or until cheese is melted. Serve in soup bowls with crusty French bread and a tossed green salad, if you wish.
COOK'S TIP: BEEF AND MACARONI INGRAM is delicious reheated. Pour into a well-greased casserole, top with cheese; bake in moderate oven (350°) 20 minutes, or until beef and macaroni are heated through and cheese is melted.

- An old short order cook's tip: Prepare bacon or sausage ahead of time, cooking halfway. Refrigerate between layers of wax paper. Finish cooking at serving time.
- Season-all, perfect for adding flavor with one shake: Combine ½ cup salt, 1 tablespoon ground pepper, 1 tablespoon paprika, 1 teaspoon garlic powder or 1 tablespoon onion powder and one teaspoon of any of the following leaf herbs, crumbled—parsley, basil, thyme, rosemary, marjoram or sage; mix well before pouring into a screwtop jar or flour shaker.
- Leftovers make quick cooking. Save leftover rice, noodles, potatoes, vegetables and meat to make casseroles and main-dish salads.
- Quick soup ideas: Heat up tomato juice or mixed vegetable juice; add leftover bits of cheese, meat, vegetables and herbs; top with popcorn, croutons or pretzels. For a cold fruit soup, purée canned fruit in container of electric blender; add wine or Sherry, if desired; serve with a dollop of sour cream and a sprinkling of sliced almonds or chopped peanuts.
- Sliced and grated vegetables take less time to cook than bigger pieces, as do cubed and ground meats.
- Quick fried rice: Brown 3 cups cooked rice with 1 small chopped onion and 1 halved, seeded and chopped green pepper in ¼ cup vegetable oil in a medium-size skillet; add 1 teaspoon salt and ½ cup diced or shredded cooked meat or chopped seafood; push to one side of skillet. Break 3 eggs into skillet; scramble until almost done; stir into rice mixture; add 2 tablespoons soy sauce and serve immediately.
- Quick hors d'oeuvre: Marinate canned mushrooms or leftover cooked vegetables in Vinaigrette Dressing; drain. Serve with toothpicks or on a bed of lettuce leaves.
- Leftover meats, starches and vegetables can work miracles when one is in a rush—so can canned and frozen foods since they cut down on preparation and cooking time.
- Canned cream soups make super spur-of-the-moment sauces, especially when mixed with Sherry or dry red or white wine.
- When chopping vegetables, especially with a food processor, prepare enough for at least 2 meals; store vegetables separately in plastic bags in the refrigerator.
- Spread hot toast or English muffins with anchovy paste or canned deviled ham; top with poached or scrambled egg and garnish with pimiento slices.
- Prepare extra amounts of potatoes, rice or pasta, to make substantial side-dish salads in a jiffy, or make the base of a quick casserole.

FAST FOOD, AMERICAN-STYLE

HOT DOG HOT POT

Frankfurters and potatoes make great winter eating that's ready in minutes.

Makes 6 servings.

- 1 pound frankfurters, sliced
- 2 tablespoons butter or margarine
- 1 cup frozen chopped onion
- 1 package (1 pound) frozen French fried potatoes
- 2 large carrots, pared and sliced
- 2 cups water
- 1 teaspoon leaf thyme, crumbled
- 1 tablespoon Worcestershire sauce
- 1 can condensed cream of mushroom soup
- 1 can (12 or 16 ounces) whole kernel corn

1. Brown frankfurters lightly in butter or margarine in an electric frypan set at 375°; push to one side. Add onion to frypan; sauté until soft.
2. Stir in potatoes, carrots, water, thyme and Worcestershire sauce. Bring to boiling; cover.
3. Lower temperature to 200°; simmer 15 minutes, or until potatoes and carrots are tender. Stir in soup, corn and liquid; heat until bubbly.

CAROLINA CHICKEN

Brunswick stew goes from pressure cooker to table in double-quick time.

Makes 6 servings.

- 2 slices bacon, diced
- 1 broiler-fryer, cut up (2½ to 3 pounds)
- 3 tablespoons all purpose flour
- 1½ teaspoons salt
- ½ teaspoon pepper
- ⅛ teaspoon cayenne pepper
- 3 medium-size onions, sliced
- 1 cup water
- 2 large ripe tomatoes, peeled and chopped
  OR: 1 can (1 pound) whole tomatoes
- 1 large red pepper, seeded and diced
- ½ teaspoon leaf thyme, crumbled
- 1 package (10 ounces) frozen lima beans
- 1 package (10 ounces) frozen whole-kernel corn
- 1 package (10 ounces) frozen cut okra
- 2 tablespoons chopped parsley
- 1 tablespoon Worcestershire sauce

1. Cook bacon until crisp in an open 6-quart pressure cooker; reserve.
2. Shake chicken pieces with flour, salt, pepper and cayenne in a plastic bag to coat well. Brown pieces, a few at a time, in bacon drippings. Stir in onions; sauté 5 minutes. Add water, tomatoes, pepper and thyme. Bring to boiling; return chicken to cooker.
3. Close cover securely; put pressure control on vent (15 pounds, if your

control has multi-pressure selections). Turn heat on high until pressure rises and control rocks, about 5 minutes.
4. Reduce heat slowly to medium-low so control rocks gently; cook 10 minutes.
5. Remove pressure cooker from heat; let cool about 5 minutes. Then place closed cooker under running water until pressure is reduced and no steam hisses; carefully remove control and cover.
6. Add lima beans, corn, okra, parsley and Worcestershire sauce; bring to boiling; cover; cook in open cooker 10 minutes, or until vegetables are tender. Sprinkle with bacon.

DENVER DINNER

Lamb shoulder and new potatoes simmer in a tomato and rosemary sauce.

Makes 6 servings.

- 2 tablespoons olive or vegetable oil
- 2 tablespoons butter or margarine
- 1 large onion, sliced
- 2 pounds boneless lamb shoulder, cut into 1-inch cubes
- ½ cup dry white wine or chicken broth
- 1 teaspoon salt
- ½ teaspoon pepper
- ½ teaspoon leaf rosemary, crumbled
- 2 large tomatoes, peeled, seeded and chopped
  OR: 1 can (1 pound) whole tomatoes
- 12 small new potatoes

1. Heat oil and butter or margarine in an open 6-quart pressure cooker; add onion and sauté until soft. Remove with slotted spoon. Brown lamb, removing cubes as they brown.
2. Add wine to cooker; boil rapidly until reduced to half. Return meat and onion; sprinkle with salt, pepper and rosemary; add tomatoes.
3. Close cover securely; put pressure control on vent (15 pounds, if your control has multi-pressure selections). Turn heat on high until pressure rises and control starts to rock, about 5 minutes. Reduce heat slowly to medium-low so control rocks gently; cook 10 minutes.
4. Remove pressure cooker from heat; let cool about 5 minutes. Then place closed cooker under running water until pressure is reduced and no steam hisses; carefully remove control and cover.
5. Add potatoes. Close cover securely; place pressure control on vent; bring up to pressure again on high heat. Lower heat; cook 4 to 5 minutes.
6. Again reduce pressure by placing closed cooker under running water until pressure is reduced and no steam hisses. Carefully remove control and cover.

HAWAIIAN PORK

A Chinese recipe inspired the flavor of this juicy pork roast. It takes time to roast, but only minutes to prepare.

Roast at 325° for 2 hours.
Makes 6 servings.

- 1 pork loin (about 4 pounds)
- ⅓ cup chopped green onion
- 1 can (6 ounces) frozen concentrate for pineapple-orange juice
- ⅓ cup soy sauce
- 3 acorn squash, halved and seeded
- 1 orange

1. Place pork, fat side up, on rack in a roasting pan. Make deep cuts (about 2 inches) with the tip of a knife into meat between each chop; fill each cut with onion, dividing evenly. If using a meat thermometer, insert bulb into center of meat without touching bone.
2. Combine pineapple-orange juice concentrate and soy sauce in a 2-cup measure. Spoon over pork; arrange squash, cut-side down, around pork.
3. Roast in slow oven (325°) 1 hour, 30 minutes. Brush pork with soy mixture. Continue roasting 30 minutes longer, brushing several times with soy mixture, or until thermometer registers 170° and pork is richly glazed.
4. Garnish roast with orange cut into wedges. Carve roast between ribs into serving-size pieces.

CHICKEN À LA KING

The chef at Delmonico's in New York named this dish for a debonair Victorian sportsman, Foxhall Keene.

Makes 4 servings.

- ¼ cup (½ stick) butter or margarine
- ¼ cup all purpose flour
- 2 tablespoons finely chopped onion
- 1 teaspoon salt
- ½ teaspoon Worcestershire sauce
- 2 cups milk
- 2 cups diced cooked chicken or turkey
- ¼ cup diced pimiento (about 4 pimientos)
- 1 can (3 or 4 ounces) sliced mushrooms
  Toast triangles

1. Melt butter or margarine in a medium-size saucepan.
2. Blend in flour, onion, salt and Worcestershire sauce. Cook, stirring constantly, until mixture bubbles; stir in milk.
3. Cook over low heat, stirring constantly, until sauce thickens and bubbles 3 minutes.
4. Stir in chicken, pimiento and mushrooms with their liquid; heat thoroughly.
5. Spoon over toast triangles and serve with an orange and carrot salad, if you wish.

Shown from left to right on pages 22 and 23 are: Pressure Cooker—Harvest Glazed Pork, Toaster Oven—Sausage Hero, Electric Wok—Ratatouille Chicken, Electric Slow Cooker—Stout-Braised Short Ribs, Electric Frypan—Vermont Ham Platter, and Microwave Oven—Barbecued Turkey. Recipes start on this page.

Pressure Cooker

HARVEST GLAZED PORK

Choose the size pork loin that fits your pressure cooker and have a fork-tender roast in less than an hour. Shown on page 22.

Makes 6 servings.

    1 pork loin (about 3 pounds)
    1 teaspoon salt
    ¼ teaspoon pepper
    1½ cups fresh cranberries (from a
        1-pound package)
    ¾ cup sugar
    ¼ cup frozen chopped onion
    1 teaspoon grated orange rind
    ¾ cup orange juice
    ½ teaspoon pumpkin pie spice
    2 packages (10 ounces each)
        frozen broccoli spears
        Poached fresh or canned pear
        halves

1. Rub pork with salt and pepper. Heat an open 6-quart pressure cooker; brown pork well on all sides in its own fat; remove and reserve.
2. Combine cranberries, sugar, onion, orange rind and juice and pumpkin pie spice in pressure cooker; bring to boiling. Return pork to pressure cooker; spoon part of cranberry glaze over to coat well.
3. Close cover securely; put pressure control on vent (15 pounds, if your control has multi-pressure selections). Turn heat on high until pressure rises and control starts to rock, about 5 minutes.
4. Reduce heat slowly to medium-low so control rocks gently; cook 50 minutes.
5. Remove pressure cooker from heat; let cool about 5 minutes. Then place closed cooker under running water until pressure is reduced and no steam hisses; carefully remove control and cover.
6. Remove pork loin to heated serving dish and keep warm. Add frozen broccoli to pressure cooker over cranberry glaze; cover pressure cooker.
7. Cook 5 minutes in open cooker, or until broccoli is crisply tender. Arrange broccoli around pork in serving dish; spoon part of cranberry glaze

over pork loin. Arrange pear halves in serving dish; fill hollows with remaining cranberry mixture.

ITALIAN CHICKEN STEW

Pungent oregano adds the classic flavor to chicken and vegetables.

Makes 4 servings.

    1 broiler-fryer, cut up (3 pounds)
    3 tablespoons olive or vegetable oil
    2 medium-size onions, sliced
    2 teaspoons salt
    ½ teaspoon pepper
    1 cup sliced celery
    2 cups diced potatoes
    1 can (8 ounces) whole tomatoes
    1 teaspoon leaf oregano, crumbled
    3 tablespoons chopped parsley
    1 cup water
    1 package (10 ounces) frozen peas

1. Brown chicken pieces, a few at a time, in oil in an open 6-quart pressure cooker; remove pieces as they brown. Add onions to pan; sauté 5 minutes. Return chicken; add salt, pepper, celery, potatoes, tomatoes, oregano, parsley and water, bring to boiling.
2. Close cover securely; put pressure control on vent (15 pounds, if your control has multi-pressure selections). Turn heat on high until pressure rises and control starts to rock, about 5 minutes.
3. Reduce heat slowly to medium-low so control rocks gently; cook 10 minutes.
4. Remove pressure cooker from heat; let cool about 5 minutes. Then place closed cooker under running water until pressure is reduced and no steam hisses; carefully remove control and cover.
5. Add peas; cook in open cooker 5 minutes, or until peas are tender. Serve hot with linguine, if you wish.

BOSTON BEEF DINNER

You don't need hours to prepare corned beef and cabbage with a pressure cooker.

Makes 6 servings.

    1 corned beef brisket (about 4
        pounds)
    1 bay leaf
    6 peppercorns
    1 onion, stuck with 2 whole cloves
    1 carrot, sliced
    1 stalk celery, sliced
    2 sprigs parsley
    1 cup apple cider
    6 carrots, pared and halved
        crosswise
    6 new potatoes, scrubbed
    1 small cabbage, cut into 6 wedges

1. Wash corned beef under cold running water. Place in a 6-quart pressure cooker; add bay leaf, peppercorns, onion with cloves, sliced carrot,

celery, parsley and apple cider. Add enough water to just cover meat. (Do not fill cooker more than ⅔ full.)
2. Close cover securely; put pressure control on vent (15 pounds, if your control has multi-pressure selections). Turn heat on high until pressure rises and control starts to rock, about 5 minutes. Reduce heat slowly to medium-low so control rocks gently; cook 30 minutes.
3. Remove pressure cooker from heat; let cool about 5 minutes. Then place closed cooker under running water until pressure is reduced and no steam hisses; carefully remove control and cover.
4. Remove corned beef to platter; keep warm. Add carrots and potatoes to cooker; cover; cook in open cooker 15 minutes. Add cabbage; cover; cook in open cooker 15 minutes longer, or until vegetables are tender.
5. Slice corned beef and arrange on platter with vegetables. Serve with Dijon mustard and gherkin pickles.

SPEEDY SWISS STEAK

Now you can serve this family favorite even on busy workdays.

Makes 6 servings.

    2 tablespoons vegetable oil
    2 pounds beef chuck steak, about
        1-inch thick
    2 teaspoons salt
    ¼ teaspoon pepper
    1 medium-size onion, chopped
        (½ cup)
    1 can (1 pound) stewed tomatoes
    1 tablespoon all purpose flour
    1 tablespoon Worcestershire sauce
    1 clove garlic, crushed
    4 large potatoes, pared and
        quartered
    1 package (10 ounces) frozen peas

1. Heat a 6-quart pressure cooker until hot; add oil; brown steak on both sides. Add salt and pepper. Sauté onion for the last few minutes.
2. Combine stewed tomatoes, flour, Worcestershire sauce and garlic; pour over steak. Add potatoes.
3. Close cover securely; place pressure control on vent (number 10, if your control has multi-pressure selections); turn heat on high until pressure rises and control starts to rock, about 5 minutes. Reduce heat slowly to medium-low so control rocks gently; cook 30 minutes.
4. Remove pressure cooker from heat; let cool about 15 minutes. Carefully remove control and cover
5. Remove steak and potatoes to heated platter and keep warm.
6. Heat sauce to boiling; add peas; cook in open pressure cooker 5 minutes; remove peas to heated platter with slotted spoon. Pass sauce in heated sauceboat.

NAPA VALLEY POT ROAST

Beef simmers in red wine with zucchini and mushrooms—so delicious, yet simple.

Makes 8 servings.

- 1 round, rump or chuck roast (4 pounds)
- 2 teaspoons salt
- ¼ teaspoon pepper
- ¼ teaspoon ground ginger
- 2 tablespoons vegetable oil
- 2 tablespoons butter or margarine
- 2 cloves garlic, minced
- 3 medium-size onions, chopped (1½ cups)
- 1 cup dry red wine
- 1 cup beef broth
- 2 medium-size zucchini, cut into chunks
- ¼ pound small mushrooms
- 1 cup pitted black olives
- ¼ cup all purpose flour
- ½ cup cold water

1. Rub roast with salt, pepper and ginger. Heat oil and butter or margarine in an open 6-quart pressure cooker; add beef; brown on all sides. Sauté garlic and onions in drippings the last 5 minutes of browning. Add wine and broth. Bring to boiling.
2. Close cover securely; put pressure control on vent (15 pounds, if your control has multi-pressure selections). Turn heat on high until pressure rises and control starts to rock, about 5 minutes. Reduce heat slowly to medium-low so control rocks gently; cook 35 minutes.
3. Remove pressure cooker from heat; let cool about 5 minutes. Then place closed cooker under running water until pressure is reduced and no steam hisses; carefully remove control and cover. Remove beef to heated platter and keep warm.
4. Add zucchini, mushrooms and olives to sauce. Simmer 15 minutes in open pressure cooker, or just until vegetables are tender. Lift vegetables from sauce with slotted spoon; arrange around roast on platter. Skim off excess fat from sauce. Combine flour and cold water in a cup until smooth; stir into bubbling sauce. Cook, stirring constantly, 3 minutes. Spoon part of sauce over meat and vegetables. Serve remaining sauce separately. Carve meat into ¼-inch slices. Serve with sourdough bread, if you wish.

PRESSURE COOKER TIPS

- Do not attempt to remove the control or cover from the pressure cooker until the pressure is reduced—by allowing pressure to drop normally of its own accord by removing pressure cooker from heat (5 to 15 minutes, depending on amount of food in cooker) or with quick-cooling by setting closed cooker under faucet of cold running water (just a few minutes).
- After reducing pressure, nudge control with tines of fork. If you hear hisses, pressure is not reduced, so continue cooling. When there are no more "hisses," remove control with tines of fork; then remove cover.
- Do not attempt to remove cover if you have to tug or use force to pry handles apart. Continue to cool under cold running water. (**Note:** Some pressure cookers have an automatic air-vent valve which rises when pressure is up and goes down when pressure is reduced.)
- Before using cooker, be sure that vent pipe is open. Clean with wooden pick or pipe cleaner. Check by looking through hole while you hold cover up against light.
- Be sure to add enough liquid to cooker so steam forms and builds up pressure. Check recipe or instruction book for amount.
- Do not fill cooker more than ⅓ full.
- Do not cook cranberries, barley, applesauce, split peas, pea soup, rhubarb, cereals, noodles, macaroni or spaghetti in pressure cooker. These foods get frothy and may block the vent pipe.
- Reduce heat after pressure is reached and control starts to rock; begin timing from this point.
- Store pressure cooker with cover inverted on top of cooker and paper towel between.

Each pressure cooker has slight design differences, so follow your manufacturer's instructions. If you have lost your instruction book, write to the manufacturer. The two major firms are: Mirro Aluminum Co., Manitowoc, Wis. 54220, and National Presto Industries, Eau Claire, Wis. 54701.

BARBECUED BEEF RIBS

They'll cheer when you serve this hearty, spicy dish on a blustery night.

Makes 6 servings.

- 5 to 6 pounds beef short ribs
- 1 cup chili sauce
- ½ cup water
- 1 medium onion, chopped (½ cup)
- 1 clove garlic, crushed
- ¼ cup firmly packed brown sugar
- 2 tablespoons wine vinegar
- 2 teaspoons salt
- 2 teaspoons prepared mustard
- ¼ teaspoon bottled red pepper seasoning
- ½ teaspoon liquid smoke (optional)
- 4 large potatoes, pared and quartered
- 4 large carrots, pared and quartered

1. Brown short ribs, part at a time, in an open 6-quart pressure cooker; remove and reserve.
2. Combine chili sauce, water, onion, garlic, brown sugar, wine vinegar, salt, prepared mustard, red pepper seasoning and liquid smoke, if used, in a medium-size mixing bowl. Add half of chili sauce mixture to pressure cooker. Add browned ribs, potatoes and carrots. Pour remainder of sauce over ribs, making sure to coat all. Close cover securely; place pressure control on vent (number 10, if your control has multi-pressure selections). Turn heat on high until pressure rises and control starts to rock, about 5 minutes.
3. Reduce heat slowly to medium-low so control rocks gently; cook 35 minutes.
4. Remove pressure cooker from heat; let cool about 5 minutes. Then place closed cooker under faucet of running water until pressure is reduced and no steam hisses. Carefully lift off control and cover; remove short ribs and vegetables to warm serving plate.
5. Skim excess fat from sauce; reheat, if necessary. Pour into warm sauceboat and pass with short ribs and vegetables.

ALMOND PORK AND BEEF

Whole almonds give the finishing touch to pork stew, Tex-Mex style.

Makes 8 servings.

- 3 tablespoons vegetable shortening
- 1½ pounds lean chuck, cubed
- 1½ pounds smoked pork butt, cubed
- 1 large onion, chopped (1 cup)
- 2 cloves garlic, minced
- 2 green chili peppers, seeded and chopped (from a 4-ounce can)
- 2 large red peppers, halved, seeded and chopped
- 2 bay leaves
- 1 teaspoon leaf oregano, crumbled
- 1 teaspoon salt
- ½ teaspoon pepper
- ½ teaspoon ground cumin
- 1 can (1 pound) whole tomatoes
- ¼ cup lemon juice
- 1 cup raisins
- 1 cup whole blanched almonds

1. Heat shortening in an open 6-quart pressure cooker. Brown beef cubes on all sides, about half at a time, removing pieces as they brown. Add pork, onion and garlic. Cook, stirring often, 5 minutes. Return beef; add chili peppers, red peppers, bay leaves, oregano, salt, pepper, cumin and tomatoes; bring to boiling.
2. Close cover securely; put pressure control on vent (15 pounds, if your control has multi-pressure selections). Turn heat on high until pressure rises and control start to rock, about 5 minutes. Lower heat to medium so control rocks gently; cook 15 minutes.

3. Remove pressure cooker from heat and let cool about 5 minutes. Place closed cooker under running water until pressure is reduced and no steam hisses. Carefully remove control and cover.

4. While meat cooks, pour lemon juice over raisins in a small bowl; allow to stand. Stir raisins and lemon juice and almonds into stew in cooker to blend. Serve over crushed corn chips or boiled rice.

POTTED VEAL SHOULDER

White wine and herbs flavor this veal dish. You can substitute boned and rolled pork.

Makes 6 servings.

- 3 pounds boneless veal shoulder, rolled and tied
- 1 clove garlic
- 1½ teaspoons salt
- ¼ teaspoon pepper
- 1 teaspoon leaf thyme, crumbled
- 1 tablespoon butter or margarine
- 1 small onion, chopped (¼ cup)
- 1 stalk celery, chopped
- 1 carrot, chopped
- 1¼ cups dry white wine
- 6 carrots, peeled and cut in half
- 8 small potatoes, with strip peeled from center
- 1 pound green beans, tipped
- 3 tablespoons all purpose flour
- ⅓ cup cold water

1. Rub veal shoulder roast with cut end of garlic, then with salt, pepper and thyme.

2. Melt butter or margarine in a 6-quart pressure cooker; brown veal on all sides. Remove and reserve.

3. Add onion, chopped celery and carrot to cooker and sauté until soft.

4. Add wine; place browned roast on chopped vegetables, basting with sauce. Close cover securely; place pressure control on vent (number 10, if your control has multi-pressure selections). Turn heat on high until pressure rises and control starts to rock, about 5 minutes. Reduce heat slowly to medium-low so control rocks gently; cook 30 minutes.

5. Remove cooker from heat; cool about 5 minutes. Place closed cooker under running water until pressure is reduced and no steam hisses. Carefully remove control and cover.

6. Add carrots, potatoes and green beans. Close cover securely; place pressure control on vent (number 15, if your control has multi-pressure selections). Turn heat on high until pressure rises and control starts to rock, about 5 minutes. Reduce heat to medium-low; cook 8 minutes.

7. Lower pressure immediately by putting cooker under cold running water for a few minutes. Carefully remove control and cover. Lift roast and vegetables to a serving platter;

keep warm.

8. Heat liquid to boiling in cooker; blend flour and cold water in a cup; stir into boiling liquid; cook, stirring constantly, until sauce thickens and bubbles 3 minutes. Serve with veal.

MELLOW BEEF BURGUNDY

Your pressure cooker makes quick work of a classic French beef dish.

Makes 8 servings.

- 5 slices bacon
- 3½ pounds beef chuck, cut into 2-inch cubes
- ½ pound mushrooms, sliced
- 2 cloves garlic, crushed
- 1 tablespoon salt
- ½ teaspoon pepper
- ⅓ cup all purpose flour
- 4 whole cloves
- 1 teaspoon leaf thyme, crumbled
- 1 bay leaf
- 1½ cups red Burgundy wine
- ¼ cup minced parsley
- 1 pound carrots, pared and cut into 2-inch pieces
- 12 small white onions, peeled
- 1 package (10 ounces) frozen peas

1. Fry bacon in open pressure cooker until crisp. Remove and reserve. Pour off all but 3 tablespoons bacon fat.

2. Brown beef, part at a time, in pan drippings; remove and reserve.

3. Add mushroom slices and garlic to cooker and sauté 2 minutes; remove mushroom slices with a slotted spoon and reserve.

4. Add beef cubes, salt and pepper to cooker; stir well. Then sprinkle flour over meat, stirring to blend well.

5. Tie cloves, thyme and bay leaf in a small piece of cheesecloth; drop into cooker. Add wine and parsley. Mix well. Crumble fried bacon and add.

6. Close cover securely. Place pressure control on vent (number 10, if your cooker has multi-pressure selections). Turn heat on high until control starts to rock, about 5 minutes. Slowly reduce heat to medium-low so control rocks gently; cook 20 minutes.

7. Remove cooker from heat immediately; place closed cooker under running water until pressure is reduced and no steam hisses. Carefully remove control and cover.

8. Add carrots and onions. Close cover securely; put pressure control on vent (number 10, if your control has multi-pressure selections); turn heat to high and bring up pressure again (when control starts to rock). Slowly reduce heat to medium-low and cook 3 minutes.

9. Again reduce pressure by placing cooker under running water. Carefully remove control and cover. Remove and discard spice and herb bag.

10. Add peas and mushrooms; cook in open cooker 3 minutes.

BEEFY VEGETABLE SOUP

You no longer have to spend the whole day preparing a stick-to-the-ribs soup.

Makes 6 servings.

- 1½ pounds beef chuck or round
- ½ pound cracked beef bones
- 6 cups water
- 1 large onion, sliced
- 2 cups sliced carrots
- 2 cups sliced celery
- ½ pound green beans, cut into 1-inch pieces
- 2 teaspoons salt
- ¼ teaspoon pepper
- 1 clove garlic, crushed
- 1 small bay leaf
- ½ teaspoon leaf thyme, crumbled
- 1 can (8 ounces) tomato sauce
- 2 cups cooked elbow macaroni
- Chopped fresh parsley

1. Place meat and bones in a 6-quart open pressure cooker; add water; bring to boiling; skim off scum.

2. Add onion, carrots, celery, green beans, salt, pepper, garlic, bay leaf, thyme and tomato sauce.

3. Close cover securely; put pressure control on vent (15 pounds, if your control has multi-pressure selections); turn heat on high until pressure rises and control starts to rock, about 5 minutes. Reduce heat slowly to medium-low so control rocks gently; cook 50 minutes.

4. Remove pressure cooker from heat; let cool about 5 minutes. Then place closed cooker under running water until pressure is reduced and no steam hisses.

5. Carefully remove control and cover. Skim fat from top of soup. Add cooked macaroni and simmer 5 minutes in open cooker. Sprinkle with chopped parsley and serve in heated soup bowls.

BEEF STEW DIJON

Just a touch of mustard and lemon gives this ragoût distinction.

Makes 4 servings.

- 1½ pounds lean chuck or round, cubed
- 2 tablespoons all purpose flour
- 2 tablespoons butter or margarine
- 2 tablespoons vegetable oil
- 2 cups sliced celery
- 4 large carrots, pared and cut into 2-inch pieces
- 1 cup beef broth
- ½ teaspoon salt
- ½ teaspoon leaf thyme, crumbled
- ½ teaspoon leaf marjoram, crumbled
- ¼ teaspoon pepper
- 1 tablespoon prepared Dijon mustard
- 2 tablespoons lemon juice
- 3 tablespoons chopped parsley

1. Shake beef with flour in a plastic

bag. Heat butter or margarine and oil in an open 4-quart pressure cooker. Add beef, part at a time; brown on all sides, removing pieces as they brown. Return all meat to cooker. Add celery, carrots, beef broth, salt, thyme, marjoram, pepper and mustard. Bring to boiling.

2. Close cover securely; put pressure control on vent (15 pounds, if your control has multi-pressure selections). Turn heat on high until pressure rises and control starts to rock, about 5 minutes. Reduce heat slowly to medium-low so control rocks gently; cook 15 minutes.

3. Remove pressure cooker from heat; let cool about 5 minutes. Then place closed cooker under running water until pressure is reduced and no steam hisses; carefully remove control and cover.

4. Let stand 10 minutes to blend flavors. Stir in lemon juice and parsley. Serve with buttered noodles or boiled new potatoes, if you wish.

LAMB À LA GRECQUE

You can brown the lamb and prepare the vegetables the evening before, then dinner is ready in minutes.

Makes 4 servings.

- 1 lemon
- 2 pounds lamb breast, cut into 4 pieces, or lamb riblets
- 2 teaspoons leaf marjoram, crumbled
- ½ teaspoon garlic salt
- ¼ teaspoon seasoned pepper
- 2 tablespoons olive or vegetable oil
- 1 medium-size onion, chopped
  Rind and juice of 2 lemons
- ½ cup water
- 4 medium-size boiling potatoes, peeled
- 1 pound green beans, tipped and cut into 1-inch pieces
- 1 tablespoon cornstarch
- ¼ cup cold water
  Fresh lemon wedges

1. Cut one-half lemon into slices and reserve. Use remaining half lemon to rub over lamb. Combine marjoram, garlic salt and pepper; rub seasonings into lamb pieces, coating evenly.

2. Heat oil in open pressure cooker and brown lamb, removing and reserving pieces as they brown. Sauté onion in remaining oil until soft. Stir in lemon rind, juice and water; bring to boiling. Replace lamb pieces; add potatoes, beans and lemon slices.

3. Close cover securely. Put pressure control on vent (15 pounds, if your control has multi-pressure selections). Turn heat on high until pressure rises and control starts to rock, about 5 minutes.

4. Reduce heat slowly to medium-low so control rocks gently; cook 10

minutes. Remove from heat; let cool about 5 minutes. Then place closed cooker under running water until pressure is reduced and no steam hisses; remove control and cover.

5. Remove lamb and vegetables to an ovenproof platter; cover loosely with aluminum foil and keep warm. Skim fat from remaining liquid. Discard lemon slices. Blend cornstarch with cold water; add to liquid in pressure cooker. Cook, stirring constantly, until sauce thickens and bubbles 1 minute. Serve over lamb and vegetables. Garnish with lemon wedges.

HAM AND BEAN SOUP

This hearty Italian-style soup starts with dried beans and a ham hock flavored with rosemary.

Makes 8 servings

- 1 package (1 pound) dried Great Northern or small lima beans
- 10 cups water
- 2 tablespoons olive or vegetable oil
- 1 large onion, chopped (1 cup)
- 1 large carrot, diced
- 1 stalk celery with top, chopped
- 2 leeks, chopped (optional)
- 1 clove garlic, minced
- ½ teaspoon leaf rosemary, crumbled
- 1 canned green chili pepper
- 1 leftover ham bone with some meat, cracked
  OR: 2 ham hocks (about 1 pound each)
- 2 teaspoons salt
- ½ teaspoon pepper
  Parmesan cheese
  Thinly sliced onion or leek

1. Pick over and wash beans; drain and combine with 6 cups of the water in a large saucepan; bring to boiling; cover. Cook 2 minutes; remove from heat; let stand 1 hour.

2. Heat oil in a 6-quart pressure cooker; add onion, carrot, celery, leeks, garlic, rosemary and chili pepper; sauté 5 to 8 minutes, or until lightly browned. Stir in beans and liquid, ham bone, salt, pepper and 2 to 4 cups water. (Do not fill pressure cooker over ⅔ full.) Bring to boiling.

3. Close cover securely; put pressure control on vent (15 pounds, if your control has multi-pressure selections). Turn heat on high until pressure rises and control starts to rock, about 5 minutes. Reduce heat slowly to medium-low so control rocks gently; cook 25 minutes.

4. Remove pressure cooker from heat; let cool about 5 minutes. Then place closed cooker under running water until pressure is reduced and no steam hisses; carefully remove control and cover.

5. Remove ham bone, returning any meat to soup. Purée about half the

beans through a sieve. Return purée to soup; heat through. Serve in heated soup bowls; garnish with cheese and onion or leek slices.

Toaster Oven

SAUSAGE HERO

Crusty hero rolls make an eatable dish for a whole-meal sandwich. Photo page 22.

Bake at 350° for 10 minutes.
Makes 4 servings.

- 1 pound sweet Italian sausages
- 1 large onion, sliced
- 1 large green pepper, halved, seeded and cubed
- ¼ pound mushrooms, sliced
  OR: 1 can (4 ounces) sliced mushrooms, drained
- 1 can (4 ounces) pimiento, drained and cut into cubes
- 1 teaspoon garlic salt
- 1 teaspoon mixed Italian herbs
- ¼ teaspoon seasoned pepper
- 2 large hero rolls
- 1 medium-size tomato, thinly sliced
- 4 slices Swiss cheese, cut into triangles

1. Prick sausages with a fork; cook slowly, turning often, in a large skillet; remove and drain on paper towels.

2. Pour off all but 3 tablespoons fat; sauté onion, green pepper, mushrooms and pimiento in skillet 5 minutes; season with garlic salt, Italian herbs and pepper.

3. Cut a thin slice from tops of hero rolls; hollow out rolls with a dinner fork. (Save tops and crumbs for a casserole topping.)

4. Spoon part of vegetable mixture into each roll; layer sliced tomatoes over, then top with remaining vegetable mixture. Arrange sausages on rolls and top with cheese triangles.

5. Bake, one hero at a time, in toaster oven set at moderate (350°) 10 minutes, or until cheese melts. Cut first hero into 4 portions and serve while second sandwich heats.

HAM-STUFFED POTATOES

Ham leftovers and chopped green onions make a savory stuffing for baked potatoes.

Bake at 400° for 1 hour,
then at 350° for 15 minutes.
Makes 4 servings.

- 4 baking potatoes, scrubbed
- 1 tablespoon butter or margarine
- 1 tablespoon all purpose flour
- 1 teaspoon salt
- ¾ cup milk
- ½ cup mayonnaise or salad dressing
- 2 cups diced cooked ham
- ½ cup diced celery
- ¼ cup chopped green onion

1. Bake potatoes in toaster oven set at hot (400°) 1 hour, or until tender

when pierced with a two-tined fork.

2. Melt butter or margarine over low heat in a medium-size saucepan; stir in flour and salt; cook, stirring constantly, until mixture bubbles.

3. Stir in milk; continue cooking and stirring until sauce thickens and bubbles 3 minutes; remove from heat. Blend in mayonnaise or dressing.

4. Cut a thin slice across top of each potato, then scoop out potato in big chunks; dice and add to sauce. Fold in ham, celery and onion. Heap mixture into potato shells.

5. Bake in toaster oven set at moderate (350°) 15 minutes.

ALL AMERICAN CASSEROLE

Boston is famous for beans; from "Ladies Choices' II," a cookbook for Carney Hospital, comes this easy and delicious recipe. To order a copy, see Buyer's Guide.

Bake at 400° for 35 minutes.
Makes 8 servings.

- 1 pound frankfurters, cut into 1-inch pieces
- 2 cans (28 ounces each) Boston-style baked beans
- ½ cup frozen chopped onion
- ½ cup chopped green pepper
- ⅔ cup bottled barbecue sauce

1. Combine frankfurters, baked beans, onion, pepper and barbecue sauce in a large bowl. Divide mixture between two 4-cup rectangular casseroles.

2. Bake, one at a time, in toaster set at hot (400°) 35 minutes, or until bubbly hot. Serve casserole with brown bread and marmalade, or cole slaw, if you wish.

GREEK OLIVE CHICKEN

Half a roasting chicken is the perfect size for a twosome.

Bake at 350° for 1 hour, 30 minutes.
Makes 2 servings.

- ½ roasting chicken (about 2½ pounds)
- 1 teaspoon salt
- ¼ teaspoon pepper
- ¼ cup olive or vegetable oil
- ¼ cup red cooking wine
- ⅓ cup pitted black olives
- 1 clove garlic
- 1 teaspoon leaf oregano, crumbled
- ½ teaspoon leaf basil, crumbled

1. Place chicken in a shallow toaster oven-size aluminum foil pan; sprinkle with salt and pepper.

2. Combine oil, cooking wine, olives, garlic, oregano and basil in container of electric blender; cover blender; process on high until smooth. Spoon over chicken to cover.

3. Bake in toaster oven set at moderate (350°) 1 hour, 30 minutes, basting several times with sauce, or until chicken is tender.

TUNA DINNER ITALIANO

Make up these foil packets early in the day. Let each family member bake his own in the electric toaster oven.

Bake at 400° for 30 minutes.
Makes 4 servings.

- 2 cans (6½ ounces each) tuna in vegetable oil
- ½ teaspoon salt
- ¼ teaspoon leaf basil, crumbled
- ¼ teaspoon pepper
- 2 teaspoons lemon juice
- 1 small eggplant, sliced ¼-inch thick
- 1 large onion, sliced
- 1 can (1 pound) tomatoes Grated Parmesan cheese

1. Mix tuna, salt, basil, pepper and lemon juice in a large bowl. Divide eggplant slices among four 12-inch foil squares. Top with tuna mixture, onion and tomatoes with liquid. Pull up ends of foil to seal foil packets. Refrigerate until serving time.

2. Bake in toaster oven set at hot (400°) 30 minutes, or until eggplant is tender. Sprinkle with Parmesan cheese, just before serving.

COOK'S TIP: Everyone arrived home at once? Then place foil packets on large cookie sheet and bake in conventional oven.

BROCCOLI-EGG BAKE

An easy and economical one-dish dinner you make without meat.

Bake at 350° for 30 minutes.
Makes 4 servings.

- 1 package (10 ounces) frozen broccoli
- 2 tablespoons butter or margarine
- 2 tablespoons all purpose flour
- ½ teaspoon salt
- ⅛ teaspoon pepper
- 1 cup milk
- ½ cup shredded process American cheese
  OR: ½ cup shredded Swiss cheese
- 6 hard-cooked eggs, shelled and sliced

1. Cook broccoli, following package directions; drain.

2. Melt butter or margarine in a small saucepan; blend in flour, salt and pepper; cook, stirring constantly, until bubbly; stir in milk.

3. Cook, stirring constantly, until sauce thickens and bubbles 3 minutes; add shredded cheese; stir until melted.

4. Arrange 2 layers each of broccoli and sliced eggs in a small shallow casserole; pour cheese sauce over.

5. Bake in toaster oven set at moderate (350°) 30 minutes, or until bubbly hot.

CURRIED HAM BAKE

Dinner's ready in minutes when you keep a few convenience foods on hand.

Bake at 400° for 10 minutes.
Makes 2 servings.

- 1 package (9 ounces) frozen small onions in cream sauce
- 1 cup frozen cut green beans (from a 1-pound bag)
- ¾ cup water
- 1 tablespoon butter or margarine
- ½ teaspoon curry powder
- 1 cup cubed cooked ham or turkey OR: 1 can (7 ounces) tuna, drained and flaked
- 1 can (5 ounces) refrigerated buttermilk flaky biscuits Sesame seeds

1. Combine frozen onions, green beans, water, butter or margarine and curry powder in a medium-size saucepan; bring to boiling; stir with a wooden spoon; cover saucepan; simmer 5 minutes.

2. Add ham, turkey or tuna and spoon into an 8x5x1-inch aluminum foil pan. Separate refrigerator biscuits into 10 pieces; overlap on top of curry mixture; sprinkle with sesame seeds.

3. Bake in toaster oven set at moderate (350°) 10 minutes, or until biscuits are golden.

CHILI CHIP CASSEROLE

This easy-on-the-cook casserole comes from "Company's Coming," a delightful cookbook published by the Ames Professional Chapter, Women In Communications, Inc. To order a copy, see Buyer's Guide.

Bake at 350° for 45 minutes.
Makes 6 servings.

- 1 pound ground beef
- 1 cup frozen chopped onion
- 1 envelope (about 1 ounce) chili seasoning mix
- 1 can (6 ounces) tomato paste
- ¾ cup water
- 1 bag (6 ounces) corn chips
- 1 can (1 pound) pinto beans, drained
- 2 cups shredded Cheddar cheese (8 ounces)

1. Brown beef in a large skillet until crumbly; stir in onion, chili seasoning mix, tomato paste and water; simmer 10 minutes.

2. Line two 4-cup rectangular casseroles with 1 cup corn chips each; spoon a quarter of the meat mixture into each casserole; sprinkle with a quarter of the pinto beans and ½ cup cheese; repeat layering with remaining meat mixture and beans; top with corn chips and cheese; cover with aluminum foil.

3. Bake, one casserole at a time, in toaster oven set at moderate (350°) 30 minutes; uncover casserole; bake 15 minutes longer, or until casserole is bubbly hot and cheese is melted.

TUNA RAMEKINS

A dish made from kitchen staples.

Bake at 400° for 15 minutes.
Makes 4 servings.

- 1 **can (7 ounces) tuna**
- 1 **pimiento, chopped**
- ½ **cup soft bread crumbs (1 slice)**
- 1 **can condensed cream of celery soup**
- ¼ **cup milk**
- 1 **cup canned peas, drained**
- 1 **package (8 ounces) refrigerator biscuits**

1. Drain tuna; break into small pieces into a medium-size bowl; add pimiento, bread crumbs, soup, milk and peas; mix well and spoon into 4 ramekins.
2. Flatten 4 biscuits; place on top of tuna in ramekins. Place remaining biscuits on a small baking pan.
3. Bake in toaster oven set at hot (400°) 15 minutes, or until biscuits are golden and tuna is hot. Bake biscuits after ramekins at 400° for 12 minutes.

DIXIE DANDY

Pantry shelf classics combine to make this hearty supper dish.

Bake at 400° for 20 minutes.
Makes 2 servings.

- 1 **cup applesauce**
- ⅛ **teaspoon ground ginger**
- ½ **can (12 ounces) pork luncheon meat**
  Whole cloves
- 1 **can (8 ounces) sweet potatoes, drained and sliced**
- ½ **cup apricot jam**
- ½ **teaspoon dry mustard**
- 1 **tablespoon water**

1. Mix applesauce and ginger in a small shallow baking dish.
2. Halve meat, lengthwise; stud each piece with cloves. Place on top of applesauce in dish; arrange sliced sweet potatoes around meat.
3. Combine jam, dry mustard and water in a 1-cup measure; spread evenly over meat and potatoes.
4. Bake in toaster oven set at hot (400°) 20 minutes, or until hot and richly glazed.

CLAM CASSEROLE

Easy and quite inexpensive.

Bake at 350° for 30 minutes.
Makes 4 servings.

- 1 **can (8 ounces) minced clams**
  Milk
- ⅓ **cup butter or margarine**
- 2 **tablespoons all purpose flour**
- 1 **egg**
- 1 **cup soft bread crumbs (2 slices)**

1. Drain liquid from clams into a 2-cup measure; add enough milk to make 1½ cups.
2. Melt half of the butter or margarine in a medium-size saucepan; stir in flour. Cook, stirring constantly, until bubbly. Stir in the 1½ cups liquid; continue cooking and stirring until mixture thickens and bubbles 3 minutes; remove from heat; cool. Beat in egg and minced clams.
3. Melt remaining butter or margarine in a small skillet; stir in bread crumbs. Heat slowly, shaking pan constantly, until crumbs are lightly toasted. Spoon half into a small shallow baking dish that will fit in toaster oven; top with clam mixture; sprinkle with remaining crumb mixture.
4. Bake in toaster oven set at moderate (350°) 30 minutes, or until heated through.

GAME HENS PROVENÇALE

Eggplant and zucchini bake along with delicate Cornish game hens in this delicious dinner for two.

Bake at 350° for 1 hour.
Makes 2 servings.

- 2 **frozen Cornish game hens, thawed (about 1 pound each)**
- 1 **teaspoon salt**
- ¼ **teaspoon pepper**
- 2 **tablespoons butter or margarine**
- 1 **cup frozen chopped onion**
- 1 **clove garlic, minced**
- ½ **small eggplant, diced**
- 2 **small zucchini, trimmed and sliced**
- 1 **medium-size tomato, diced**
- 1 **teaspoon mixed Italian herbs, crumbled**

1. Sprinkle hens with salt and pepper; brown in butter or margarine in a large skillet; remove to a small shallow baking dish.
2. Sauté onion and garlic until soft in pan drippings; add eggplant, zucchini, tomato and Italian herbs. Cook 2 minutes; add to baking dish; cover with aluminum foil.
3. Bake in toaster oven set at moderate (350°) 1 hour, or until hens and vegetables are tender.

PEPPER-BEAN CUPS

If all the family won't be home at once, bake for 20 minutes, then finish baking as they come home.

Bake at 350° for 30 minutes.
Makes 4 servings.

- 4 **large green peppers**
- 1 **pound ground beef**
- 1 **can (1 pound) pork and beans in tomato sauce**
- 1 **can (about 4 ounces) French fried onion rings**
- ½ **cup catsup**
- 1 **teaspoon prepared mustard**

1. Cut a thin slice from top of each pepper; scoop out seeds and membrane. Parboil peppers in a small amount of boiling salted water 10 minutes; drain well. Stand in an 8x5x1-inch aluminum foil pan.
2. Shape ground beef into a large patty in a skillet; brown 5 minutes on each side, then break into chunks.
3. Stir in pork and beans, half of the onion rings, catsup and mustard. Spoon into pepper cups, dividing evenly.
4. Bake in a toaster oven set at moderate (350°) 20 minutes; top with remaining onion rings. Bake 10 minutes longer, or until onions are hot and crisp.

Electric Wok

RATATOUILLE CHICKEN

Electric woks are great for stir-frying dishes in various international flavors. This dish captures the taste of Southern France. Shown on page 22.

Makes 4 servings.

- 4 **chicken fillets, cut into 1-inch pieces (see Cook's Tip)**
- 3 **tablespoons vegetable oil**
- 1 **clove garlic, minced**
- 1 **large onion, sliced**
- 1 **small zucchini, trimmed and cut into sticks**
- 1 **small yellow squash, trimmed and cut into sticks**
- 1 **small eggplant, cut into 1-inch pieces**
- 1 **large green pepper, halved, seeded and cut into cubes**
- 1 **large red pepper, halved, seeded and cut into cubes**
- ½ **pound mushrooms, sliced (see Cook's Tip)**
- 1 **can (1 pound) tomato wedges, drained**
- 2 **teaspoons salt**
- 1 **teaspoon mixed Italian herbs, crumbled**
- ¼ **teaspoon seasoned pepper**

1. Heat electric wok to 375°. Brown chicken in oil and garlic; remove and reserve.
2. Stir-fry onion rings in wok 2 minutes; add zucchini, yellow squash, eggplant, peppers and mushrooms; stir-fry 3 minutes, or until vegetables are shiny and bright.
3. Return chicken to wok; add tomato wedges, salt, Italian herbs and pepper; stir-fry gently, just to blend; cover wok; lower temperature to 225°.
4. Steam 5 minutes, or just until vegetables are crisply tender. Serve with hot French bread, if you wish.
COOK'S TIP: Chicken fillets are sometimes labelled as boneless breast of chicken. To slice mushrooms neatly and quickly, use an egg slicer.

SHREDDED BEEF AND BEANS

A little meat goes a long way in this vegetable-meat combo.

Makes 6 servings.

- 2 tablespoons peanut or vegetable oil
- 1 pound beef round, cut into very thin strips
- 1 clove garlic, minced
- 2 cups sliced green beans
- 3 carrots, pared and thinly sliced
- 2 small zucchini, sliced
- 1 can (5 ounces) water chestnuts, sliced
- 2 teaspoons salt
- ⅛ teaspoon pepper
- 3 tablespoons soy sauce
- 1 cup water
- 1 tablespoon cornstarch
- 1 tablespoon dry Sherry
- 4 cups hot cooked rice
  Toasted sliced almonds

1. Heat oil in an electric wok set at 360°; add beef; stir-fry until color turns from pink to brown.
2. Add garlic, beans, carrots, zucchini, water chestnuts, salt, pepper, soy sauce and ¾ cup of the water. Cover; lower temperature; simmer 5 minutes, or until vegetables are crisply tender.
3. Combine cornstarch, Sherry and remaining ¼ cup water in a cup; add to skillet; cook and stir gently just until sauce thickens and bubbles.
4. Spoon hot rice onto serving platter; spoon mixture over; sprinkle with toasted almonds.

CHINESE WOK DINNER

Stir-fry cooking is the way to serve a delicious dinner in a short time.

Makes 4 servings.

- 1 pound round steak
  OR: 2 whole chicken breasts (about 12 ounces each)
- ⅓ cup soy sauce
- ⅓ cup sake, dry Sherry or chicken broth
- 4 tablespoons peanut or vegetable oil
- 1 clove garlic, halved
- 1 small acorn squash, halved, seeded, cubed and cooked 5 minutes
- 1 cup cut green beans
- 1 small yellow squash, tipped and sliced
- 1 cup sliced mushrooms
- 1 package (6 ounces) frozen Chinese snow peas, thawed
- 1 package (10 ounces) fresh spinach, washed and trimmed
- 3 cups shredded Chinese cabbage

1. Cut beef into thin strips or remove skin and bones from chicken and cut into 1-inch pieces. Combine beef or chicken with soy sauce and sake, Sherry or chicken broth in a glass bowl; marinate 15 minutes.
2. Turn electric wok to 375° and add 2 tablespoons of the oil; heat until sizzling; add garlic and cook 2 minutes; remove and discard garlic.
3. Remove beef or chicken from marinade and drain on paper towels, reserving marinade. Cook meat quickly in hot oil, stirring constantly; remove and keep warm.
4. Add remaining 2 tablespoons oil and heat; add acorn squash and green beans; toss until glistening with oil; push to one side; add yellow squash and mushrooms; toss in oil, then push to side; add snow peas, spinach and Chinese cabbage and toss.
5. Return meat to wok with reserved marinade and toss to blend well; lower temperature to 200° and cover wok.
6. Simmer 5 minutes, or until vegetables are crisp but tender. Serve with boiled rice, if you wish.

COOK'S TIP: The vegetables can be prepared ahead of time and arranged in a decorative pattern on a large flat tray; cover with plastic wrap, and chill in refrigerator with marinating beef or chicken, until ready to cook.

TORI SUKIYAKI

This one-pot chicken and vegetable dish is a Japanese classic prepared at the table—each diner cooks his own food in a simmering mixture of sugared soy sauce and sake.

Makes 4 servings.

- 2 whole chicken breasts (about 12 ounces each)
- 1 bunch green onions
- 1 large onion
- ½ pound mushrooms
- 1 package (10 ounces) fresh spinach
  OR: 2 cups shredded Chinese cabbage
- 1 package (4 ounces) thread noodles (harusame) (optional)
- 1 can (8 ounces) bamboo shoots (optional)
- 2 tablespoons peanut vegetable oil
- ½ cup soy sauce
- 2 tablespoons sugar
- 2 cakes soybean curd (tofu), cut into 1-inch cubes (optional)
- ½ cup sake or Sherry
- ½ teaspoon monosodium glutamate

1. Remove skin and bones from chicken; slice into thin strips.
2. Trim green onions and cut into 3-inch pieces; cut onion into ½-inch slices and separate into rings; cut mushrooms into ¼-inch slices; wash and drain spinach well; remove stems and break into small pieces.
3. If using harusame, bring 1 cup water to boiling; drop in harusame, return to boiling, then drain and cut noodles into thirds.
4. If using bamboo shoots, pare and cut in half, lengthwise; cut into thin slices, crosswise, and wash under running water; drain.
5. Arrange chicken, vegetables and harusame in neat rows on a large platter; cover platter with plastic wrap and refrigerate until serving time.
6. Preheat an electric wok set at 425° for several minutes. Rub part of oil over bottom.
7. Place ¼ of the chicken in wok; pour in 2 tablespoons of the soy sauce and sprinkle with part of the sugar. Cook 1 minute, stirring and turning, then push to one side.
9. Add ¼ each of green onions, onion, mushrooms, spinach, tofu, harusame and bamboo shoots, if used; sprinkle with 2 tablespoons of the sake or dry Sherry and monosodium glutamate. Cook, stirring often, 4 to 5 minutes, or until vegetables are crisp and tender. (If food begins to stick or burn, lower temperature and add a drop or two of cold water to wok.) Divide among 4 serving dishes; eat, then continue cooking and enjoying.

CHICKEN ALMOND

An Oriental favorite of white meat, delicate vegetables and toasted nuts.

Makes 6 servings.

- 3 whole chicken breasts, split (about 12 ounces each)
- 2 tablespoons peanut or vegetable oil
- 1 large onion, sliced
- 1½ cups chopped celery
- 1 package (6 ounces) frozen Chinese snow peas
  OR: 1 package (10 ounces) frozen peas
- ½ pound mushrooms, sliced
  OR: 1 can (3 or 4 ounces) sliced mushrooms
- 2 cups chicken broth
- 1½ teaspoons salt
- 2 tablespoons cornstarch
- ½ teaspoon ground ginger
- ¼ cup soy sauce
  Toasted slivered almonds

1. Remove chicken from bones; slice into thin strips. Brown chicken strips quickly in oil in an electric wok set at 360°; remove chicken from wok and keep warm.
2. Sauté onion in oil 2 minutes; push to side. Stir in celery and sauté 2 minutes; push to side. Place snow peas or peas, mushrooms and liquid and chicken strips in pan; pour in broth; add salt and cover. Lower temperature to 200° and steam 10 minutes, or until peas are tender.
3. Blend cornstarch and ginger with soy sauce in a cup; stir in 2 tablespoons water until smooth; stir into liquid in pan. Cook, stirring constantly, until sauce thickens and bubbles 3 minutes. Sprinkle with almonds.

CHICKEN SCARPARIELLO

"Scarpariello" in Italian means the shoe repair man, or this inexpensive dish with regal flavor.

Makes 6 servings.

- 3 whole chicken breasts (about 12 ounces each)
- ⅓ cup olive or vegetable oil
- 2 teaspoons salt
- ½ teaspoon freshly ground pepper
- 3 large zucchini, sliced
- 1 clove garlic, minced
- 2 tablespoons chopped chives or green onions
- ¾ cup diced mushrooms
- 1½ cups dry white wine
- ½ cup chicken broth
- 2 tablespoons minced parsley

1. Remove chicken from bones; cut into 1-inch pieces.
2. Heat oil in an electric wok set at 360°; sauté chicken until browned; sprinkle with salt and pepper. Add zucchini and toss to coat with oil. Mix in garlic and chives or green onions, then add mushrooms, wine and broth.
3. Bring to boiling; lower temperature to 200° and cover wok. Cook 10 minutes, or until chicken is tender. Sprinkle with parsley, before serving.

WOK ARROZ CON POLLO

Spanish dishes, too, can be part of an electric wok's repertoire.

Makes 6 servings.

- 3 whole chicken breasts (about 12 ounces each)
- 3 tablespoons vegetable oil
- 1 large onion, chopped (1 cup)
- 2 cloves garlic, minced
- 2 cups tomato juice
- 1 cup water
- 3 tomatoes, peeled and chopped
- 1 bay leaf
- ½ teaspoon ground saffron (optional)
- 1½ teaspoons salt
- ¼ teaspoon pepper
- 3 cups packaged precooked rice
- 1 medium-size green pepper, halved, seeded and diced
- 1 pimiento, sliced
- ¼ cup dry Sherry

1. Remove chicken from bones; and cut into 1-inch pieces. Brown quickly in oil in an electric wok set at 360°; remove chicken from wok and keep warm in a covered dish.
2. Add onion and garlic to wok; sauté until soft.
3. Return chicken to wok; add tomato juice, water, tomatoes, bay leaf, saffron, if used, salt and pepper. Cover; lower temperature to 200° and simmer 10 minutes.
4. Add rice, green pepper, pimiento and Sherry. Cover; cook 10 minutes, or until chicken is tender and liquid is absorbed.

POLYNESIAN FISH

Any evening you can turn your home into a Polynesian restaurant with this simple, delicious dish.

Makes 6 servings

- 2 packages (12 ounces each) frozen haddock or cod fillets
- 3 tablespoons soy sauce
- 3 tablespoons peanut or vegetable oil
- 2¼ cups pineapple juice
- ¼ cup cornstarch
- 1 can (8½ ounces) pineapple chunks in syrup
- 2 cans (3 or 4 ounces each) sliced mushrooms
- ½ teaspoon salt
- 1 package (6 ounces) frozen Chinese snow peas
  OR: 1 package (10 ounces) frozen peas
- 6 cups shredded Chinese cabbage
  Hot cooked rice

1. Cut fish into cubes on a wooden board with a heavy French knife.
2. Place soy sauce in pie plate; marinate fish in sauce 15 minutes.
3. Remove fish from marinade, reserving sauce; brown quickly in oil in an electric wok set at 360°.
4. Stir ½ cup pineapple juice into cornstarch in a cup to make a smooth paste; reserve.
5. Stir remaining pineapple juice, pineapple chunks, reserved marinade and mushrooms with liquid into chicken in pan; bring to boiling.
6. Stir in cornstarch mixture and salt; cook, stirring constantly, until sauce bubbles 1 minute. Cover; lower temperature to 200°; simmer 5 minutes.
7. Stir in snow peas or peas; arrange cabbage on top. Cover; cook 4 minutes, or until peas and cabbage are tender. Serve over hot cooked rice and with toasted almonds, if you wish.

JAMAICA STYLE RICE

Caribbean cooking goes Oriental style.

Makes 4 servings.

- 1 pound chicken livers, halved
- ¼ cup vegetable oil
- 1 medium-size onion, chopped (½ cup)
- ½ cup diced green pepper
- 1 clove garlic, minced
- 1½ cups packaged precooked rice
- 1½ cups tomato juice
- 1 can (6 ounces) sliced mushrooms
- 1 small can (4 ounces) pimiento, diced
- 1 teaspoon salt
  Dash freshly ground pepper
  Sliced green or black olives

1. Brown chicken livers in oil in an electric wok set at 360°; remove and keep warm.
2. Sauté onion, green pepper and

garlic in oil 3 minutes.
3. Return chicken livers to wok; add rice, tomato juice, mushrooms and liquid, pimiento, salt and a generous grind of a pepper mill.
4. Bring to boiling; turn off heat; let rice stand until all liquid is absorbed, about 5 minutes.
5. Fluff rice and garnish with olive slices.

TERIYAKI CHICKEN

Pork or shrimp can be substituted for the chicken in this recipe.

Makes 4 servings.

- 2 whole chicken breasts (about 12 ounces each)
- 3 tablespoons teriyaki or soy sauce
- 3 tablespoons peanut or vegetable oil
- 2 medium-size yellow squash, trimmed and sliced
- 1 package (9 ounces) frozen cut green beans
- 2 cups water
- 2 tablespoons dry Sherry or sake
- 1 can (8½ ounces) pineapple chunks in syrup
- 2 tablespoons cornstarch
- 1 can (5 ounces) water chestnuts, sliced

1. Remove chicken from bones; slice into thin strips.
2. Marinate chicken in teriyaki or soy sauce in a bowl 15 minutes.
3. Heat oil in an electric wok set at 360°; remove chicken from sauce, reserving sauce; brown chicken quickly in hot oil. Add squash and green beans. Sauté, stirring gently, 3 minutes, or just until shiny and moist. Add reserved teriyaki or soy sauce, water and Sherry or sake; cover wok and lower temperature to 200°; steam 5 minutes.
4. While vegetables steam, drain syrup from pineapple into small cup; stir in cornstarch to make a smooth paste.
5. Stir into bubbling liquid; cook, stirring constantly, 3 minutes; add pineapple chunks and water chestnut slices; cook 2 minutes. Serve over Chinese noodles, if you wish.

Electric Slow Cooker

STOUT-BRAISED SHORT RIBS

Guinness stout adds an Irish touch to fork-tender beef ribs; substitute beer or beef broth, if you wish.

Cook on 190° to 200° for 8 hours, or on 290° to 300° for 4 hours.
Makes 6 servings.

- 3 pounds beef short ribs
- 1 large onion, chopped (1 cup)
- 1 package (1 pound) carrots, pared and cut into 4-inch pieces
- 1 pound green beans, tipped

1 cup stout, beer or beef broth
1 bay leaf
2 teaspoons salt
¼ teaspoon pepper
3 tablespoons all purpose flour
⅓ cup cold water
¼ cup chopped parsley

1. Brown short ribs in their own fat in a large skillet or an electric slow cooker with a browning unit; remove and reserve; brown onion, carrots and green beans in pan drippings.
2. Place short ribs in slow cooker with vegetables; add stout, beer or beef broth; add bay leaf, salt and pepper; cover.
3. Cook on low (190° to 200°) 8 hours, or on high (290° to 300°) 4 hours, or until short ribs are tender; remove meat and vegetables to a heated serving platter and keep warm.
4. Turn heat control to high (290° to 300°); combine flour and cold water in a cup; stir into cooker with parsley; cover; cook 15 minutes. Spoon part of gravy over meat and vegetables and pass remainder in a heated gravy boat. Serve with Irish soda bread.

COQ AU LEEK

Delicate chicken and leeks combine with wine and herbs to make a memorable meal.

Cook on 190° to 200° for 8 hours, or on 290° to 300° for 4 hours.
Makes 4 servings.

1 broiler-fryer, cut up (2½ pounds)
2 tablespoons peanut or vegetable oil
1 large onion, chopped (1 cup)
1 clove garlic, minced
1 bunch leeks, washed and cut into 2-inch pieces
1 package (1 pound) carrots, pared and cut into 2-inch pieces
1 teaspoon leaf marjoram, crumbled
1 bay leaf
¼ teaspoon lemon pepper
½ cup white cooking wine
2 tablespoons cornstarch
¼ cup white cooking wine

1. Brown chicken in oil in a large skillet or an electric slow cooker with a browning unit; remove and reserve. Sauté onion and garlic until soft.
2. Place chicken, onion and garlic in slow cooker; add leeks, carrots, marjoram, bay leaf, lemon pepper and the ½ cup white wine; stir to blend; cover.
3. Cook on low (190° to 200°) 8 hours, or on high (290° to 300°) 4 hours, or until chicken is tender. Remove chicken and vegetables to a heated platter with a slotted spoon and keep warm.
4. Turn heat control to high (290° to 300°). Combine cornstarch and the ¼ cup wine in a cup; stir into liquid in slow cooker until well blended; cover; simmer 15 minutes. Spoon sauce over chicken and serve sprinkled with chopped parsley.

BUSY DAY POT ROAST

You don't brown the meat, and the vegetables are frozen—so ingredients are ready for the slow cooker in minutes.

Cook on 190° to 200° for 10 hours, or on 290° to 300° for 5 hours.
Makes 8 servings.

1 boneless rump or chuck pot roast (about 4 pounds)
2 bags (1 pound each) frozen vegetables for stew
1 cup red cooking wine OR: 1 cup tomato juice
1 teaspoon seasoned salt
½ teaspoon seasoned pepper
¼ cup all purpose flour
½ cup cold water

1. Place pot roast in an electric slow cooker; add frozen vegetables, wine or tomato juice, seasoned salt and pepper; stir to blend; cover cooker.
2. Cook on low (190° to 200°) 10 hours, or on high (290° to 300°) 5 hours, or until meat is tender when pierced with a two-tined fork. Remove meat and vegetables to a heated platter and keep warm.
3. Turn heat control to high (290° to 300°). Combine flour with cold water in a cup; stir into liquid in slow cooker until well blended; cover; simmer 15 minutes. Pass gravy in a heated gravy boat. Serve with mountains of fluffy mashed potatoes.

TUSCAN VEAL

Boneless veal breast and a trio of Italian vegetables make a super sauce for spaghetti.

Cook on 190° to 200° for 8 hours, or on 290° to 300° for 4 hours.
Makes 8 servings.

1 boneless veal breast (about 2 pounds)
2 tablespoons olive or vegetable oil
1 large onion, chopped (1 cup)
1 clove garlic, minced
1 small eggplant, diced (about 1 pound)
3 large zucchini, cut into 1-inch pieces
1 jar (15½ ounces) spaghetti sauce with mushrooms
1 teaspoon salt
1 teaspoon leaf oregano, crumbled
¼ teaspoon pepper

1. Brown veal in oil in a large skillet or an electric slow cooker with a browning unit; remove and reserve. Sauté onion and garlic in pan drippings until golden.
2. Place veal in slow cooker with onion and garlic; add eggplant, zucchini, spaghetti sauce, salt, oregano and pepper; stir to blend; cover.
3. Cook on low (190° to 200°) 8 hours, or on high (290° to 300°) 4 hours, or until veal is tender when pierced with a two-tined fork. Serve over hot spaghetti, if you wish.

MOLASSES BEAN MEDLEY

Pork chops and two varieties of beans bubble in a spicy sauce.

Cook on 190° to 200° for 8 hours, or on 290° to 300° for 4 hours.
Makes 6 servings.

6 link sausages (from a 1-pound package)
6 thin pork chops (about 1½ pounds)
2 large onions, sliced
2 large green peppers, halved, seeded and cut into strips
1 package (10 ounces) frozen Fordhook lima beans, thawed
1 can (1 pound) red kidney beans
1 can (1 pound) stewed tomatoes
⅓ cup dark molasses
2 tablespoons spicy prepared mustard
¾ teaspoon salt

1. Brown sausages in a large skillet or an electric slow cooker with a browning unit; remove and reserve. Brown pork chops in pan drippings; remove and reserve. Sauté onion and green peppers until soft.
2. Place sausages, pork chops, onion and green peppers in a slow cooker; add lima beans, kidney beans, stewed tomatoes, molasses, mustard and salt, stir to blend; cover cooker.
3. Cook on low (190° to 200°) 8 hours, or on high (290° to 300°) 4 hours, or until chops are tender. Serve with salad greens and a fruit plate, if you wish. Tall glasses of Sangria would go well with this meal.

DEVILED LAMB SHANKS

Meaty lamb shanks simmer in a mustardy onion sauce.

Cook on 190° to 200° for 8 hours, or on 290° to 300° for 4 hours.
Makes 4 servings.

4 lamb shanks (about 3½ pounds)
12 small white onions, peeled
1 clove garlic, minced
1 pound green beans, tipped
1 teaspoon leaf rosemary, crumbled
1 can condensed cream of onion soup
¼ cup water
2 tablespoons Dijon mustard

1. Trim excess fat from lamb shanks. Brown lamb shanks, two at a time, in a large skillet or an electric slow cooker with a browning unit; remove and reserve. Brown onions and garlic 5 minutes in pan drippings.
2. Place lamb shanks, onions, garlic and green beans in slow cooker; add rosemary, soup, water and mustard; stir to blend; cover cooker.
3. Cook on low (190° to 200°) 8 hours, or on high (290° to 300°) 4 hours, or until lamb shanks are very tender. Serve with crusty French bread, if you wish.

DIXIE HAM AND LIMAS

Dried lima beans and smoky ham bake in one big flavorful supper dish.

Cook on 190° to 200° for 10 hours,
   or on 290° to 300° for 5 hours.
Makes 8 servings.

 1 pound dried large lima beans
 4 cups cold water
 1 large onion, chopped (1 cup)
 1 can (1 pound) tomatoes
 3 cups diced cooked ham
 1 cup sliced celery
 1 cup pared shredded carrots
 2 teaspoons salt
 1 teaspoon leaf basil, crumbled
 ½ teaspoon leaf thyme, crumbled

1. Pick over beans and rinse. Combine beans and cold water in a large saucepan; cover. Bring to boiling; cook 2 minutes; remove from heat; let stand, stirring beans once, for 1 hour. (Or cover beans with water in slow cooker and soak overnight at room temperature.)
2. Pour beans with water into slow cooker; add onion, tomatoes, ham, celery, carrots, salt, basil and thyme; stir to blend; cover cooker.
3. Cook on low (190° to 200°) 10 hours, or on high (290° to 300°) 5 hours, or until beans are tender. Serve with toasted cornbread, if you wish.

SOUTHERN LAMB STEW

When you cook this economy cut of lamb, the tender meat falls off the bones.

Cook on 190° to 200° for 8 hours,
   or on 290° to 300° for 4 hours.
Makes 6 servings.

 4 pounds lamb riblets or breast of
    lamb, cut into serving-size
    pieces
12 small white onions, peeled
 3 large sweet potatoes, pared and
    cut into 1-inch pieces
 1 leek, washed and sliced
 2 cups water
 1 tablespoon salt
 1 tablespoon Worcestershire
    sauce
 1 teaspoon leaf rosemary,
    crumbled
 ¼ teaspoon pepper
 ¼ cup all purpose flour
 ½ cup cold water

1. Heat a large skillet or an electric slow cooker with a browning unit; brown lamb, a few pieces at a time, in pan; remove and reserve; brown onions in pan drippings.
2. Place lamb, onions, sweet potatoes and leek in slow cooker; add water, salt, Worcestershire sauce, rosemary and pepper; stir to blend; cover.
3. Cook on low (190° to 200°) 8 hours, or on high (290° to 300°) 4 hours, or until lamb is very tender. Remove meat and vegetables to a heated platter; keep warm.

4. Turn heat control to high (290° to 300°). Combine flour with cold water in a cup; stir into liquid in slow cooker until well blended; cover; simmer 15 minutes. Pass gravy in a heated gravy boat. Sprinkle meat with chopped fresh mint, if you wish.

CHILI BEAN SUPPER

Red pepper seasoning and chili powder give a South-of-the-Border flavor to beans.

Cook on 190° to 200° for 10 hours,
   or on 290° to 300° for 5 hours.
Makes 8 servings.

 1 package (1 pound) dry lima beans
 4 cups water
 2 cups cubed cooked ham
 1 can (1 pound) stewed tomatoes
 1 can (1 pound) whole kernel corn
 1 large onion, chopped (1 cup)
 1 tablespoon chili powder
 1 tablespoon Worcestershire sauce
    Few drops bottled red pepper
    seasoning

1. Pick over beans and rinse. Cover beans with water in a large kettle; bring to boiling; cover; cook 2 minutes; remove from heat; let stand 1 hour. (Or cover beans with water in slow cooker and soak overnight at room temperature.)
2. Pour beans and liquid into slow cooker; add ham, stewed tomatoes, whole kernel corn, onion, chili powder, Worcestershire sauce and red pepper seasoning; stir to blend; cover.
3. Cook on low (190° to 200°) 10 hours, or on high (290° to 300°) 5 hours, or until beans are tender. Serve with an avocado and romaine salad, if you wish.

SICILIAN BEANBAKE

Use hot or sweet Italian sausages, according to how hot you like your dishes.

Cook on 190° to 200° for 10 hours,
   or on 290° to 300° for 5 hours.
Makes 6 servings.

 1 package (1 pound) dried Great
    Northern beans
 6 cups water
 1 pound hot or sweet Italian
    sausages, sliced
 1 large onion, chopped (1 cup)
 1 clove garlic, minced
 1 can (1 pound) Italian tomatoes
 1 bay leaf
 2 teaspoons mixed Italian herbs,
    crumbled
 2 teaspoons salt
 ½ teaspoon freshly ground pepper

1. Pick over beans and rinse. Cover beans with water in a large kettle; bring to boiling; cover; cook 2 minutes; remove from heat; let stand 1 hour. Pour into an electric slow cooker. (Or cover beans with water in slow cooker and soak overnight at

room temperature.)
2. Brown sausages in a large skillet; push to one side; sauté onion and garlic in same pan until soft; stir in Italian tomatoes, bay leaf, mixed Italian herbs, salt and pepper; bring to boiling; stir into beans; cover cooker.
3. Cook on low (190° to 200°) 10 hours, or on high (290° to 300°) 5 hours, or until beans are tender. Serve with an antipasto salad, if you wish.

WEST COAST BEEF STEW

Pungent with spice, rich with a tomato-wine sauce, this stew is outstanding.

Cook on 190° to 200° for 8 hours,
   or on 290° to 300° for 4 hours.
Makes 6 servings.

 1½ pounds boneless beef chuck,
     cubed
  2 tablespoons all purpose flour
  1 teaspoon salt
  ½ teaspoon celery salt
  ½ teaspoon garlic powder
  ½ teaspoon ground ginger
  ¼ teaspoon pepper
  2 tablespoons vegetable oil
  2 large onions, sliced
  6 large carrots, pared and cut into
     2-inch pieces
  1 can (16 ounces) tomatoes
  ¼ cup dry red wine
  ¼ cup dark molasses
  ½ cup water
  ¼ cup raisins

1. Shake beef cubes in a plastic bag with flour, salt, celery salt, garlic powder, ginger and pepper to coat.
2. Heat oil in a large skillet or an electric slow cooker with a browning unit; brown meat cubes on all sides; remove and reserve. Sauté onion and carrots in pan drippings until golden.
3. Place beef, onion, carrots and tomatoes in slow cooker; add wine, molasses and water; stir to blend; cover cooker.
4. Cook on low (190° to 200°) 8 hours, or on high (290° to 300°) 4 hours, or until meat is very tender. Stir raisins into sauce and cook 5 minutes. Serve with fluffy mashed potatoes, if you wish.

PIQUANT POT ROAST

Dark molasses and spicy ginger add just the right touch of flavor to beef.

Cook on 190° to 200° for 10 hours,
   or on 290° to 300° for 5 hours.
Makes 8 servings.

 1 boneless chuck roast
    (about 4 pounds)
 1 teaspoon salt
 ¼ teaspoon freshly ground pepper
 ¼ cup (½ stick) butter or margarine
 1 package (1 pound) carrots, pared
    and cut into 2-inch pieces
 2 large onions, sliced
 ½ cup dark molasses

⅓ cup cider vinegar
1 can (13¾ ounces) beef broth
1 can (6 ounces) tomato paste
½ teaspoon ground ginger
⅓ cup all purpose flour
⅔ cup cold water

1. Trim excess fat from roast; rub with salt and pepper. Melt butter or margarine in a large skillet or an electric slow cooker with a browning unit; brown meat on all sides; remove and reserve. Sauté carrots and onion slices in pan drippings until vegetables are golden.
2. Place meat, carrots and onions in slow cooker; add molasses, vinegar, beef broth, tomato paste and ginger; stir to blend; cover cooker.
3. Cook on low (190° to 200°) 10 hours, or on high (290° to 300°) 5 hours, or until meat is very tender. Remove to a carving board; keep hot while finishing sauce.
4. Turn heat control to high (290° to 300°). Combine flour with cold water in a cup; stir into liquid in slow cooker until well blended; cover; simmer 15 minutes. Serve with hot buttered noodles, if you wish.

Electric Frypan

VERMONT HAM PLATTER

Maple-flavored pancake syrup adds the final touch to a smoky ham steak. Shown on page 23 with spinach-stuffed tomatoes and watermelon pickles.

Makes 4 servings.

1 ready-to-eat ham steak (about 1 pound)
3 tablespoons butter or margarine
1 tablespoon prepared mustard
1 can (1 pound) sweet potatoes, drained
4 small tomatoes
1 package (10 ounces) frozen creamed spinach, cooked
¼ cup maple-flavored pancake syrup

1. Brown ham steak in butter or margarine in an electric frypan set at 350°; stir prepared mustard into pan drippings; turn steak over in mixture to coat.
2. Add sweet potatoes to frypan and coat with pan drippings. Turn temperature control to 225°; cover frypan. Cook ham and vegetables for 15 minutes.
3. While steak cooks, hollow out tomatoes, saving tomato pulp for soup. Fill tomatoes with creamed spinach. Arrange tomatoes in frypan with ham and sweet potatoes. Brush ham and sweet potatoes with pancake syrup.
4. Cook 10 minutes, or until ham is nicely glazed. Serve with watermelon pickles, if you wish.

SKILLET LAMB AND LEEKS

Soup makes the sauce—leeks give the flavor.

Makes 6 servings.

1 tablespoon vegetable oil
6 shoulder lamb chops, ¾-inch thick (about 2 pounds)
1 can condensed tomato rice soup
½ cup water
½ teaspoon salt
¼ teaspoon caraway seeds
⅛ teaspoon pepper
1 bunch leeks or green onions, trimmed and halved, lengthwise

1. Heat oil in an electric frypan set at 350°; brown chops on both sides. Drain off drippings. Add soup, water, salt, caraway seeds and pepper.
2. Cover frypan and turn control to simmer. Cook 15 minutes. Add leeks or green onions and cover; cook 30 minutes longer. Serve with hot cooked rice, if you wish.

ELECTRIC FRYPAN CHICKEN

Don't have a slow cooker, but want to make recipes in this section? Use your electric frypan and follow the cooking directions in this recipe as a general guide.

Cook on "simmer" for 8 hours.
Makes 4 servings.

1 broiler-fryer, cut up (2½ pounds)
4 medium-size boiling potatoes, pared and quartered
8 small white onions, peeled
6 small zucchini, cut into 1-inch pieces
1½ cups water
2 envelopes or teaspoons instant chicken broth
2 teaspoons salt
1 teaspoon dillweed
½ pound mushrooms, quartered OR: 1 can (3 or 4 ounces) sliced mushrooms
¼ cup all purpose flour
½ cup cold water

1. Find "simmer" on your electric frypan by pouring 2 cups cold water into frypan and turning heat control to about 200°. (If there is no marking for 200°, try some place between the lowest setting on the control and the first temperature marking.) Allow water to heat until tiny pin-point bubbles begin to form on the bottom of the frypan. This is the simmer point. If water begins to boil, lower temperature control a little. (You want the pin-point bubbles, but not the rolling boil.) Pour out water and mark the simmer spot on heat control with red paint or nail polish.
2. Place chicken, potatoes, onions, zucchini, water, instant chicken broth, salt and dillweed in electric frypan; stir to blend well. (Don't worry that the water level is so low; the steam will baste the food.) Cover with frypan dome, making sure vents

are closed.
3. Turn heat control to "simmer" and cook 8 hours, or until chicken and vegetables are tender.
4. Turn heat control to 250° and add mushrooms; cook 5 minutes. Combine flour and cold water in a cup; stir into liquid in frypan; cover; cook 15 minutes.
COOK'S TIP: Recipes that have been tested on a higher setting (250°) of the electric frypan cook much more quickly than on the setting (290° to 300°) of the slow cooker. So it is wisest to follow only the "simmer" setting on the electric frypan for the low setting of the slow cooker recipes in this section.
Suggested Variations: One-and-a-half pounds cubed boneless lamb shoulder or pork shoulder can be substituted for the chicken in this recipe.

WESTWOOD SKILLET DINNER

Meatballs with a garden full of vegetables.

Makes 8 servings.

2 pounds ground meatloaf mixture
2 eggs
1 cup soft bread crumbs (2 slices)
¼ cup chopped parsley
2 teaspoons salt
1 large onion, chopped (1 cup)
1 medium-size head cabbage (about 2 pounds)
1 cup sliced pared carrots
1 cup mixed vegetable juice (see Cooks' Guide)
1 teaspoon leaf basil, crumbled
¼ teaspoon pepper
1 package (10 ounces) frozen Fordhook lima beans
1 package (10 ounces) frozen peas

1. Mix meatloaf mixture lightly with eggs, bread crumbs, chopped parsley and 1 teaspoon of the salt until well blended; shape meat mixture into 48 small balls.
2. Brown meat, half at a time, in an electric frypan set at 375°; remove and reserve.
3. Pour all but 3 tablespoons drippings from pan. Stir in onion and sauté just until soft.
4. Cut cabbage in half; slice one half into 8 wedges, then shred other half finely to make about 6 cups. Stir shredded cabbage into onion in pan; cook 2 minutes, or just until cabbage is wilted.
5. Stir in carrots, mixed vegetable juice, remaining teaspoon salt, basil and pepper. Arrange cabbage wedges around edge; cover. Bring to boiling, lower temperature to simmer, then cook 15 minutes.
6. Stir limas and peas into vegetables in frypan; top with meatballs; cover. Cook 15 minutes longer, or until limas are tender and meatballs are heated through.

DUCHESS MEATLOAF PIE

A variation of "meat and potatoes" with a hint of onion.

Makes 6 servings.

- 1 envelope onion soup mix
- ½ cup water
- 2 pounds ground beef
- 1 can (1 pound) stewed tomatoes
  Hot mashed potatoes

1. Stir soup mix into water in a 2-cup measure.
2. Measure out ¼ cup soup mixture and blend into ground beef in a large bowl. Shape mixture into a thick 8-inch round patty in an electric frypan; cut into 6 wedges.
3. Pour remaining soup mixture, then tomatoes, over meatloaf; cover.
4. Set temperature at 250° and cook 25 minutes, or until beef is done as you like it.
5. Spoon hot mashed potatoes into a mound on top of meat; dip gravy from bottom of frypan with a spoon and drizzle over.

RISOTTO ALLA MILANESE

This Italian specialty can be ready for the table in less than 30 minutes.

Makes 4 servings.

- 4 slices bacon, diced
- 1 pound chicken livers, halved
- ¼ cup all purpose flour
- 1 teaspoon salt
- ¼ teaspoon pepper
- 1 large onion, chopped (1 cup)
- 2 cups packaged precooked rice
- 2 envelopes or teaspoons instant chicken broth
- 1 teaspoon leaf basil, crumbled
- 1 bay leaf
- 2½ cups water
  Chopped parsley

1. Cook bacon until crisp in an electric frypan set at 360°; remove with a slotted spoon and reserve.
2. Shake chicken livers in a plastic bag with flour, salt and pepper.
3. Brown chicken livers in bacon drippings; remove with slotted spoon and reserve.
4. Sauté onion in drippings until soft. (If there is no fat remaining in wok, add 2 tablespoons vegetable oil.) Stir in rice, chicken broth, basil, bay leaf and water.
5. Bring to boiling; lower heat. Stir rice mixture well; return chicken livers; cover.
6. Lower temperature to 200°; simmer 10 minutes, or until liquid is absorbed and rice is tender; remove bay leaf. Sprinkle with reserved bacon and chopped parsley.

COOK'S TIP: If you have an electric wok and like to cook at the table, this recipe will work well in it.

HARVEST PORK CHOPS

Soy and ginger add zip to the pineapple-orange sauce.

Makes 6 servings.

- 1 can (6 ounces) frozen pineapple-orange juice concentrate
- 3 tablespoons soy sauce
- 2 teaspoons ground ginger
- 1 teaspoon salt
- ½ teaspoon leaf marjoram, crumbled
- 6 shoulder pork chops, cut 1-inch thick
- 2 acorn squash
- 3 pickled sweet red peppers, halved

1. Combine fruit juice, soy sauce, ginger, salt and marjoram in a 2-cup measure; let stand while browning chops.
2. Trim excess fat from chops; brown chops well in an electric frypan set at 375°; drain fat from pan; pour fruit juice mixture over chops.
3. Slice acorn squash into 1-inch-thick rings; remove seeds; halve rings; arrange with chops in pan; cover, being sure vents are closed.
4. Lower temperature to 225°; simmer, brushing chops and squash with glaze once or twice, 45 minutes, or until chops are tender.
5. Add pickled red peppers to pan 5 minutes before chops are done to heat thoroughly. Serve with boiled potatoes sprinkled with chopped parsley, if you wish.

30-MINUTE MEDLEY

First one home can have this skillet specialty ready in minutes.

Makes 4 servings.

- ¾ cup packaged precooked rice
- 1 can condensed cream of celery soup
- ¾ cup water
- 1 tablespoon butter or margarine
- 1 package (10 ounces) frozen peas, separated
- 1 can (3 ounces) sliced mushrooms
- 4 eggs
- 1 cup shredded Swiss cheese (4 ounces)
  Chopped parsley

1. Combine rice, soup, water and butter or margarine in an electric frypan; cover.
2. Set heat control to 350°; bring mixture to boiling; reduce heat to simmer; simmer 5 minutes.
3. Stir in frozen peas and simmer 5 minutes; stir in mushrooms.
4. Make 4 indentations in rice mixture. Break an egg into each indentation. Cover and continue cooking on simmer until eggs are almost set, about 3 to 5 minutes. Sprinkle with cheese. Cover and cook until eggs are set and cheese melts; about 5 minutes. Garnish with parsley.

CONFETTI SKILLET SUPPER

Flecks of tomato, corn and lima beans add color to this flavorful rice dish.

Makes 4 servings.

- 1 cup regular rice
- 1 cup frozen chopped onion
- 2 tablespoons butter or margarine
- 1 can (1 pound) stewed tomatoes
- 1 package (10 ounces) frozen baby lima beans
- 1 package (10 ounces) frozen whole kernel corn
- 2 teaspoons salt
- 1 teaspoon leaf oregano, crumbled
- ¼ teaspoon pepper
- 1 pound frankfurters

1. Sauté rice and onion in butter or margarine until onion is soft in an electric frypan set at 350°; add in tomatoes, lima beans, corn, salt, oregano, pepper and franks.
2. Lower temperature to 200°; simmer 30 minutes, or until liquid is absorbed and rice is tender. Fluff rice with fork just before serving.

COUNTRY SKILLET BEEF

Pot roast takes next to no time to fix when your electric frypan does most of the work.

Makes 8 servings.

- 1 blade- or round-bone chuck roast (4 pounds)
- 1 medium-size onion, sliced
- ½ cup dry red wine or water
- 1 teaspoon salt
- 6 peppercorns
- 1 bay leaf
- 8 medium-size potatoes, pared and halved
- 6 small zucchini, sliced
- 1 red pepper, sliced in rings and seeds removed
- ¼ cup all purpose flour
- ½ cup cold water

1. Brown beef in its own fat in an electric frypan set at 350°; remove and reserve. Drain all but 2 tablespoons fat from frypan.
2. Sauté onion until soft; add wine or water, salt, peppercorns and bay leaf. Return meat to frypan; cover.
3. Lower temperature to 225°; simmer 1 hour. Arrange potatoes around meat; cover; simmer 30 minutes. Place zucchini on meat; cover; simmer 15 minutes. Add pepper rings; simmer 10 minutes, or until meat and vegetables are tender.
4. Remove meat and vegetables to heated platter; keep hot.
5. Combine flour and ½ cup cold water in a 2-cup measure until smooth. Increase temperature to 350°; when liquid in frypan bubbles, stir in flour mixture. Cook, stirring constantly, until sauce thickens and bubbles 3 minutes. Pass sauce in a heated gravy boat.

SANTA CLARA CHICKEN

Apricots from sunny California give tang to skillet chicken with carrots and potatoes.

Makes 4 servings.

- 1 broiler-fryer, quartered (about 2½ pounds)
- 2 tablespoons vegetable oil
- 1 cup frozen chopped onion
- 1½ teaspoons seasoned salt
- 1 can (5½ ounces) apricot nectar
- 2 tablespoons lemon juice
- 1 can (15 ounces) whole carrots, drained
- 1 package (10 ounces) frozen potato puffs

1. Brown chicken, skin-side down, in oil in an electric frypan set at 375°. Turn to brown second side. Push chicken to one side; sauté onion 3 minutes; sprinkle with seasoned salt.
2. Add apricot nectar and lemon juice to frypan; bring to boiling, stirring up browned bits. Cover. Lower temperature to 200°; simmer 15 minutes. Spoon some sauce over chicken; open vent of frypan; continue cooking 15 minutes, or until chicken is tender. Remove chicken to heated serving platter and keep warm.
3. Bring sauce to boiling; cook 2 minutes, or until slightly thickened. Add carrots and potatoes; cook until hot and glazed; spoon over chicken. Serve with a romaine and chicory salad, if you wish.

WESTERN TURKEY SCRAMBLE

Turkey and ham combine with rice, tomatoes and chili powder in this cooksaver super supper dish.

Makes 6 servings.

- 1 medium-size onion, sliced
- 1 clove garlic, minced
- 2 tablespoons peanut or vegetable oil
- 1 teaspoon salt
- 1 to 3 teaspoons chili powder
- ⅛ teaspoon pepper
  Dash cayenne pepper
- 2 cans (1 pound each) stewed tomatoes
- 2 cups diced cooked turkey
- 2 cups diced cooked ham or bologna
- 2 cups packaged precooked rice
- 3 tablespoons chopped parsley
- 1 bay leaf

1. Sauté onion and garlic in oil until soft in an electric wok set at 360°. Stir in salt, chili powder, pepper and cayenne; cook 2 minutes.
2. Stir in tomatoes, turkey, ham or bologna, rice, parsley and bay leaf; lower temperature to 200°; cover.
3. Simmer 5 minutes, or until rice is tender and liquid is absorbed. Remove bay leaf. Serve with chilled pear halves on leaf lettuce with bottled blue cheese dressing, if you wish.

SKILLET BEAN BAKE

Lima beans are the quick-cooking choice in this minute-timed version of a classic.

Makes 4 servings.

- 4 pieces cut-up chicken (about 1 pound)
- ½ teaspoon salt
- 2 tablespoons vegetable oil
- 4 smoky link sausages (from a 6-ounce package)
- 1 large onion, chopped (1 cup)
- 1 clove garlic, minced
- 2 envelopes or teaspoons instant chicken broth
- ¾ cup water
- ½ teaspoon leaf marjoram, crumbled
- 2 packages (10 ounces each) frozen Fordhook lima beans

1. Sprinkle chicken with salt. Brown in vegetable oil in electric frypan set at 325°; add sausages when chicken is half browned. Add onion and garlic; sauté until soft.
2. Add instant chicken broth, water and marjoram; bring to boiling. Add limas and return to boiling.
3. Cover frypan; lower temperature to simmer; cook 20 minutes, or until chicken and lima beans are tender.

LAMB AND NOODLE STEW

Make this family-satisfying dish in less than an hour in an electric frypan.

Makes 6 servings.

- 6 lamb neck slices (about 1-inch thick)
- 2 tablespoons vegetable oil
- 3½ cups water
- 1 envelope (1⅜ ounces) onion soup mix
- 1 teaspoon Worcestershire sauce
- 1 package (8 ounces) medium egg noodles
- ⅓ cup all purpose flour
- ½ cup dry white wine
- 1 package (9 ounces) frozen French style green beans, thawed
- 1 teaspoon salt
- ¼ teaspoon pepper
- ½ cup grated Parmesan cheese
- ¼ cup toasted slivered almonds

1. Brown neck slices in hot oil in an electric frypan. Add water, onion soup mix and Worcestershire sauce. Bring to boiling; turn heat to simmer; cover frypan, cook 50 minutes. Meanwhile, cook noodles al dente (barely tender, still firm), following package directions.
2. Combine flour with wine in a cup until smooth; add to bubbling lamb mixture. Cook, stirring constantly, until sauce thickens and bubbles. Add noodles and green beans; mix gently. Season with salt and pepper. Top with Parmesan cheese and almonds.
3. Cover and simmer 10 minutes, or until heated through.

CAJUN STEW

Our version of this Louisiana favorite is ready in less than half an hour.

Makes 4 servings.

- 2 chicken leg quarters
- 1 tablespoon vegetable oil
- ⅓ cup frozen chopped onion
- ¼ cup frozen chopped green pepper
- 1 clove garlic, minced
- 1 tablespoon chili powder
- ¼ teaspoon ground cumin
- ¾ cup water
- ½ cup uncooked regular rice
- 1¼ teaspoons salt
- 1 package (8 ounces) frozen deveined shelled shrimp
- 1 can (1 pound) whole tomatoes
- 1 package (10 ounces) frozen whole okra
- ¼ cup chopped parsley

1. Cut chicken quarters into 2 pieces. Heat oil in an electric frypan. Add chicken pieces and brown well. Add onion, green pepper, garlic, chili powder and cumin. Sauté 2 minutes, or until onion is soft.
2. Stir in water, rice and salt. Bring to boiling. Cover, reduce heat and simmer 5 minutes.
3. Stir in shrimp and tomatoes. Return to simmering, cover and cook 15 minutes. Add okra and cook 5 minutes longer. Stir in parsley, just before serving.

QUICK FRENCH CASSOULET

Tastes like the classic version, but takes only minutes.

Makes 4 servings.

- 1 package (1 pound) pork sausages
- 4 slices bacon, cut into 1-inch pieces
- 1½ cups frozen chopped onions
- 2 cups water
- 1 can condensed beef broth
- 1 can (8 ounces) stewed tomatoes
- 1 teaspoon salt
- 1 bay leaf
- ¾ teaspoon leaf basil, crumbled
- ½ teaspoon leaf thyme, crumbled
- ¼ teaspoon garlic powder
- ⅛ teaspoon pepper
- 2 packages (10 ounces each) frozen lima beans

1. Brown sausages in an electric frypan; drain and pour off fat. Push sausages to one side; add bacon and cook until crisp. Add onions and sauté 2 minutes.
2. Stir in water, beef broth, tomatoes, salt, bay leaf, basil, thyme, garlic powder and pepper; bring to boiling.
3. Add lima beans. Return to boiling, cover; reduce heat and simmer 30 minutes, or until beans are tender. Mash a few beans against side of pan for thicker consistency.

SAUSAGE IN BEEF ROLLS

Sausage links make a savory filling for these round steak roll-ups.

Makes 8 servings.

- 2 pounds beef round steak, cut about ½-inch thick
  - OR: 2 pounds cubed steaks or beef for braciola
- 1 package (8 ounces) pork sausages
- 1 jar (14 ounces) spaghetti sauce
- ¾ cup red wine or water
- 2 packages (10 ounces each) frozen broccoli spears
  - Cooked linguine or spaghetti

1. Trim fat from steak; cut meat into eight even-sized pieces. Pound each slice beef with mallet or rolling pin to ¼-inch thickness. (If using meat for braciola, omit this step.)
2. Brown sausages for 5 minutes in an electric frypan set at 375°; drain.
3. Roll each steak around a sausage; fasten with wooden picks.
4. Brown rolls, a few at a time, in drippings; drain on paper towels. Pour all fat from skillet.
5. Pour spaghetti sauce and wine or water into skillet; bring to boiling, scraping up browned bits. Lower temperature to 200°; add beef rolls; turn to coat with sauce; cover; simmer 30 minutes. Add broccoli; cook 15 minutes longer, or until meat is tender. Remove wooden picks; serve over hot linguine or spaghetti.

BARBECUED LAMB SHANKS

No need to wait for summer in order to enjoy the barbecue flavor.

Makes 4 servings.

- 4 lamb shanks, cut in half
- ½ cup all purpose flour
- 1 teaspoon salt
- ¼ teaspoon pepper
- ¼ cup vegetable oil
- 3 medium-size onions, chopped (1½ cups)
- 1 bottle (12 ounces) chili sauce
- 1 cup water
- ¼ cup cider vinegar
- 1 teaspoon prepared mustard
- ½ teaspoon salt
- 2 tablespoons Worcestershire sauce
- 2 acorn squash, sliced and seeded

1. Shake lamb in flour, salt and pepper in a plastic bag.
2. Preheat electric frypan to 360°. Heat oil in skillet and add lamb shanks. Brown on all sides; push to one side; sauté onions until soft.
3. Combine chili sauce, water, vinegar, mustard, salt and Worcestershire sauce in a 4-cup measure; add to lamb; add acorn squash slices.
4. Cover; simmer at 200° 2 hours, 30 minutes, or until lamb is tender.

GOURMET SCRAMBLE

Chicken livers are quick to cook and delicious, too.

Makes 4 servings.

- ½ pound chicken livers
- 3 tablespoons butter or margarine
- 1 medium-size onion, chopped (½ cup)
- ½ cup sliced celery
- 6 eggs
- ½ teaspoon salt
  - Dash pepper
- 1 package (3 ounces) cream cheese, cubed
  - Chopped parsley

1. Cook chicken livers in butter or margarine in an electric frypan set at 325° until browned; push to one side; sauté onion and celery in same pan until tender.
2. Mix eggs, salt and pepper with a fork in a medium-size bowl. Pour over liver in pan. Add cream cheese.
3. Draw pancake turner completely across the bottom and sides of skillet, forming large soft curds, until eggs are set, but do not stir constantly. Sprinkle with chopped parsley just before serving.

Microwave Oven

BARBECUED TURKEY

Frozen whole turkey breast makes economical and delicious eating; microwave cooking makes it quick to fix. Shown on page 23.

Defrost for 20 minutes.
Microwave for 60 minutes.
Makes 6 servings plus leftovers.

- 1 frozen whole turkey breast (about 5 pounds)
- 2 tablespoons butter or margarine, melted
  - Salt and pepper
- 2 whole acorn squash
- 1 can (8 ounces) tomato sauce
- ½ cup frozen chopped onion
- 1 clove garlic, minced
- 2 tablespoons soy sauce
- 1 tablespoon honey
- 1 teaspoon prepared mustard
  - Dash cayenne pepper (optional)

1. Place frozen turkey breast, on its side, in a microwave-safe casserole; cover with wax paper.
2. Defrost 10 minutes; turn to other side; defrost 10 minutes longer.
3. Stand turkey breast upright in casserole; brush with part of the melted butter or margarine; season with salt and pepper; cover turkey breast with wax paper.
4. Microwave at medium power 30 minutes. Wash and cut acorn squash into slices; remove seeds; halve slices.
5. Combine tomato sauce, onion, garlic, soy sauce, honey, mustard and cayenne in a small bowl.

6. Spoon barbecue mixture generously over turkey breast; arrange squash slices around turkey; brush with remaining melted butter and season with salt and pepper. Cover only squash slices with wax paper.
7. Microwave at medium power 30 minutes, or until turkey and squash slices are tender. Allow to stand 10 minutes before serving.

MICROWAVE DO'S AND DON'T'S

- Never operate oven with door open.
- Never operate oven if it is damaged in any way.
- Avoid metal cooking containers—pots and pans; foil-lined paper bags, boxes and baking trays; skewers; foil trays. They reflect microwaves and therefore interfere with the cooking process.
- Only use utensils suitable for the microwave oven—ovenproof glass or glass ceramic oven baking dishes (without metallic trim or signatures on the outside); paper cups, plates, towels and wax paper (best for defrosting or heating foods); dishwasher-safe plastics (best for re-heating foods). Many companies now label containers and utensils that are "microwave-safe."
- Round-shaped containers are best for even heating.
- Don't leave meat or candy thermometers in food when microwave cooking, unless they are specifically designed for microwave use.
- Some foods do not microwave well. Don't microwave eggs in shells, popcorn, pancakes (except to reheat), large food loads, such as a dozen potatoes or a 25-pound turkey.
- Do not attempt to deep-fry or can foods in microwave oven. Canning necessitates prolonged high temperatures and deep-fat frying may cause burns.
- Do not heat bottles with narrow necks—they may shatter.
- Arrange foods of equal size in a ring, leaving the center empty, so that all sides are exposed to the microwave energy.
- Arrange foods, such as chicken drumsticks, with the thicker portion to the outside of the dish, letting them cook through without overcooking the thinner areas.
- Quick-to-heat foods, such as rolls, are placed near the center of a dish; slower-cooking foods are placed near the outside of the dish.
- Prick potatoes in their skins, egg yolks and chicken livers before cooking, to prevent bursting.
- Plastic wrap and plastic cooking pouches can be used in the microwave oven; make a small slit with a two-tined fork when cooking food that steams, to prevent bursting.

GROUND BEEF DINNER

The All-American favorite, meat and potatoes, ready for serving in half an hour.

Microwave for 20 minutes.
Makes 4 servings.

1 pound ground chuck
1 cup frozen chopped onion
1 can (1 pound) lima beans
4 medium-size potatoes, pared and thinly sliced
3 tablespoons all purpose flour
3 tablespoons butter or margarine
3 tablespoons milk
1 teaspoon salt
1 teaspoon leaf thyme, crumbled
½ teaspoon paprika
¼ teaspoon seasoned pepper

1. Brown ground chuck and onion in an 8-cup microwave-safe casserole. (The microwave browning dish is perfect.) Stir frequently; drain off fat.
2. Drain liquid from lima beans and sprinkle limas over meat; layer potato slices over; dust with flour; dot with butter or margarine and drizzle milk over; season with salt, thyme, paprika and pepper. Cover casserole loosely with plastic wrap.
3. Microwave at full power 20 minutes, rotating dish several times, or until potatoes are tender when pierced with a two-tined fork.

FLORIDA SNAPPER

Flounder, haddock or cod can be used in place of red snapper in this pungent Caribbean speciality.

Microwave 16 minutes.
Makes 6 servings.

2 pounds fresh or frozen red snapper fillets
1 small tomato, chopped
1 cup frozen chopped onion
1 small green pepper, halved, seeded and chopped
1 can (3 or 4 ounces) mushroom pieces, drained
1 clove garlic, minced
1 teaspoon leaf oregano, crumbled
Dash bottled red pepper seasoning
½ cup bottled Italian salad dressing
3 medium-size zucchini, trimmed and cut into 2-inch pieces
¼ cup chili sauce
Salt and pepper

1. Defrost fish, if frozen, in a 13x9x2-inch microwave-safe casserole for 5 minutes; remove fish from dish.
2. Combine tomato, onion, green pepper, mushrooms, garlic, oregano and red pepper seasoning in same dish; stir in salad dressing to blend well; cover with plastic wrap.
3. Microwave at full power 6 minutes. Place fish over sauce, spooning part over; arrange zucchini around fish; spread chili sauce on top of fish and vegetables; cover.

4. Microwave 6 minutes. Turn dish; microwave 4 minutes. Taste sauce; season with salt and pepper, if necessary. Let stand 4 minutes before serving.

ZESTY STUFFED PEPPERS

Old-fashioned family favorites can still be served—even when time is short—if you use your microwave oven.

Microwave for 30 minutes.
Makes 4 servings.

4 large green peppers
1 pound ground meatloaf mixture or ground beef
1 cup cooked rice
1 cup frozen chopped onion
1½ teaspoons garlic salt
¼ teaspoon pepper
1 can condensed tomato soup
½ cup red cooking wine
1 cup shredded Provolone cheese

1. Cut a ½-inch slice from tops of peppers; remove seeds.
2. Combine meat, rice, onion, garlic salt and pepper in a medium-size bowl; spoon into green peppers, dividing evenly.
3. Place peppers in a 10-cup microwave-safe casserole. Combine tomato soup and cooking wine in a small bowl; spoon over peppers; cover casserole with plastic wrap.
4. Microwave at full power 30 minutes; sprinkle tops with cheese; let stand 5 minutes before serving.

ARIZONA CHILI

Hearty as the stew made over campfires in the Old West, yet ready in less than an hour.

Microwave for 45 minutes.
Makes 6 servings.

1½ pounds ground beef
1 cup frozen chopped onion
1 can (2 pounds, 3 ounces) Italian tomatoes in tomato purée
2 cans (about 1 pound each) red kidney beans
1 large green pepper, halved, seeded and chopped
1 to 3 teaspoons chili powder
2 teaspoons salt
Corn chips
Shredded Cheddar cheese

1. Crumble beef into a 10-cup microwave-safe casserole; add onion.
2. Microwave at full power 3 minutes; stir mixture; microwave 2 minutes longer.
3. Stir in tomatoes in purée, kidney beans and liquid, green pepper, chili powder and salt until well blended. Cover casserole with plastic wrap.
4. Microwave at full power 40 minutes; stir chili; allow to stand 10 minutes. Top with crushed corn chips and shredded Cheddar cheese just before serving.

RHODE ISLAND FILLETS

White wine and lemon slices add the crowning touch to this delicate fish dish.

Microwave for 15 minutes.
Makes 4 servings.

1 package (1 pound) frozen cod or haddock, thawed
1 teaspoon salt
½ teaspoon fines herbes, crumbled
¼ teaspoon pepper
¼ cup chopped shallots
OR: 1 small onion, chopped (¼ cup)
1 large lemon, thinly sliced
1 package (9 ounces) cut green beans
1 can condensed cream of mushroom soup
½ cup dry white wine

1. Season fish with salt, fines herbes and pepper; arrange in a 12-cup microwave-safe casserole. Cover dish with plastic wrap.
2. Microwave at full power 5 minutes; sprinkle with shallots; layer with lemon slices. Arrange green beans around fish. Combine soup and wine in a bowl; pour over fish. Cover with plastic wrap.
3. Microwave 5 minutes; rotate dish; microwave 5 minutes longer. Allow to stand 10 minutes before serving.

POLYNESIAN CHICKEN

Sweet and spicy, this modern-day version of a South Seas classic is extra easy when made in a microwave oven.

Microwave for 23 minutes.
Makes 4 servings.

1 broiler-fryer, cut up (2½ pounds)
½ cup soy sauce
½ cup dry white wine
1 tablespoon Worcestershire sauce
1 clove garlic, minced
1 teaspoon ground ginger
Dash bottled red pepper seasoning
1 bag (1 pound) frozen carrots
1 bag (1 pound) frozen French fried potatoes

1. Place chicken pieces in a deep glass bowl. Combine soy sauce, wine, Worcestershire sauce, garlic, ginger and red pepper seasoning in a small bowl; pour over chicken. Cover bowl with plastic wrap; marinate in refrigerator at least 2 hours, or overnight.
2. Arrange chicken pieces in a 12-cup shallow microwave-safe casserole. (Place large pieces in corners and smaller ones in the center.) Pour sauce into dish; cover with plastic wrap.
3. Microwave at full power 13 minutes, rotating dish several times; arrange carrots and potatoes around chicken; spoon sauce over; cover. Microwave 10 minutes longer, or until chicken is tender. Allow to stand 5 minutes before serving.

ZURICH ZUCCHINI

The Swiss are famous for their savory meatless supper dishes. This one combines eggs, cheese and squash.

Microwave for 15 minutes.
Makes 4 servings.

- 2 **large zucchini, trimmed and cut into 1-inch pieces**
- 1 **cup frozen chopped onion**
- 4 **eggs**
- 1½ **cups shredded Swiss cheese (6 ounces)**
- 1 **teaspoon salt**
- 1 **teaspoon leaf basil, crumbled**
- ¼ **teaspoon seasoned pepper**

1. Combine zucchini and onion in a greased 6-cup shallow microwave-safe casserole; cover lightly with plastic wrap.
2. Microwave at full power 7 minutes; drain all liquid from dish and save for soup or sauce.
3. Beat eggs in a medium-size bowl with a wire whip until foamy; stir in cheese, salt, basil and pepper until well blended. Pour over zucchini in casserole, stirring to mix well. Cover casserole with a paper towel.
4. Microwave at medium power 5 minutes; remove paper towel; microwave 3 minutes longer, or until egg mixture in center is set.

WASHINGTON PORK CHOPS

Chips of rosy red apple and savory stuffing make pork super delicious.

Microwave for 35 minutes.
Makes 4 servings.

- 4 **pork chops, cut 1-inch thick (about 2 pounds)**
- ½ **cup orange juice**
- 1 **large apple, quartered, cored and chopped**
- 2 **tablespoons butter or margarine**
- 1½ **cups packaged stuffing mix (from an 8-ounce package)**
- ¼ **cup crab apple jelly**
- 2 **tablespoons dry white wine**
- ½ **teaspoon salt**
- ½ **teaspoon ground cinnamon**
- 1 **package (10 ounces) frozen broccoli spears**

1. Cut a deep pocket into center of each pork chop.
2. Combine orange juice, chopped apple and butter or margarine in a large saucepan; bring to boiling; stir in packaged stuffing mix until well blended.
3. Divide stuffing among chops, filling each chop generously. Arrange chops in a 10-cup shallow microwave-safe casserole, placing bones toward center and pockets at corners of dish.
4. Combine jelly, wine, salt and cinnamon in a small saucepan; heat until jelly melts; brush half over chops. Cover casserole with wax paper.
5. Microwave at medium power 15 minutes; give casserole a half-turn; arrange broccoli around chops. Microwave 20 minutes longer, or until chops are tender. Allow to stand 5 minutes. Brush chops with remaining glaze just before serving.
COOK'S TIP: To make cutting pockets in pork chops easier, put uncooked chops in the freezer for 10 minutes to firm up meat.

MONTEREY LAMB CHOPS

Rosy tomatoes and bright green pepper make a colorful sauce for this easy-on-the-cook microwave recipe.

Microwave 21 minutes.
Makes 4 servings.

- 4 **shoulder lamb chops (about 1½ pounds)**
- 3 **tablespoons all purpose flour**
- 1 **teaspoon salt**
- 1 **teaspoon paprika**
- 1 **teaspoon leaf thyme, crumbled**
- ¼ **teaspoon seasoned pepper**
- 3 **tablespoons vegetable oil**
- 2 **large tomatoes, chopped OR: 1 can (1 pound) Italian tomatoes**
- 1 **medium-size green pepper, halved, seeded and coarsely chopped**
- ¼ **pound mushrooms, chopped**
- 1 **cup white wine or chicken broth**

1. Season lamb chops with a mixture of flour, salt, paprika, thyme and seasoned pepper.
2. Arrange lamb chops in a 12-cup shallow microwave-safe casserole; drizzle with oil; sprinkle tomatoes, green pepper and mushrooms over; pour wine or broth in; cover with plastic wrap.
3. Microwave at full power 8 minutes; rotate dish; microwave 8 minutes; uncover; cook 5 minutes longer. Serve with hot cooked rice, if you wish.

PIE PLATE MEATLOAF

Savory vegetables and cheese are layered in our family-pleasing meatloaf.

Microwave for 30 minutes.
Makes 6 servings.

- 1½ **pounds ground beef**
- 1½ **cups soft white bread crumbs (3 slices)**
- ½ **cup tomato juice**
- 2 **teaspoons garlic salt**
- ¼ **teaspoon lemon pepper**
- 1 **package (10 ounces) frozen mixed vegetables**
- 1 **cup frozen chopped onion**
- 1 **cup shredded mozzarella cheese (4 ounces)**
- ½ **cup chili sauce**

1. Combine ground beef, 1 cup of the bread crumbs, tomato juice, garlic salt and lemon pepper in a large bowl; mix lightly until well blended. Pat half the mixture into a 9-inch glass pie plate.
2. Cook mixed vegetables, following label directions; drain; stir in remaining ½ cup bread crumbs, onion and cheese until well blended. Spoon over meat layer to within ½-inch of edge.
3. Pat remaining meat mixture over vegetable layer. Brush with chili sauce. Cover plate with plastic wrap.
4. Microwave at full power 30 minutes; allow to stand 10 minutes; cut into wedges to serve.

SOUTH SEA CHICKEN

Sweet potatoes and pineapple make the perfect accompaniments for chicken.

Microwave for 20 minutes.
Makes 4 servings.

- 1 **broiler-fryer, cut up (3 pounds)**
- 1 **teaspoon salt**
- ¾ **teaspoon leaf rosemary, crumbled**
- ¼ **teaspoon seasoned pepper**
- 2 **tablespoons chopped shallots OR: ¼ cup frozen chopped onion**
- 1 **can (8¼ ounces) crushed pineapple in syrup**
- 1 **teaspoon ground ginger**
- 1 **can (1 pound) sweet potatoes**
- 1 **package (10 ounces) broccoli spears, thawed**

1. Rub chicken pieces with salt, rosemary and pepper; arrange chicken pieces in a 12-cup shallow microwave-safe casserole. (Place large pieces in corners and small ones in the center.) Sprinkle shallots or onion over.
2. Combine crushed pineapple, syrup and ginger in a small bowl; spoon over chicken. Cover with plastic wrap.
3. Microwave at full power 10 minutes, rotating dish several times. Arrange sweet potatoes and broccoli around chicken; spoon part of sauce over; microwave 10 minutes, or until chicken is tender. Allow to stand 4 minutes before serving.

Here are a few general guidelines for adapting your favorite one-dish recipes to a slow cooker:
- Uncooked meat and vegetable combinations will require 8 to 10 hours on low (190° to 200°) or 4 to 5 hours on high (290° to 300°).
- One hour of simmering on the range or baking at 350° in the oven is equal to 8 to 10 hours on low (190° to 200°), or 4 to 5 hours on high (290° to 300°).
- Reduce the liquid in your recipe to about 1 cup since the slow cooker method of simmering foods saves all the food's natural juices.
- Use canned soups and broths, wine or water as the liquid in your slow cooker.
- Don't add dairy products, such as milk, sour cream, or cream until the final 30 minutes of cooking.

Dried beans, or legumes, have always played an important role in society. In Greco-Roman elections, they were used to count votes—a white bean meant "yes" and a black one, "no." Cultivated in the Americas since prehistoric times, beans were one of the first forms of money, as well as a favorite food among the Indians.

Today, beans are as popular as ever, both here and abroad. For those who want to cut down on meat, beans provide an excellent source of protein when combined with small amounts of meat or cheese. Yet, they are inexpensive. And their versatility makes it possible to enjoy them in many ways.

Although usually associated with homey casseroles, stews and soups, beans are also wonderful in salads and dips or as a hearty side dish. Their subtle flavors blend well with such stronger ones as smoked meats, onions, chili powder, tomatoes and a variety of fresh and dried fruits.

Presoak beans in one of two ways before cooking: Soak them overnight in water to cover. Alternately, boil them in water to cover for 2 minutes; let stand, off heat, 1 hour, then proceed with recipe. Use soaking liquid in cooking, because it contains vitamins. To test for doneness, taste or blow on a few—if their skins burst, they are done.

Whether you simmer them on top of the stove, in a slow cooker, or in the oven, 1 cup of dried beans will become 2-2½ cups cooked, or enough to serve 3 to 4 persons. Dried beans keep almost indefinitely if stored in a jar with a close-fitting lid or a tightly-closed plastic bag set in a cool, dry place.

Casseroles and stews made with beans seem to improve if made one day before serving time, and then reheated, so they are perfect for meals you prepare in advance. The photo below shows just a few of the many shapes, sizes and colors available.

PINTO beans have brown speckles on a pink background.

BLACK-EYED beans are oval shaped and have a spot of black or yellow.

RED KIDNEY beans go into chili, with or without meat. Burgundy-colored.

GARBANZO beans, or chick peas, are nutty and used in stews.

GREEN SPLIT PEAS make wholesome soups, especially with ham.

GREAT NORTHERN beans are white and a fundamental ingredient in cassoulet stew.

beans&

For more than half the world's population, rice is the most important food. It's hard to imagine an Indian or Chinese meal without a steaming bowl of this starchy grain accompanying it. Known since around 3,000 B.C., rice probably originated in India. Today, it's grown on almost every continent, with the U.S. as the largest producer.

Most American stores stock several of the more than 6,000 varieties of rice. Although it exists in a myriad of colors, white and brown are the two kinds most available in this country.

Long grain white rice—whether Carolina-type, converted, minute-type or quick—is the most widely used. When it's milled, the bran skin under the husk is removed, making it easier to store and quicker to cook.

- Both Carolina-type and converted (processed before milling) rices are excellent as side dishes or in entrée pilafs; converted rice in particular has fluffy, separate grains.
- Quick (parboiled) and minute-type (or packaged precooked) rices are good choices when you want to save time and ensure uniform results.
- Short-grain white rice makes creamy Italian risottos and sweet puddings, as it is very absorbent and needs slow cooking and more liquid.
- Try brown rice when you want to add a nutty flavor to casseroles, soups and side dishes; because only its husk is removed, it takes longer to cook and stays chewier, but also has more protein and natural minerals and vitamins.
- Wild rice is actually a water grass, but it often comes packaged with long grain rice and is a wonderful accompaniment to game dishes. And don't hesitate to try the many packaged flavored rice and rice and vermicelli mixes.

Rice can be simmered on top of the stove or oven baked and is delicious served many ways. Toss it with butter, or use grated cheese, toasted almonds and poppy seeds, sautéed mushrooms or chopped parsley. Toasting it in oil before adding liquid gives rice a richer flavor (see page 80). Or mold it in a ring, ready to hold creamed entrées or vegetables: Toss cooked rice in melted butter or well-seasoned vinaigrette dressing; pack loosely into a ring mold or angel food tube pan and smooth top. Set mold in a flameproof baking dish; place baking dish on top of the stove and fill half-way with boiling water. Cover with aluminum foil and simmer 10-15 minutes. Center a heated serving dish on top of the mold and invert both. Fill center with creamed or curried chicken or seafood. Leftover rice is tasty in soup, stuffed pepper and cabbage or as the main ingredient in fried rice. It makes an elegant salad when mixed with leftover bits of vegetables and meat in a vinaigrette or mayonnaise-based dressing. For a quick and satisfying dessert, fold cooked rice into sweetened whipped cream and top with a dab of jam or jelly.

Follow package or recipe directions for cooking methods and times, adding different liquids, herbs and spices for variety. Check half-way through cooking time and add more liquid, if necessary. Rice is done when grains are tender and liquid is absorbed; then fluff with a fork.

Prepare about 1 cup uncooked regular rice or 2 cups packaged pre-cooked rice for 4-6 servings.

Whether plain or mixed with other freezable foods, rice keeps in the freezer 6-8 months. To reheat, add 2 tablespoons liquid for each cup rice; simmer 4-5 minutes in a covered saucepan.

Uncooked rice keeps well if stored in a covered container in a cool, dry place.

rice&pasta

Pasta is almost synonymous with Italy, where some believe it originated. Yet it is featured in the cuisines of many other countries. Since Thomas Jefferson introduced it to the United States, pasta has become a national favorite.

A product of durum wheat flour, water and sometimes egg or spinach, pasta is usually made commercially; it's easy and delicious to prepare at home, too (see page 66). There seems to be no end to the enormous variety of pasta shapes and sizes—from barley-shaped orzo to large hollow manicotti—though most are made from the same basic dough.

• Egg noodles are a bit richer and wonderful with stews containing sour cream, such as beef stroganoff.

• Spinach noodles—pasta verdi—are a pleasant change; when mixed with regular pasta, they make a dish called "hay and straw."

• Look in the health food section of your market for whole wheat noodles, a relative newcomer to the pasta scene.

Shaped into strips, threads, wagon wheels and other shapes, filled or not, pasta is dried before storing and cooking. In Italy, it is served as the "first plate" before the main course. But in other parts of Europe and in the United States, pasta is usually prepared as the center of the meal. There are many other ways to enjoy pasta besides serving it with tomato sauce and grated cheese, as good as that can be.

Stuffed manicotti, ravioli or large shells are all nourishing entrées, served with meat sauce or plain tomato sauce. Lasagna has been a popular dish for years and is especially tasty when made with a combination of ricotta or cottage cheese and mozzarella cheese. Try hot noodles with freshly grated cheese, butter and cream to make noodles Alfredo, a perfect main dish when served with a salad or an unusual accompaniment to lighter meat dishes. Add pasta, particularly the light, smaller varieties, to soups. Or prepare a noodle pudding, with meat and pot cheese, or fruit and cottage cheese for dessert.

Cooking time varies with the size, shape and freshness of the pasta, so read package or recipe directions and watch the kettle carefully. Bring plenty of salted water to the boiling.

• Add pasta slowly so water keeps boiling.

• Don't break long spaghetti into pieces; lower them slowly into boiling water, curving them around the pot as they soften.

• Boil pasta, uncovered, stirring occasionally to prevent sticking.

• Test for doneness 1 to 2 minutes before time given in directions. Either taste a piece—it should be firm but tender (al dente)—or press a bit against the side of the kettle with a fork. If it breaks easily and smoothly, it's done.

• Don't overcook pasta. Drain well and at once in a colander. Serve immediately or keep warm: Place in a colander over simmering water; cover top with aluminum foil or pot cover and keep warm for up to 1 hour. To keep for more than 1 hour, cook pasta al dente, drain and toss with vegetable oil to coat. Just before serving, plunge pasta into boiling water 1 minute, drain and toss with melted butter or other sauce.

• While grated Parmesan and Romano cheeses are the classic toppings for pasta, other cheeses lend themselves well to sprinkling, too. Try grating bits of Cheddar, Gruyere or Swiss for a taste change.

Allow 2 ounces uncooked pasta for side dishes and 4 ounces for entrées per serving.

Unopened, pasta keeps fresh for months in a cool dry place. Opened, it should be placed in a covered container.

From the multitude of rice and pasta varieties, several kinds shown below, from left to right: Large shells, cavatelli ("5 bumps"), long grain white rice, rigatoni, brown rice, pasta verdi (spinach noodles), rotelle (spaghetti twists) and quick or packaged precooked rice.

Parsley Dumplings steam up light and fluffy with garden-fresh flavor.

Nutty Poppy Seed Biscuits get their tangy flavor and tenderness from buttermilk.

In a hurry? Roll up a batch of Cheddar Cheese Pinwheels, using refrigerated rolls.

Weave a lattice of pastry dough to make a Crisscross Top that's golden brown and flaky.

top it off!

Change the character of any casserole, stew or fricassee by topping it in a new and different way. The choices are almost endless—make dumplings or main dish pastry, or use refrigerated rolls and biscuits for a quick and easy finish. They're a great way to serve leftovers, too, because they satisfy even the heartiest of appetites. Recipes and variations start on page **97**, but don't hesitate to vary them even further with ingredients you have on hand. Try deviled ham pinwheels, sesame biscuits or chive dumplings, to name just a few. Whatever you choose to make, remember to have the stew or casserole bubbling hot before adding topping. Otherwise, the results will be soggy, not properly cooked. And don't be tempted to peek when you make dumplings if you want them to be light and fluffy!

Five different cheeses in our Pasta Con Cinque Formaggi prove that variety is the spice of life—and mealtime! A truly delicious meatless main dish.

Recipe is on page 69.

EASY AS PIE

It's no wonder that hearty meat pies have long been popular in English households. Melton Mowbray Pie combines pork and veal in a golden, flaky crust for a satisfying one-dish meal.

To give a shiny finish to any pastry, or to attach decorative trims, brush uncooked crust with a mixture of egg and water just before baking.

Recipe is on page 98.

Sour cream
sauce won't curdle
if you spoon part of
the hot pan liquid
into sour cream,
then stir mixture
into skillet. *Never* let
sour cream sauce boil.

Imaginative seasonings characterize the
OLD WORLD FLAVOR
robust flavor of classic German cooking.

ESSEN POTATO SCALLOP

A showy recipe that makes the most of leftover ham or tongue.

Bake at 350° for 15 minutes.
Makes 6 servings.

- 6 medium-size potatoes
- ¼ cup chopped green onions
- 2 tablespoons butter or margarine
- 2 tablespoons all purpose flour
- 1½ teaspoons salt
- ¼ teaspoon pepper
- 1 cup milk
- ½ cup mayonnaise or salad dressing
- 4 teaspoons prepared mustard
- 1 teaspoon Worcestershire sauce
- 1 cup frozen peas (from a 1-pound bag)
- 12 slices cooked tongue or ham
- 1 tablespoon white corn syrup

1. Cook potatoes in boiling salted water in a large saucepan 20 minutes, or until tender; drain. Cool till easy to handle; peel and slice; place in a large bowl; add onions.
2. While potatoes cook, melt butter or margarine in a small saucepan; stir in flour, salt and pepper; cook, stirring constantly, just until bubbly.
3. Stir in milk; continue cooking and stirring until sauce thickens and bubbles 3 minutes; remove from heat. Stir in mayonnaise or dressing, 3 teaspoons of the mustard and Worcestershire sauce.
4. Pour hot sauce over potatoes and onions; toss lightly until potatoes are coated. Spoon into a large, ovenproof platter or 8-cup casserole.
5. Cook peas in boiling salted water in a small saucepan 5 minutes; drain.
6. Overlap meat in a ring on potatoes; spoon peas into center.
7. Mix corn syrup and 1 teaspoon mustard in a cup; brush over meat.
8. Bake in moderate oven (350°) 15 minutes, or until potatoes are hot and the meat is lightly glazed.

Noodles and pickled red cabbage surround the veal in Paprika Schnitzel, a classic dish from Germany. Recipe is on this page.

BEEF IN HORSERADISH SAUCE

Revive leftover meat in a spicy sauce.

Makes 6 servings.

- 1 cup chopped celery
- 1 medium-size onion, chopped (½ cup)
- 2 tablespoons butter or margarine
- 1 teaspoon curry powder
- ½ teaspoon ground ginger
- ½ teaspoon pepper
- 1½ cups leftover gravy
  OR: 1 can (10½ ounces) beef gravy
- ¼ cup red cooking wine
- 1 tablespoon Worcestershire sauce
- 1 teaspoon prepared horseradish
- 3 cups diced cooked beef
- 1 container (8 ounces) dairy sour cream
- 1 tablespoon chopped parsley
  Mashed potatoes

1. Sauté celery and onion in butter or margarine until soft in a large skillet.
2. Stir in curry powder, ginger and pepper; cook 1 to 2 minutes. Stir in gravy, wine, Worcestershire sauce, horseradish and beef; bring to boiling; cover. Simmer 10 minutes to blend flavors.
3. Stir about 1 cup hot sauce into sour cream in a small bowl, then stir back into meat mixture in pan. Heat slowly until hot, but do not boil; stir in parsley. Serve over mashed potatoes.

PAPRIKA SCHNITZEL

Rosy paprika and sour cream are classic ingredients with veal in savory German cooking. Photo is on page 56.

Makes 6 servings.

- 6 slices bacon, diced
- 6 slices veal for scallopine (about 1½ pounds)
- ¼ cup all purpose flour
- ½ teaspoon salt
- ¼ teaspoon pepper
- 1 large onion, sliced
- 1 cup beef broth
- 1 package (1 pound) noodles, cooked
- 1 jar (1 pound) pickled red cabbage, heated
- 1 tablespoon paprika
- 1 container (8 ounces) dairy sour cream

1. Brown bacon until crisp in a large skillet; remove with a slotted spoon and reserve.
2. Sprinkle veal with a mixture of flour, salt and pepper on wax paper. Brown veal in bacon drippings; push to one side; add onion rings; sauté until golden; add beef broth; cover skillet; simmer 5 minutes.
3. Line a heated serving platter with noodles; spoon a ring of pickled cabbage over noodles. Place veal, folding slices in half and onions in center of platter; sprinkle with crisp bacon; keep warm.
4. Stir paprika into liquid in skillet and cook 2 minutes; remove skillet from heat; stir ½ cup hot liquid into sour cream in a small bowl; stir into skillet. Return skillet to heat and cook, stirring constantly, until sauce heats through, but do not allow to boil; spoon sauce over veal.

WARSAW-TREAT PEA SOUP

Poland contributes this robust soup with chunks of potato simmered along with split peas and savory sausage.

Makes 8 servings.

- 1 package (1 pound) green or yellow split peas
- 6 cups water
- 1 large leek, chopped
  OR: 1 large onion, chopped (1 cup)
- 2 teaspoons salt
- 1 kielbasa (Polish sausage) (about 1 pound), scored
- 2 medium-size boiling potatoes, pared and diced
- 2 cups chopped celery and leaves
- 1 teaspoon leaf savory, crumbled
- ½ teaspoon pepper

1. Pick over split peas and rinse under running water. Combine peas and water in a large heavy kettle.
2. Bring to boiling; stir in leek or onion and salt; cover kettle; lower heat. Simmer 30 minutes; add kielbasa; simmer 1 hour.
3. Add potatoes, celery and leaves, savory and pepper; simmer 45 minutes longer, or until soup is thick and potatoes are tender. Remove kielbasa; cut into chunks; return to kettle. Ladle soup into heated soup bowls and serve with pumpernickel bread, if you wish.

SKILLET SAUERBRATEN

A fast version of the popular classic.

Makes 6 servings.

    2 pounds ground beef
    2 teaspoons salt
    ¼ teaspoon pepper
    ¼ teaspoon ground cloves
    ¼ cup wine vinegar
    1 carrot, pared and sliced
    1 medium-size onion, peeled and
       sliced
    1 stalk celery, sliced
    1 bay leaf
    ¾ cup water
    ½ cup wine vinegar
    2 tablespoons brown sugar
    1 package (1 pound) frozen whole
       baby carrots
    3 gingersnaps
    ½ cup hot water
      Hot buttered noodles

1. Mix ground beef lightly with salt, pepper, cloves and the ¼ cup vinegar; shape into a big patty in a skillet.
2. Place carrot, onion, celery and bay leaf around meat. Mix water, the ½ cup vinegar and brown sugar; pour over meat; cover.
3. Simmer, basting often, 45 minutes; add carrots, simmer 15 minutes longer. Remove meat to heated platter; keep hot.
4. Soften gingersnaps in hot water; stir into drippings in pan. Heat, stirring constantly, just until gravy thickens; remove bay leaf. Pour over meat or pass separately to spoon over individual servings.

YORKVILLE BEEF PLATTER

Caraway seeds, paprika and onion season beef the Old World way; sauerkraut serves as "sauce."

Makes 6 servings.

    1 round, rump or boneless chuck
       roast (about 4 pounds)
    1 cup water
    ¼ cup chili sauce
    1 envelope (2 to a package) onion
       soup mix
    1 tablespoon caraway seeds
    1 tablespoon paprika
    ¼ teaspoon pepper
    1 can (1 pound, 11 ounces)
       sauerkraut, drained
    ¼ cup firmly packed brown sugar
    1 container (8 ounces) dairy sour
       cream

1. Brown beef in its own fat in a Dutch oven or electric fry pan; stir in water, chili sauce, onion soup mix, caraway seeds, paprika and pepper; cover, keeping vents closed.
2. Simmer, turning meat once or twice, 1 hour; skim off all fat. Mix sauerkraut and brown sugar in a medium-size bowl; stir into liquid around meat; cover again. Simmer 1

hour longer, or until meat is tender. Remove to carving board; keep hot.
3. Stir about ½ cup hot sauerkraut mixture into sour cream in a medium-size bowl, then stir back into remaining sauerkraut mixture in pan. Heat very slowly until hot, but do not boil.
4. Spoon sauerkraut into a deep serving platter. Carve meat into ¼-inch-thick slices; place on top. Serve with noodles, and pickled beets.

CHEESE BLINTZES

This versatile recipe can be served as a main dish for brunch or lunch.

Makes 12 servings.

Batter
    5 eggs
    2 cups all purpose flour
  2½ cups milk
    ⅓ cup vegetable oil
Cheese Filling
    1 container (2 pounds) cream-style
       cottage cheese
    2 eggs
    ⅓ cup sugar
  1½ teaspoons vanilla
    ⅓ cup butter or margarine
Topping
    1 can (1 pound, 5 ounces) cherry
       pie filling
    1 container (16 ounces) dairy sour
       cream

1. Prepare batter: Beat eggs just until blended in a large bowl; sift flour over the eggs and beat in just until smooth; stir in milk and oil. Cover; chill for at least 2 hours.
2. Make cheese filling: Combine cottage cheese, eggs, sugar and vanilla in a large bowl. Beat until smooth; set aside.
3. Heat a heavy 8-inch skillet slowly; test temperature by sprinkling on a few drops of water. When drops bounce about, the temperature is right. Grease skillet lightly with part of the butter or margarine.
4. Measure batter, a scant ¼ cup at a time, into skillet, tilting it to cover the bottom completely.
5. Cook blintz 1 to 2 minutes, or until top is set and underside is golden; remove to a plate. Repeat with remaining batter to make 24 blintzes. Layer each blintz with a piece of foil or waxed paper to keep separated.
6. Place 3 tablespoons cheese filling down the center of the browned side of each blintz. Overlap two opposite sides over filling, then fold up ends toward middle on seam side.
7. Melt remaining butter or margarine in a large skillet. Brown blintzes, seam-side down, turning to brown on other side. Keep warm until all blintzes have been browned. Serve warm, topped with cherry pie filling and sour cream.

SALMON CHOWDER

A meal in itself, delicious with a loaf of crusty rye bread and cucumber salad.

Makes 8 servings.

    3 medium-size potatoes, pared
       and diced
    1 large onion, chopped (1 cup)
    1 cup thinly sliced celery
    ¼ cup (½ stick) butter or margarine
    ⅓ cup all purpose flour
    6 cups milk
    1 bag (2 pounds) frozen peas and
       carrots
    1 can (1 pound) salmon
    1 teaspoon caraway seeds
  1½ teaspoons salt
    ¼ teaspoon seasoned pepper
      Chowder crackers

1. Cook potatoes, in boiling salted water to cover in a medium-size saucepan 15 minutes, or just until tender; set aside.
2. Sauté onion and celery in butter or margarine until soft in a kettle. Blend in flour; cook, stirring constantly, until bubbly. Stir in milk; continue cooking and stirring until mixture thickens and bubbles 1 minute.
3. Add peas and carrots; bring slowly to boiling; cover. Simmer 5 minutes, or until vegetables are tender.
4. Drain salmon; remove skin and bones; break salmon into large chunks. Stir into vegetable mixture with potatoes and liquid, caraway seeds, salt and pepper. Heat slowly, stirring several times, just until hot.
5. Ladle into a tureen or heated bowls. Serve with chowder crackers.

BRATWURST IN SOUR CREAM

Germans love sausages and know many imaginative ways to prepare them. This sweet-sour style is perfect with noodles.

Makes 6 servings.

    2 packages (12 ounces each)
       cooked bratwurst
      OR: 2 packages (1 pound each)
       knackwurst
    2 tablespoons butter or margarine
    2 medium-size onions, thinly
       sliced
    3 tablespoons all purpose flour
    ½ teaspoon salt
  1½ cups apple cider or beer
    1 container (8 ounces) dairy sour
       cream
      Hot buttered noodles

1. Brown sausages well on all sides in butter or margarine in a large skillet; remove sausages from skillet.
2. Sauté onion slices until soft in same skillet. Stir in flour and salt; blend well. Stir in apple cider or beer; cook until bubbly. Return sausages to skillet; cover.
3. Lower heat and simmer sausages for 15 minutes.

4. Spoon sour cream into a small bowl; gradually blend in 1 cup of hot sauce; stir mixture back into skillet. Cook, stirring constantly, until sauce is hot, but do not allow to boil. Serve with hot buttered noodles.

HAMBURG RAGOÛT

Cooked cucumber adds a different flavor to this meatball and vegetable casserole.

Bake at 350° for 30 minutes.
Makes 6 servings.

- 1 pound ground beef
- ½ pound ground veal
- 1 cup soft bread crumbs (2 slices)
- 1 egg
- ½ cup evaporated milk
- 1 small onion, grated
- 1 teaspoon grated lemon rind
- 1 teaspoon salt
- ¼ cup vegetable shortening
- 6 medium-size potatoes, pared and cut into French-fries
- 1 medium-size cucumber, halved lengthwise and sliced ¼ inch thick
- 1 can (12 or 16 ounces) whole-kernel corn
- 1 tablespoon all purpose flour
- ½ teaspoon salt
- ⅛ teaspoon pepper
- 1 container (8 ounces) dairy sour cream

1. Mix beef, veal, bread crumbs, egg, evaporated milk, onion, lemon rind and the 1 teaspoon salt in large bowl; shape into 36 small balls. Brown in shortening in a medium-size skillet; place in mound in one-third of a greased 12-cup casserole.
2. Cook potatoes in small amount of boiling salted water in a large saucepan 5 minutes; transfer with slotted spoon to dish, piling in mound to fill second third of dish; reserve potato water.
3. Cook cucumber slices in small amount of boiling salted water 3 minutes; drain, adding liquid to potato water. Drain corn, adding liquid to potato-cucumber water, if needed, to make 1 cup. Toss corn with cucumbers; spoon into remaining space in dish.
4. Blend flour, the ½ teaspoon salt, and pepper into drippings in pan; stir in reserved vegetable liquid. Cook, stirring constantly, until gravy thickens and boils 1 minute. Stir sauce into sour cream in a small bowl; pour into pan; heat just to boiling. Pour over potatoes and meat; tip dish gently from side to side so gravy flows to bottom; cover.
5. Bake in moderate oven (350°) 30 minutes, or until bubbly hot.
COOK'S TIP: For entertaining, you might like to cut the potatoes into fancy sticks with a ripple-edge vegetable cutter.

BEER-BRAISED LOIN OF PORK

Tender, juicy pork simmers long and lazily in dark beer. No watching necessary.

Bake at 350° for 2 hours.
Makes 8 servings.

- 1 loin of pork (about 4 pounds)
- 1 large onion, chopped (1 cup)
- 1 pound carrots, pared and diced
- 1 bottle or can (12 ounces) dark beer
- 2 teaspoons salt
- ¼ teaspoon pepper
- 1 bay leaf
- 5 whole cloves

1. Brown pork loin well on all sides in a kettle or Dutch oven; remove from pan. (Or, brown meat in a roasting pan on surface burners.)
2. Drain all but 3 tablespoons drippings from pan. Sauté onions and carrots in pork drippings until golden. Stir in beer, salt, pepper, bay leaf and whole cloves. Return pork to kettle and cover. (If using roasting pan, cover tightly with aluminum foil.)
3. Bake in moderate oven (350°) 2 hours, or until pork is tender when pierced with a 2-tined fork. Place pork on platter and keep warm.
4. Pour cooking liquid from kettle into a large bowl. Skim off fat; remove bay leaf. Place in container of electric blender; cover and process at low speed until smooth (or press through a sieve). Pour sauce into saucepan. Bring to boiling, stirring often. Stir in a little gravy coloring, if you wish. Spoon sauce generously over the pork slices.

RHINELAND BOILED BEEF

Serve with a nippy horseradish sauce for a favorite German family dinner.

Makes 8 servings.

- 1 rump roast (about 5 pounds)
- 1 medium-size onion, halved
- 2 medium-size carrots, pared and sliced
- 1 stalk celery, sliced
- 1 bay leaf
- 1 teaspoon salt
- ½ teaspoon peppercorns
- 8 medium-size potatoes, pared
- 1 yellow turnip, pared and diced
  Cold Horseradish Sauce
  (recipe follows)

1. Place beef in a kettle or Dutch oven; add onion, carrots, celery, bay leaf, salt, peppercorns and water just to cover meat. Bring to boiling; reduce heat; cover. Simmer 2 hours, add potatoes and turnips; cook 30 minutes longer, or until meat is tender when pierced with a two-tined fork.
2. Serve beef and vegetables on a heated platter, accompanied by COLD HORSERADISH SAUCE. Strain broth to use for a soup or gravy base.

COLD HORSERADISH SAUCE: Makes 2 cups. Combine ½ cup fresh bread crumbs, ¼ cup milk, 2 tablespoons prepared horseradish and ¼ teaspoon salt; let stand 15 minutes, or until bread crumbs are soft. Beat ½ cup heavy cream until stiff in a small bowl; fold in horseradish mixture; refrigerate until serving time.

BAVARIAN STUFFED CABBAGE

Caraway seeds and cooked beef make a savory stuffing for a whole cabbage.

Makes 6 servings.

- 1 large cabbage
- ¼ teaspoon salt
- 2 tablespoons butter or margarine
- 1 medium-size onion, chopped (½ cup)
- ½ cup chopped celery with leaves
- ¼ cup chopped parsley
- 2 cups finely chopped cooked beef
- 2 cups diced cooked potatoes
- ⅛ teaspoon salt
- ¼ teaspoon pepper
- 1 teaspoon caraway seeds, crushed
  Creamy Horseradish Sauce
  (recipe follows)

1. Remove coarse outer leaves from cabbage. Place cabbage in a large kettle with boiling salted water to cover. Cover and simmer 5 minutes. Remove from water, drain and cool.
2. Peel back 6 outer leaves carefully. Cut out center of cabbage from the top, making a hole 3 inches wide and 2-inches deep. Sprinkle cavity with the ¼ teaspoon salt. Chop removed cabbage to measure ½ cup; reserve.
3. Melt butter or margarine in a large skillet. Add onion and sauté until tender. Remove from heat. Add celery and leaves, parsley, beef, potatoes, the ½ teaspoon salt, pepper, caraway seeds and reserved ½ cup chopped cabbage; mix well. Pack into cavity of cabbage. Reshape turned back leaves to cover opening; wrap cabbage in cheesecloth. Place on a rack in a kettle. Add boiling water to a depth of 1 inch.
4. Cover kettle and simmer over low heat 30 minutes. Remove cabbage with 2 slotted spoons; drain over kettle; place on heated platter; remove cheesecloth. Serve with CREAMY HORSERADISH SAUCE.

CREAMY HORSERADISH SAUCE: Makes 2 cups. Melt ¼ cup (½ stick) butter or margarine in a medium-size saucepan; stir in ¼ cup all purpose flour, 1 teaspoon salt and ¼ teaspoon white pepper; cook, stirring constantly, until mixture bubbles. Stir in 2 cups milk and cook, stirring constantly, until sauce thickens and bubbles 3 minutes. Stir in 1 tablespoon prepared horseradish.

SAUSAGE CHOWDER

A hearty dish made in minutes.

Makes 8 servings.

- 1 package (12 ounces) smoked sausage links
- 2 tablespoons butter or margarine
- 1 large onion, chopped (1 cup)
- 2 packages (10 ounces each) frozen mixed vegetables
- 1 cup water
- 6 cups milk
- 1 tablespoon prepared mustard
- 2 teaspoons salt
- ¼ teaspoon pepper
- 1 cup dry instant mashed potatoes

1. Cut sausages into 1-inch-thick pieces; brown in butter or margarine in a heavy kettle; remove and set aside. Stir onion into drippings; sauté until soft.
2. Stir in mixed vegetables and water; cook, following label directions. Stir in milk, mustard, salt, pepper and sausages. Bring slowly to boiling, stirring several times.
3. Slowly stir in dry potatoes until mixture thickens slightly. Ladle into heated soup bowls.

CABBAGE ROULADEN

These German roll-ups have a meatloaf filling in a beefy sauce.

Bake at 375° for 45 minutes.
Makes 4 servings.

- 8 large cabbage leaves (from a medium-size head)
- 1 pound ground beef
- ¼ cup quick-cooking rolled oats
- 1 small onion, chopped (¼ cup)
- 1 tablespoon chopped parsley
- 1 egg
- 1 can condensed beef broth
- 1 teaspoon salt
- ⅛ teaspoon pepper
- 1 tablespoon butter or margarine
  Hot cooked noodles

1. Trim base of cabbage and carefully break off 8 whole leaves. (Save remaining cabbage for another meal.)
2. Place leaves in a large saucepan; pour in water to a depth of 1 inch; cover. Heat to boiling; remove from heat. Let stand 5 minutes, or until leaves wilt; drain well.
3. Mix ground beef lightly with rolled oats, onion, parsley, egg, ⅔ cup of the beef broth, salt and pepper.
4. Lay cabbage leaves flat on counter top; spoon meat mixture onto middle of each, dividing evenly. Fold edges of each leaf over filling and roll up; fasten with wooden picks. Arrange rolls in a single layer in a greased 6-cup shallow casserole.
5. Pour remaining broth over cabbage rolls; dot with butter or margarine; cover.

6. Bake in moderate oven (375°) 45 minutes, or until cabbage is tender. Lift onto a heated serving platter with a slotted spoon; remove picks. Serve over hot cooked noodles.
COOK'S TIP: Trim thick rib of wilted cabbage leaves with a sharp paring knife for ease in rolling up leaves.

BREMEN HAMBURGER JUMBLE

An easy oven casserole with ground beef, noodles and a medley of vegetables.

Bake at 350° for 40 minutes.
Makes 6 servings.

- 1 pound ground round or chuck
- 2 cups uncooked noodles
- 1 can (1 pound) tomatoes
- 2 cups shredded cabbage
- 1 cup pared sliced raw carrots
- 1 can condensed cream of vegetable soup
- 1 cup water
- 1 teaspoon instant minced onion
- ½ teaspoon salt

1. Shape ground beef into a large patty in a large skillet; brown 5 minutes on each side, then break up into small chunks. Spoon into an 8-cup casserole.
2. Stir noodles, tomatoes, cabbage, carrots, soup, water, instant minced onion and salt into skillet and blend well. Spoon into dish and cover.
3. Bake in moderate oven (350°) 40 minutes, or until noodles and vegetables are tender.

BALTIC BAKED SHRIMP

Shrimp baked under a buttery crumb topping.

Bake at 325° for 25 minutes.
Makes 4 servings.

- 1 bag (1 pound) frozen shelled deveined raw shrimp
- ½ cup (1 stick) butter or margarine, melted
- 1 cup fine dry bread crumbs
- ¼ cup grated Parmesan cheese
- ½ teaspoon salt
- ½ teaspoon pepper
- 2 tablespoons lemon juice
- 2 tablespoons dry Sherry

1. Place frozen shrimp in an 8x8x2-inch baking pan; brush each one lightly with part of the melted butter or margarine. Heat in a slow oven (325°) while preparing crumb topping.
2. Blend remaining butter or margarine with bread crumbs, cheese, salt, pepper, lemon juice and dry Sherry in small bowl; spoon mixture evenly over shrimp.
3. Bake in slow oven (325°) 25 minutes, or until topping is golden. Serve with grated zucchini lightly sautéed in butter just until tender.

DUTCH PEA SOUP

From Germany's neighbor comes this hearty main-dish soup, flavored with salt pork, carrot, celery and green onion.

Makes 6 servings.

- 1 package (1 pound) dried green or yellow split peas
- 8 cups water
- ¼ pound lean salt pork, in one piece
- 1 large carrot, pared and diced
- 1 large stalk celery, diced
- 5 green onions, trimmed and sliced
- 2 teaspoons salt
- ¼ teaspoon freshly ground pepper

1. Pick over peas; wash; place in a large heavy kettle; add water and salt pork. Bring to boiling over moderate heat; cover; simmer 1 hour, 30 minutes.
2. Add carrot, celery, green onions, salt and pepper; cover and simmer 30 minutes. Uncover; turn heat to lowest point and simmer very slowly 1 hour longer, stirring occasionally, until quite thick (it should be about the consistency of gravy). Taste for salt, adding more if needed.
3. Ladle into soup bowls and serve with buttered brown bread, and cucumber salad, if you wish.

HAMBURG MACARONI

Though Germans are great potato lovers, they enjoy pasta, too.

Bake at 350° for 30 minutes.
Makes 6 servings.

- 1 package (8 ounces) small twist or elbow macaroni
- 1 small onion, peeled and sliced
- 1 tablespoon butter or margarine
- 1 pound ground beef
- 2 tablespoons all purpose flour
- 3 teaspoons paprika
- ½ teaspoon salt
- 1 envelope or teaspoon instant beef broth
- 1 cup milk
- 1 can (3 or 4 ounces) chopped mushrooms
- ½ cup water
- 1 container (8 ounces) dairy sour cream
- ¼ cup chopped parsley
- 1 cup buttered bread crumbs

1. Cook macaroni, following label directions; drain, then return to kettle.
2. Sauté onion lightly in butter or margarine in a large skillet; push to one side. Shape ground beef into a large patty in same pan; brown 5 minutes on each side, then break up into chunks.
3. Blend in flour, 2½ teaspoons of the paprika and salt; add instant beef broth, milk, mushrooms and their liquid, and water. Cook, stirring constantly, until mixture thickens and boils 1 minute.

4. Blend about ½ cup of the hot mixture into sour cream, then stir back into pan. Stir into cooked macaroni; add parsley.

5. Spoon into a greased 8-cup casserole; sprinkle with buttered bread crumbs and remaining ½ teaspoon paprika.

6. Bake in moderate oven (350°) 30 minutes, or until bubbly hot and crumbs are golden. Serve with tomato and cucumber salad, if you wish.

MUENSTER AND EGGS

A meatless main dish with soufflé topping.

Bake at 325° for 45 minutes.
Makes 4 servings.

- 2 cups bread cubes (4 slices)
- ½ cup (1 stick) butter or margarine
- 2 packages (10 ounces each) frozen chopped spinach
- 1 medium-size onion, chopped (½ cup)
- 1 cup cubed Muenster cheese (4 ounces)
- 2 teaspoons salt
- ⅛ teaspoon pepper
- ⅛ teaspoon ground nutmeg
- ¼ cup all purpose flour
- 1 cup milk
- ⅓ cup grated Parmesan cheese
- 8 eggs

1. Sauté bread cubes in 2 tablespoons of the butter or margarine in a medium-size skillet till golden; place in the bottom of a lightly greased 6-cup casserole. Sauté onion until tender in same skillet in 2 more tablespoons butter; reserve.

2. Cook spinach in medium-size saucepan, following label directions; drain very well. Return to saucepan; add onion, Muenster cheese, salt, pepper and nutmeg. Spoon over bread.

3. Melt remaining butter or margarine in a small saucepan; stir in flour; cook, stirring constantly, just until mixture bubbles. Stir in milk slowly; continue cooking and stirring until sauce thickens and bubbles 3 minutes. Remove from heat.

4. Stir in Parmesan cheese. Cool.

5. Separate 4 of the eggs. Beat egg whites in a medium-size bowl just until they form soft peaks.

6. Beat egg yolks in a large bowl until thick and fluffy, then beat in cooled white sauce mixture, small amount at a time. Carefully fold in egg whites until no streaks of white remain.

7. With spoon, make 4 indentations in the spinach mixture, 1 inch from edge of dish. Carefully break remaining 4 eggs, one into each indentation. Spoon soufflé mixture completely over top, right to the edge.

8. Bake in moderate oven (325°) for 45 minutes, till puffy, firm and golden. Serve at once.

SAUSAGE AND POTATO SALAD

Sausages team with potatoes in a mellow, sweet-and-sour dressing.

Makes 6 servings.

- 9 medium-size potatoes (about 3 pounds), pared and diced
- 1 small onion, chopped (¼ cup)
- 1 cup thinly sliced celery
- ½ cup thinly sliced dill pickle
- 2 cans (about 4 ounces each) Vienna sausages, sliced
- 2 tablespoons butter or margarine
- 2 tablespoons brown sugar
- 2 tablespoons cider vinegar
- 2 tablespoons water
- ½ teaspoon dry mustard
- ¼ teaspoon salt

1. Cook potatoes in boiling salted water just until tender in a medium-size saucepan; drain. Stir in onion, celery and pickle.

2. Sauté Vienna sausages lightly in butter or margarine in large skillet; mix in brown sugar, cider vinegar, water, dry mustard and salt; bring just to boiling.

3. Pour over potato mixture in saucepan; toss lightly. Serve hot.

PORK-STUFFED CABBAGE

Paprika flavors and colors the sauce for this delightful dish.

Makes 6 servings.

- 1 large cabbage (about 4½ pounds)
- 1½ pounds ground pork
- 1 large onion, chopped (1 cup)
- 1 hard roll, soaked in water, squeezed dry and crumbled
- 1½ cups cooked rice
- 1 clove garlic, chopped
- 2 eggs
- 1½ teaspoons salt
- ½ teaspoon leaf marjoram, crumbled
- 1 teaspoon paprika
- 6 slices bacon, chopped
- 1 can (13¾ ounces) chicken broth
- 1 container (8 oz) dairy sour cream
- 1 tablespoon all purpose flour
- 2 teaspoons paprika

1. Core cabbage and cover with boiling water in a large kettle. Simmer 10 minutes, then drain and cool. Separate into large leaves. Slice off the tough rib on back of each leaf.

2. Mix pork, onion, roll, rice, garlic, eggs, salt, marjoram and the 1 teaspoon paprika in a large bowl until well blended.

3. Place ⅓ cup of mixture on a cabbage leaf. Roll, turning ends in and rolling up; secure with wooden picks. Repeat until all of mixture is used. Shred remaining cabbage.

4. Fry bacon until crisp in a nonstick Dutch oven (see Buyer's Guide). Add half the shredded cabbage. Top with

cabbage rolls and remaining shredded cabbage. Pour chicken broth over top; cover tightly. Simmer 1 hour. Remove cabbage rolls to a heated platter and keep warm.

5. Combine sour cream, flour and paprika in a small bowl; stir a cup of pan juices into sour cream, then pour into Dutch oven. Cook over low heat until mixture thickens; do *not* boil. Pour over cabbage and serve at once.

CHICKEN BAVARIA

Chicken and beans in sour cream sauce, topped with crunchy pretzels.

Bake at 350° for 20 minutes.
Makes 6 servings.

- 2 packages (9 ounces each) frozen whole green beans
- 1 clove garlic, sliced
- 3 cups cubed cooked chicken
- ¼ teaspoon seasoned pepper
- 1 container (8 ounces) dairy sour cream
- 2 tablespoons butter or margarine
- 1 package (3 ounces) pretzels, crushed

1. Cook green beans with sliced garlic, following label directions; drain; remove garlic. Place in a 4-cup casserole; top with chicken. Stir seasoned pepper into sour cream and spoon over chicken.

2. Melt butter or margarine in a small saucepan; add pretzels and toss to coat well. Sprinkle over sour cream.

3. Bake in moderate oven (350°) 20 minutes, or until pretzels are golden and sauce bubbles.

CHICKEN ROMANOFF

One of the most popular of all ways with noodles. Cottage and Parmesan cheeses blend with sour cream for the sauce.

Bake at 350° for 30 minutes.
Makes 4 servings.

- 1 package (8 ounces) noodles
- 1 cup cubed cooked chicken
- 1 container (8 ounces) cream-style cottage cheese
- 1 container (8 ounces) dairy sour cream
- ½ cup grated Parmesan cheese
- 1 teaspoon grated onion
- 1 teaspoon Worcestershire sauce

1. Cook noodles in boiling salted water in a kettle, following label directions; drain; return to kettle.

2. Stir in chicken, cottage cheese, sour cream, Parmesan cheese, onion and Worcestershire sauce; spoon into a 6-cup casserole.

3. Bake in moderate oven (350°) 30 minutes, or until hot. Sprinkle with chopped parsley, if you wish. Serve with pickled cucumber slices.

GERMAN

CAULIFLOWER SOUFFLÉ

Classified as an expensive vegetable, cauliflower becomes bargain fare when stretched with noodles.

Broil for 3 to 4 minutes.
Makes 6 servings.

- 1 large cauliflower, separated into flowerets
- 1 package (8 ounces) fine noodles
- ⅓ cup chopped parsley
- 2 cups finely diced Muenster cheese (8 ounces)
- 3 tablespoons butter or margarine
- ¼ teaspoon salt
- ½ cup mayonnaise or salad dressing
- 1 tablespoon grated onion
- 1 tablespoon lemon juice
  Dash cayenne pepper
- 1 egg white, stiffly beaten
- ¼ cup grated Parmesan cheese

1. Cook cauliflower in lightly salted boiling water in a large saucepan 15 minutes, or until tender; drain; keep hot.
2. Cook noodles; drain; mix with half the parsley; add Muenster cheese, butter or margarine and salt; turn into an 8-cup flameproof casserole; top with cauliflower.
3. Combine mayonnaise or salad dressing, remaining parsley, onion, lemon juice and cayenne pepper; fold into beaten egg white; spoon over hot cauliflower-noodle mixture. Sprinkle Parmesan cheese evenly over all.
4. Broil, 4 inches from heat, 3 to 4 minutes, until top is puffed and browned.

OLD-WORLD SAUERBRATEN

Sauerbraten means "our pot roast" in German. You marinate it for 2 to 3 days.

Makes 8 servings.

- 5 to 6 pounds beef round, rump, sirloin tip or boneless chuck roast
- 2 cups wine vinegar or cider vinegar
- 2 cups water
- ¼ cup firmly packed brown sugar
- 1 tablespoon salt
- ½ teaspoon pepper
- ½ teaspoon ground cloves
- 1 bay leaf
- 3 medium-size onions, chopped (1½ cups)
- 2 large carrots, diced (1½ cups)
- 1½ cups diced celery
- 2 tablespoons bacon drippings or vegetable shortening
- 8 gingersnaps, crumbled

1. Place meat in a large glass or ceramic bowl; pour mixture of vinegar, water, brown sugar, salt, pepper, cloves, bay leaf, onions, carrots and celery over. Cover; store in refrigerator 2 to 3 days, turning meat several times to marinate on all sides.
2. When ready to cook, remove meat from marinade and pat dry; brown in hot drippings or shortening in heavy kettle or Dutch oven. Strain vegetables from marinade; add to meat in kettle, then pour in liquid to a depth of 1 inch.
3. Cover kettle tightly; simmer 3 hours, or until meat is very tender. Remove to heated serving platter; keep hot while making gravy.
4. Strain broth into a 4-cup measure; let stand 1 minute, or until fat rises to top. Skim off fat, returning 4 tablespoons to kettle.
5. Add water to broth, if needed, to make 2 cups; stir back into kettle; sprinkle crumbled gingersnaps over. Cook, stirring constantly, until gravy thickens and bubbles.
6. Slice meat; serve with hot gravy, noodles and carrots, if you wish.

SMOKED PORK PLATTER

A budget dinner with continental flavor.

Makes 6 servings.

- 1 smoked pork shoulder roll (about 3 pounds)
- 2 tablespoons brown sugar
- 1 tablespoon mixed pickling spices
- 6 medium-size fresh beets
- 6 medium-size potatoes, pared
- 12 small carrots, pared
- 1 small cabbage, cut into 6 wedges (about 1 pound)
  Horseradish-Mustard Sauce (recipe follows)

1. Place shoulder roll, brown sugar and pickling spices in a kettle; add water to cover. Cover and simmer 1 hour, 15 minutes, or until meat is almost tender.
2. While meat cooks, cut leafy tops to within 1 inch of beets. (This helps beets keep their rich color.) Cook beets in boiling salted water in a medium-size saucepan 45 minutes, or until tender; drain. Run under cold water; slip off skins. Cut beets in quarters; return to saucepan; keep hot.
3. When meat is almost tender, arrange potatoes and carrots around meat in kettle; cover and cook 30 minutes. Place cabbage wedges on top; cook 15 minutes longer, or until all vegetables are tender.
4. Lift out vegetables with a slotted spoon; place with beets in separate rounds around the edge of a heated large serving platter.
5. Slice part of meat; place all in middle of platter. Pass HORSERADISH-MUSTARD SAUCE.

HORSERADISH-MUSTARD SAUCE: Makes 1 cup. Blend together 1 container (8 ounces) dairy sour cream, 2 tablespoons prepared horseradish, 2 tablespoons dry mustard and 1 teaspoon salt in a bowl; cover. Chill.

CHOUCROUTE GARNIE

This cents-saving Alsatian dish combines sauerkraut, pork hocks and knackwurst.

Makes 6 servings.

- 2 cans (1 pound, 11 ounces each) sauerkraut
- 6 pork hocks (about 3 pounds)
- 2 cups dry white wine
- 1 bay leaf
- 6 whole cloves
- 1 medium-size onion
- 1½ pounds knackwurst
- 1 red apple, quartered, cored and sliced
- 12 new potatoes (about 1¼ pounds)

1. Soak sauerkraut 5 minutes in cold water in a large bowl; drain well.
2. Place pork hocks in a Dutch oven. Add drained sauerkraut, wine and bay leaf. Press cloves into onion; press onion down into sauerkraut. Bring to boiling; reduce heat; cover. Simmer very slowly 1 hour, 30 minutes, tossing with a fork once or twice, or until pork hocks are almost tender.
3. Score knackwurst with a sharp knife; place on sauerkraut; simmer about 20 minutes longer. Add apple slices, pushing them down into sauerkraut. Cook 10 minutes longer.
4. Scrub potatoes well; cook in boiling salted water to cover in a large saucepan 20 minutes, or until done.
5. Arrange meat and sauerkraut mixture with potatoes on a large deep platter. Serve with whole-wheat bread and mustard, if you wish.

BRESLAU TURKEY

Roast turkey was a favorite Sunday dinner choice in this former German city, now part of Poland.

Makes 6 servings.

- 1 packaged frozen boneless turkey roast (about 2 pounds)
- 2 tablespoons vegetable oil
- ½ teaspoon monosodium glutamate
- ½ teaspoon seasoned salt
- ¼ teaspoon seasoned pepper
- 1 envelope or teaspoon instant beef broth
- 1 medium-size onion, chopped (½ cup)
- 1 cup water
- 1 can (1 pound) cut green beans
- 2 cups thinly sliced celery
- 1 cup elbow macaroni

1. Remove thawed turkey roast from foil package. Brown slowly in vegetable oil in a Dutch oven or electric skillet.
2. Stir in monosodium glutamate, seasoned salt and pepper, instant beef broth, onion and water. Bring to boiling; cover; lower heat.
3. Simmer, turning meat once or twice, 2 hours, or until tender. Remove to a cutting board; keep warm

while cooking vegetables and pasta.

4. Pour liquid from Dutch oven into a 4-cup measure; drain liquid from green beans into same cup. Add water, if needed, to make 4 cups. Return to Dutch oven; bring to boiling.

5. Stir in celery, macaroni and beans. Cook, stirring several times, 10 minutes, or until macaroni and celery are tender and almost all of the liquid has evaporated. Spoon vegetables onto a heated large deep platter.

6. Carve turkey into ¼-inch-thick slices; arrange slices, overlapping, on top of vegetables on serving platter. Sprinkle lightly with chopped parsley, if you wish.

SILESIAN OXTAIL SOUP

A treasured winter dish in western Poland, old-fashioned oxtail soup goes splendidly with a garnish of Eggs Mimosa.

Bake at 450° for 45 minutes.
Makes 6 servings.

3 pounds oxtails, cut up
3 teaspoons salt
⅛ teaspoon pepper
1 large onion, chopped (1 cup)
2 carrots, pared and sliced
1 parsnip, pared and sliced
1 turnip, pared and sliced
2 tablespoons brandy
6 cups water
½ teaspoon leaf savory, crumbled
1 bay leaf
Eggs Mimosa (recipe follows)
Chopped parsley

1. Spread oxtails in a single layer in a shallow roasting pan. Sprinkle with 2 teaspoons of the salt and pepper.

2. Roast in very hot oven (450°) 45 minutes, or until oxtails are nicely browned. Drain off fat, reserving 2 tablespoons.

3. Sauté onion, carrots, parsnip and turnip in reserved fat in kettle or Dutch oven 10 minutes, or until soft. Add browned oxtails. Drizzle brandy over; ignite carefully with a lighted match. Add water and remaining 1 teaspoon of salt to roasting pan in which oxtails were browned. Heat, stirring constantly, to dissolve browned bits; pour over oxtails and vegetables in Dutch oven; add savory and bay leaf. Bring to boiling; reduce heat; cover; simmer slowly 2 hours, or until meat separates easily from bones.

4. Ladle into soup bowls. Carefully place a half Egg Mimosa in each bowl; sprinkle with parsley. Serve with a loaf of crusty French bread, if you wish.

EGGS MIMOSA: Makes 6 servings. Cut 3 hard-cooked eggs in half, lengthwise. Carefully remove yolks, keeping whites whole. Press yolks through a sieve; spoon into the whites, mounding slightly.

BAKED FISH DANZIG

Sour cream and buttered bread cumbs make this dish special.

Bake at 350° for 55 minutes.
Makes 6 servings.

2 packages (1 pound each) frozen cod, haddock, or flounder fillets
OR: 2 pounds fresh cod, haddock or flounder fillets
4 tablespoons all purpose flour
2 teaspoons salt
¼ teaspoon pepper
1 cup milk
2 cups coarse soft bread crumbs (4 slices)
¼ cup (½ stick) butter or margarine
1 tablespoon chopped parsley
1 container (8 ounces) dairy sour cream
1 package (10 ounces) frozen peas, cooked, drained and seasoned
Lemon slices
Chopped parsley

1. Cut frozen or fresh fillets into serving-size pieces; coat with mixture of flour, salt, and pepper. Arrange in single layer in a 13x9x2-inch baking dish; pour milk over.

2. Bake in moderate oven (350°) 45 minutes.

3. Toast crumbs lightly in butter or margarine in a medium-size skillet, stirring often. Stir parsley into sour cream. Remove fish from oven; spoon sour cream mixture over; top with toasted crumbs.

4. Bake 10 minutes longer, or until sour cream is set. Prepare peas and season, following label directions; spoon at either end of fish. Garnish fish with lemon slices and chopped parsley; if you wish.

GERMAN STUFFED PEPPERS

Though the recipe calls for ground beef, you can substitute 2 cups of leftover chopped roast beef, lamb or pork.

Makes 6 servings.

1 small onion, diced (¼ cup)
1 tablespoon butter or margarine
¼ cup uncooked long grain rice
1½ cups water
1 pound ground round or chuck
1 teaspoon salt
¼ teaspoon pepper
6 medium-size green peppers
¼ cup (½ stick) butter or margarine
2 tablespoons all purpose flour
2 teaspoons sugar
1 can (1 pound) tomato purée

1. Sauté onion in the 1 tablespoon butter or margarine until soft in a large skillet. Add rice; cook over low heat, stirring constantly, 1 minute. Stir in ½ cup of the water; cook until rice is almost tender (about 10 minutes).

2. Remove skillet from heat; add

meat, ½ teaspoon of the salt and ⅛ teaspoon of the pepper, mixing thoroughly.

3. Wash green peppers; cut off tops; scoop out seeds and membranes being careful to keep skin intact. Stuff loosely with rice-meat mixture.

4. Melt the ¼ cup butter or margarine in a small heavy kettle or Dutch oven. Stir in flour, sugar, remaining ½ teaspoon salt and ⅛ teaspoon pepper. Slowly stir in tomato purée and remaining 1 cup water. Simmer over low heat, stirring constantly, until sauce is smooth.

5. Stand filled peppers upright in tomato sauce; cover. Simmer over low heat 30 minutes, or until peppers are tender and heated through. Serve with crusty French bread and butter, if you wish.

TUNA-CHEESE IMPERIAL

Cream cheese, Muenster cheese and sliced olives give this economical tuna-noodle casserole an expensive taste.

Bake at 350° for 30 minutes.
Makes 6 servings.

1 package (8 ounces) wide noodles
½ cup (1 stick) butter or margarine
5 tablespoons all purpose flour
1 teaspoon salt
¼ teaspoon pepper
2½ cups milk
1 package (8 ounces) cream cheese
1 can (about 6½ ounces) tuna, drained and flaked
½ cup sliced pimiento-stuffed olives
2 tablespoons cut chives
1 package (6 ounces) sliced Muenster cheese
1½ cups soft bread crumbs (3 slices)

1. Cook noodles, following label directions; drain.

2. Melt 5 tablespoons of the butter or margarine in a medium-size saucepan; stir in flour, salt and pepper; cook, stirring constantly, until bubbly. Stir in milk; continue cooking and stirring until sauce thickens and bubbles 3 minutes. Slice cream cheese into sauce; stir until melted, then stir in tuna, olives and chives. Stir to mix ingredients well and then remove saucepan from heat.

3. Pour about ¾ cup sauce into a greased 10-cup casserole. Layer half of the noodles, half of the remaining sauce, 2 slices Muenster cheese, remaining noodles, remaining Muenster cheese and remaining sauce.

4. Melt remaining 3 tablespoons butter or margarine in a small saucepan; add bread crumbs; toss lightly with a fork just to moisten. Sprinkle over casserole.

5. Bake in moderate oven (350°) 30 minutes, or until bubbly. Serve with a mixed green salad, if you wish.

SAUCISSE CHOUCROUTE

A classic combination from Alsace, the contested region of Germany and France.

Bake at 350° for 2 hours.
Makes 6 servings.

1 can (1 pound, 12 ounces)
  sauerkraut
3 potatoes, pared and diced
3 carrots, pared and diced
1 medium-size onion, chopped
  (½ cup)
1 can condensed chicken broth
1 cup Rhine wine
1 pound bratwurst
1 pound knackwurst

1. Drain sauerkraut; rinse with cold water. Squeeze out excess water.
2. Combine sauerkraut, potatoes, carrots, onion, chicken broth and wine in a 10-cup casserole. Top with bratwurst and knackwurst; cover casserole.
3. Bake in moderate oven (350°) 2 hours, or until liquid is absorbed.
COOK'S TIP: While the Choucroute is baking, why not core some cooking apples, fill with raisins, brown sugar and butter and bake along with main dish?

ALPINE ONION TARTS

Tiny pies with Swiss cheese inside and out —even to the peaks on top. Round out your meal with a spinach salad.

Bake at 450° for 5 minutes,
then at 325° for 25 minutes.
Makes 6 servings.

1 package piecrust mix
1 medium-size onion, chopped
  (½ cup)
2 tablespoons butter or margarine
4 eggs, separated
1½ cups dairy sour cream (from a
  16-ounce container)
¼ teaspoon salt
⅛ teaspoon pepper
½ pound Swiss cheese, cut into ½-
  inch cubes
2 tablespoons grated Parmesan
  cheese
½ cup shredded Swiss cheese
1 tablespoon chopped parsley

1. Prepare piecrust mix, following the label directions, or make pastry from your favorite two-crust recipe. Roll out, half at a time, ⅛-inch thick, on lightly floured pastry cloth or board; cut 3 six-inch rounds from each half. (A saucer makes a good pattern.) Fit each round into a 4-inch tart-shell pan, pressing pastry firmly against bottom and side. Trim overhang to ½ inch; turn edge under, flush with rim; flute to make a stand-up edge. Prick shells all over with fork.
2. Bake in very hot oven (450°) 5 minutes; remove from oven. Lower oven temperature to 325°.
3. Sauté onion in butter or margarine until soft in a small skillet, spoon into partly baked shells, dividing evenly.
4. Beat egg yolks slightly in a medium-size bowl; stir in sour cream, salt, pepper, cubed Swiss and Parmesan cheese. Spoon over onion in tart shells.
5. Bake in slow oven (325°) 15 minutes.
6. While tarts bake, beat egg whites until they form soft peaks in a medium-size bowl. Remove tarts from oven; spoon beaten egg whites over each, swirling with back of spoon. Top with shredded Swiss.
7. Bake 10 minutes longer, or until tops are golden. Sprinkle with parsley.

BEEF MIROTON

The frugal Germans have a grand way with leftover beef.

Makes 6 servings.

2 tablespoons butter or margarine
2 large onions, sliced
½ cup dry white wine
¼ cup catsup or chili sauce
1 can condensed beef broth
2 teaspoons aromatic bitters
3 cups leftover cooked beef,
  thinly sliced
½ cup sliced sour gherkins
½ cup sliced pitted black olives
4 cups hot cooked noodles
¼ cup grated Parmesan cheese

1. Melt butter or margarine over high heat in a large skillet. Add onions and sauté, stirring constantly, until onions brown. Add wine, catsup, beef broth and bitters. Bring to boiling; lower heat and simmer 2 minutes.
2. Stir in beef, gherkins and olives. Cook 1 minute, or until piping hot and bubbly. Spoon into serving dish and surround with hot noodles. Sprinkle with grated Parmesan cheese. Serve with a romaine salad, if you wish.

HUNGARIAN SZÉKELY GULYÁS

A hearty, economical dish from Germany's neighbor.

Makes 6 servings.

2 pounds pork, cut into 1-inch cubes
2 tablespoons butter or margarine
1 large onion, chopped (1 cup)
1 tablespoon paprika
1 can condensed chicken broth
1 cup water
1 teaspoon caraway seeds
2 teaspoons salt
  Dash pepper
1 can (1 pound, 11 ounces)
  sauerkraut
2 tablespoons all purpose flour
¼ cup water
1 container (8 ounces) dairy sour
  cream
  Chopped parsley

1. Brown pork, part at a time, in butter or margarine in a heavy kettle or Dutch oven. Sauté onion until golden in same pan, about 5 minutes, adding more butter or margarine, if needed. Stir in paprika; cook 1 minute longer. Return all meat.
2. Stir in chicken broth, the 1 cup water, caraway seeds, salt and pepper. Bring to boiling; lower heat and cover. Simmer 1 hour, 15 minutes.
3. Drain and rinse sauerkraut; stir into stew. Simmer 30 minutes longer, or until meat is tender.
4. Blend flour and the ¼ cup water in a small cup; stir into simmering stew. Cook and stir until gravy thickens and bubbles 3 minutes.
5. Lower heat; stir 1 cup hot sauce into sour cream in a small bowl until well blended; stir back into kettle. Heat just until heated through. *Do not boil.* Sprinkle with parsley.

TZIMMES

An easily assembled dish, often made for the Friday Sabbath dinner. It is shown on page 65 served with pumpernickel bread.

Bake at 350° for 2 hours, 30 minutes.
Makes 8 servings.

1 package (11 ounces) mixed
  dried fruit
1 chuck, brisket or shoulder roast
  (about 3 pounds)
1 tablespoon all purpose flour
2 teaspoons salt
¼ teaspoon pepper
4 carrots, pared and quartered
4 sweet potatoes or yams, peeled
  and quartered
½ lemon, thinly sliced
½ lime, thinly sliced
2 cups water
1 cup orange juice
4 tablespoons honey

1. Rinse dried fruit in running water and soak in cold water 1 hour; drain.
2. Sprinkle meat with flour, salt and pepper; brown over medium heat in a 12-cup flameproof casserole or Dutch oven. Arrange dried fruit, carrots, potatoes and lemon and lime slices around it. Mix water, orange juice and honey in a medium-size bowl; pour over all; cover casserole.
3. Bake in moderate oven (350°) 2 hours, 30 minutes, or until meat and vegetables are tender when pierced with a two-tined fork.
COOK'S TIP: TZIMMES is even better when reheated the next day.

☞

Tzimmes is a brisket of beef, seasoned with honey and baked in a mingling of fruits and vegetables. Recipe is on this page.

If you've never experienced the spirited taste of Italy at home, your time has come. Cannelloni

DELIZIOSO!

Italiana, with its homemade pasta, is definitely one dish to add to your repertoire. But don't take our word for it—Mangia!

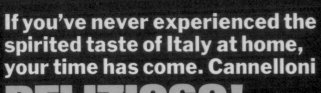

Roll pasta dough so thin you can see the grain of your wooden board. Spoon filling from corner to corner.

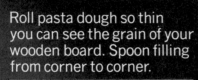

Grease a large cookie sheet with oil. Pat yeast dough out to a 14 x 11-inch rectangle with your hands, making edges thicker.

SICILIAN PIZZA

This is the thicker, more bread-like crust with a trio of toppings and lots of cheese. Photograph is on page 68.

Bake at 400° for 40 minutes.
Makes one 14x11-inch pizza.

Pizza Dough (recipe follows)
1 pound sweet Italian sausages
2 large onions, sliced
1 clove garlic, minced
½ pound mushrooms, sliced
1 teaspoon salt
1 teaspoon leaf oregano, crumbled
¼ teaspoon pepper
2 large green peppers, halved, seeded and cubed
2 cups Zesty Tomato Sauce (recipe, page 70)
1 package (8 ounces) mozzarella cheese

1. Prepare PIZZA DOUGH.
2. Prick sausages with a table fork; brown in a large skillet, turning often, until cooked; remove and drain on paper towels; cut into 1-inch slices.
3. Drain and reserve all but 3 tablespoons fat from skillet; sauté onions and garlic until soft in skillet; add mushrooms and sauté 2 minutes; sprinkle with half the salt, oregano and pepper; remove and reserve.
4. Add 2 tablespoons reserved fat to skillet; sauté green peppers 3 minutes; sprinkle with remaining salt, oregano and pepper.
5. Spoon ZESTY TOMATO SAUCE over prepared PIZZA DOUGH; arrange sausage, onion-mushroom mixture and green peppers in strips down dough.
6. Bake in hot oven (400°) 30 minutes. Cut cheese into thick slices; arrange in strips on top of pizza. Bake 10 minutes longer, or until crust is golden and cheese melts.

PIZZA DOUGH

Makes one 14 x 11-inch rectangle.

1 envelope active dry yeast
½ teaspoon sugar
1 cup very warm water
3½ cups all purpose flour
1 teaspoon salt

1. Sprinkle yeast and sugar into very warm water in a large bowl. ("Very warm" water should feel comfortably warm when dropped on wrist.) Stir until well blended and allow to stand 10 minutes, or until mixture begins to bubble.

Sicilian Pizza combines three toppings, mozzarella cheese and a zesty tomato sauce on a thick, bread-like crust. Recipe is on this page.

2. Stir flour and salt into bowl until a stiff dough is formed.
3. Turn dough out onto a lightly floured pastry cloth or board. Knead until smooth and elastic, about 5 minutes, using only enough flour needed to keep dough from sticking.
4. Place in a greased large bowl; turn to coat all over with shortening. Cover with a clean towel. Let rise in a warm place, away from draft, 30 minutes, or until double in bulk.
5. Punch dough down. Grease a large cookie sheet and grease hands lightly. Place dough in pan and stretch dough to form a 14x11-inch rectangle, keeping dough slightly thicker on edges.

PASTA CON CINQUE FORMAGGI

Try a new pasta shape and toss it with five special cheeses. Photo, page 530.

Makes 6 servings.

1 package (1 pound) mostaccioli, ziti, rigati or elbow macaroni
¼ cup (½ stick) butter or margarine
1 cup shredded Swiss cheese (4 ounces)
1 cup shredded Bel Paese cheese (4 ounces)
1 cup shredded mozzarella cheese (4 ounces)
1 cup shredded Provolone cheese (4 ounces)
1 cup heavy cream
¼ teaspoon pepper
¼ cup grated Parmesan cheese

1. Cook and drain pasta in a large kettle, following label directions, and keeping 1 cup cooking liquid in kettle; return pasta to kettle.
2. Toss pasta with butter or margarine, Swiss cheese, Bel Paese, mozzarella, Provolone, heavy cream and pepper over low heat, until cheeses melt evenly and coat pasta. Spoon into a heated dish; sprinkle with Parmesan cheese and serve.

RISOTTO BOLOGNESE

This Italian-style rice dish with ground beef and bacon is so quick, yet hearty.

Makes 6 servings.

4 slices bacon, diced
1 pound ground beef
1 teaspoon salt
¼ teaspoon pepper
1 large onion, chopped (1 cup)
1 green pepper; seeded and chopped
1 cup regular rice
2 envelopes or teaspoons instant chicken broth
1 teaspoon leaf basil, crumbled
1 bay leaf
2½ cups water
Chopped parsley

1. Cook bacon until crisp in a large skillet. Remove bacon; drain.

2. Form ground beef into a large patty; brown on both sides in bacon drippings in skillet; drain fat.
3. Break beef up into chunks; sprinkle with salt and pepper. Remove and reserve.
4. Sauté onion and green pepper in same skillet until soft. (If no fat remains in the skillet, add 2 tablespoons vegetable oil.) Stir in rice, instant chicken broth, basil, bay leaf and water.
5. Bring to boiling. Lower heat; stir rice mixture well; cover.
6. Simmer 10 minutes. Spoon browned beef over rice. Return cover and simmer 20 minutes longer, or until liquid is absorbed and rice is tender; remove bay leaf. Sprinkle with reserved bacon and chopped parsley. Garnish with bacon curls, if you wish.

CANNELLONI ITALIANA

Delicate squares of homemade pasta are filled with a ricotta and prosciutto mixture and doubly sauced—delizioso! Shown on page 66 just before being baked.

Bake at 350° for 40 minutes.
Makes 8 servings.

Pasta Dough (recipe, page 70)
1 container (1 pound) ricotta cheese or dry cottage cheese
1 pound mozzarella cheese, shredded
¼ pound prosciutto or boiled ham, finely chopped
3 egg yolks
1 teaspoon salt
Freshly ground pepper
3 cups Zesty Tomato Sauce (recipe, page 70)
Béchamel Sauce (recipe, page 112)

1. Cook PASTA DOUGH, a quarter of the squares at a time, in a large kettle of boiling salted water 5 minutes; remove with slotted spoon to a large bowl of cold water.
2. Combine ricotta or cottage cheese, mozzarella, prosciutto or ham, egg yolks, salt and pepper in a medium-size bowl; stir until well blended.
3. Spread ZESTY TOMATO SAUCE in a 12-cup shallow casserole.
4. Remove pasta squares, one at a time, from water; drain on paper towels; spoon part of the cheese mixture diagonally from one corner to another (see picture, page 66); fold opposite corners over and place over tomato sauce in casserole. Repeat to make 16 cannelloni.
5. Spoon BÉCHAMEL SAUCE down the center of the cannelloni.
6. Bake in moderate oven (350°) 40 minutes, or until bubbly hot.
HOSTESS TIP: Casserole can be prepared ahead of time and refrigerated. Bake in moderate oven (350°) 1 hour, or until bubbly hot.

PASTA DOUGH

Makes about 1½ pounds.

- **3 cups all purpose flour**
- **2 teaspoons salt**
- **3 eggs**
- **2 tablespoons olive or vegetable oil**
- **¼ cup lukewarm water**

1. Sift flour and salt onto a large wooden board; make a well in center; add eggs, oil and water. Work liquids into flour with fingers to make a stiff dough. (Or make dough in a large bowl, but it's not as much fun.)
2. Knead dough on board (do not add additional flour) 10 minutes, or until dough is smooth and soft.
3. Wrap dough in plastic wrap. Let stand 20 minutes. Cut into quarters; keep dough you are not working with wrapped, or it will dry out.
4. Roll out dough quarter on wooden board to an 8x8-inch square. (Do not use additional flour, but if dough really sticks, sprinkle board lightly with cornstarch.) This takes a lot of pressure. Repeat with remaining dough.
5. Cut dough into 4 x 4-inch squares and lay in a single layer on clean towels to dry for 1 hour; repeat with remaining dough.

PINWHEEL GNOCCHI

Tender green spinach and potatoes pinwheel together to make this Italian favorite.

Bake at 400° for 25 minutes.
Makes 4 servings.

- **1 package (10 ounces) frozen chopped spinach**
- **1 cup ricotta cheese (from a 1-pound container)**
- **1 cup grated Parmesan cheese**
- **¼ teaspoon ground nutmeg**
- **¼ teaspoon salt**
- **¼ teaspoon pepper**
- **6 medium-size potatoes, pared**
- **2 eggs, beaten**
- **3 cups sifted all purpose flour**
- **2 tablespoons butter or margarine, melted**

1. Cook spinach, following label directions; squeeze and press all water out of the spinach; spread on paper towels. Chop very fine.
2. Combine the spinach, ricotta, ½ cup of the Parmesan cheese, nutmeg, salt and pepper in a small bowl. Refrigerate until ready to use.
3. Cook potatoes in boiling salted water until tender in a large saucepan; toss over very low heat 2 minutes to dry potatoes.
4. Mash potatoes until smooth in a large bowl; beat in the eggs. Blend in 2¾ cups of the flour to make a soft dough. Knead on lightly floured pastry cloth, adding only enough of the remaining ¼ cup flour to keep dough from sticking. Roll out to a 14-

inch square and spread with spinach filling; roll up, jelly-roll fashion. Wrap in plastic wrap; refrigerate for at least 1 hour.
5. Carefully cut dough into 1-inch slices. Place them; overlapping, in a greased 9x9x2-inch casserole. Spoon melted butter over the top and sprinkle with the remaining Parmesan.
6. Bake in hot oven (400°) 25 minutes, or until golden.

ZITI CASSEROLE

Ziti are the long, hollow, tube-shaped pasta that fill so nicely with savory sauce.

Bake at 350° for 40 minutes.
Makes 8 servings.

- **1 package (1 pound) ziti**
- **1 container (1 pound) ricotta cheese OR: 1 container (1 pound) cream-style cottage cheese**
- **¼ pound mozzarella cheese, diced**
- **½ cup grated Parmesan cheese**
- **1 egg**
- **¾ teaspoon salt**
- **¼ teaspoon pepper**
- **6 cups Zesty Tomato Sauce (recipe follows)**

1. Cook ziti and drain, following label directions.
2. Combine ricotta or cottage cheese, mozzarella, Parmesan, egg, salt and pepper in a large bowl.
3. Layer ziti, cheese mixture and ZESTY TOMATO SAUCE in a 13x9x2-inch casserole, starting and ending with meat sauce.
4. Bake in moderate oven (350°) 40 minutes, or until bubbly hot.

ZESTY TOMATO SAUCE

Makes 10 cups.

- **1 large onion, chopped (1 cup)**
- **2 cloves garlic, minced**
- **¼ cup olive or vegetable oil**
- **2 cans (2 pounds, 3 ounces each) Italian tomatoes**
- **2 cans (6 ounces each) tomato paste**
- **2 tablespoons sugar**
- **1 tablespoon leaf oregano, crumbled**
- **1 tablespoon leaf basil, crumbled**
- **1 tablespoon salt**
- **½ teaspoon pepper**
- **¼ cup grated Parmesan cheese**

1. Sauté onion and garlic in oil until soft in a large skillet.
2. Stir in tomatoes, tomato paste, sugar, oregano, basil, salt and pepper. Simmer, uncovered, stirring frequently, 45 minutes, or until sauce thickens. Stir in Parmesan cheese; cool.
COOK'S TIP: You can freeze recipe-size portions of this sauce in plastic freezer containers, if you wish. And by making a big batch of this hearty home-style sauce, you're ready to make dozens of classic Italian dishes.

NOODLES NAPOLI

Skillet-quick to mix, this hearty dish is ready in minutes.

Makes 6 servings.

- **1 pound ground beef**
- **½ pound sausage meat**
- **1 medium-size onion, chopped (½ cup)**
- **1 clove garlic, minced**
- **1 package (8 ounces) noodles, cooked**
- **1 can (1 pound) Italian tomatoes**
- **1 green pepper, quartered, seeded and chopped**
- **1½ teaspoons salt**
- **1 cup grated Provolone cheese (4 ounces)**

1. Mix ground beef and sausage meat; shape into a large patty in a large skillet; brown 5 minutes on each side; break up into chunks. Remove and reserve.
2. Pour off all but 3 tablespoons drippings; stir in onion and garlic; sauté just until soft. Add noodles.
3. Stir in tomatoes, green pepper, salt and browned meat; cover.
4. Simmer, stirring often, 10 minutes; stir in cheese; cover again. Cook 10 minutes longer, or until cheese melts.

PORK STEW ITALIANO

It's surprising how closely pork can resemble veal when treated this way.

Makes 6 servings.

- **2 pounds pork shoulder, cubed**
- **2 tablespoons olive or vegetable oil**
- **1 large onion, chopped (1 cup)**
- **2 cloves garlic, minced**
- **1 can (2 pounds, 3 ounces) Italian tomatoes**
- **1 tablespoon salt**
- **2 teaspoons mixed Italian herbs, crumbled**
- **½ teaspoon pepper**
- **1 bay leaf**
- **1 cup dry red wine**
- **3 medium-size zucchini, cut into 1-inch pieces**
- **¼ cup all purpose flour**
- **½ cup dry red wine**

1. Brown pork, a few pieces at a time, in oil in a large kettle or Dutch oven; remove and reserve. Sauté onion and garlic in pan drippings; return pork to pan; add tomatoes, salt, Italian herbs, pepper, bay leaf and the 1 cup wine.
2. Bring slowly to boiling; lower heat; cover kettle; simmer 1 hour. Add zucchini; cook 30 minutes longer, or until meat and zucchini are tender. Remove bay leaf.
3. Stir flour into the ½ cup wine in a cup until smooth; stir into bubbling liquid. Cook, stirring gently, until sauce thickens and bubbles 3 minutes. Serve over hot spaghetti and top with grated Parmesan cheese, if you wish.

EGGPLANT PARMIGIANA

It's always been a favorite.

Bake at 350° for 50 minutes.
Makes 8 servings.

- 1½ pounds ground beef
- 1 cup frozen chopped onion
- 1 clove garlic, minced
- 2 tablespoons olive or vegetable oil
- 1 envelope (1½ ounces) spaghetti sauce mix
- 1 can (8 ounces) tomato sauce
- ¾ cup water
- ¾ cup dry red wine
- 1½ teaspoons leaf basil, crumbled
- 1 teaspoon leaf oregano, crumbled
- 1 medium-size eggplant, peeled and sliced (about 1 pound)
- ½ cup olive or vegetable oil
- ½ cup grated Parmesan cheese
- 1 pound mozzarella cheese, thickly sliced

1. Brown beef with onion and garlic in the 2 tablespoons oil in a large saucepan; add spaghetti sauce mix, tomato sauce, water, wine, basil and oregano. Cover; simmer 15 minutes.
2. Sauté eggplant slices, part at a time, in part of the ½ cup oil, adding more oil as needed, in a large skillet until limp and golden. Transfer eggplant to a 12-cup shallow casserole.
3. Spoon meat sauce over eggplant. Sprinkle Parmesan cheese evenly over. Top with mozzarella.
4. Bake in moderate oven (350°) 50 minutes, or until sauce is bubbly hot, and cheese is melted.

ITALIAN SQUASH BOWLS

Pizza-flavored ground beef fills acorn squash shells.

Bake at 375° for 1 hour, 45 minutes.
Makes 6 servings.

- 3 medium-size acorn squash
- 2 tablespoons butter or margarine, melted
- 1½ pounds ground beef
- 1½ cups soft bread crumbs (3 slices)
- 1 egg
- ⅓ cup catsup
- 1 teaspoon salt
- 1 teaspoon leaf oregano, crumbled
- 2 tablespoons grated Parmesan cheese

1. Halve squash; scoop out seeds and membrane. Brush hollows with melted butter or margarine; sprinkle lightly with salt and pepper. Place in a shallow baking pan.
2. Combine ground beef with bread crumbs, egg, catsup, salt and oregano until well blended. Heap into squash halves, dividing evenly. Sprinkle with Parmesan cheese.
3. Bake in moderate oven (375°) 45 minutes; cover with aluminum foil. Bake 1 hour longer, or until squash are tender.

HAM-STUFFED ZUCCHINI

An easy and imaginative way to turn leftover ham into something special.

Bake at 325° for 45 minutes.
Makes 8 servings.

- 8 small zucchini
- 2 teaspoons salt
- 4 cups ground cooked ham
- 2 eggs
- ¼ teaspoon pepper
- 1 teaspoon leaf basil, crumbled
- ½ cup chopped pimiento
- ½ cup chopped green pepper
- ¼ cup shredded Swiss cheese
- 1 tablespoon vegetable oil

1. Cut off the ends of the zucchini; hollow out with an apple corer, removing all of the pulp and leaving only the shell. Sprinkle the insides with 1 teaspoon of the salt.
2. Combine ground ham, remaining teaspoon of salt, eggs, pepper, basil, pimiento, green pepper and cheese in a medium-size bowl. Pack ½ cup of filling into each shell, using your fingers or a teaspoon.
3. Place zucchini in a greased large baking dish. Brush with oil.
4. Bake in moderate oven (350°) 50 minutes, or until sauce is bubbly hot and cheese is melted.

FISH AND SHELLS ITALIANO

Flavorful cod and tender macaroni shells are baked in a zippy tomato sauce.

Bake at 375° for 30 minutes.
Makes 6 servings.

- 1 package (1 pound) macaroni shells
- 1 medium-size onion, chopped (½ cup)
- ½ teaspoon leaf basil, crumbled
- 2 tablespoons olive or vegetable oil
- 1 envelope (about 1½ ounces) spaghetti sauce mix
- 1 can (2 pounds) Italian tomatoes
- 1 package (1 pound) frozen cod fillets, cut into cubes
- ⅓ cup grated Parmesan cheese
- 1 package (8 ounces) mozzarella cheese, sliced

1. Cook macaroni shells, following label directions; drain.
2. While shells cook, sauté onion with basil in oil in large saucepan; stir in spaghetti sauce mix and tomatoes. Cover; simmer for 10 minutes; add the fish cubes; simmer 10 minutes longer.
3. Spoon half the macaroni shells into a 12-cup casserole; sprinkle with half the Parmesan cheese; top with half the fish-tomato sauce. Repeat layers; arrange mozzarella cheese slices on top.
4. Bake in moderate oven (375°) 30 minutes, or until bubbly hot.
COOK'S TIP: If made in the morning and chilled, take from refrigerator and let stand at room temperature 30 minutes before baking.

FARFALLE LEONARDO

Tiny egg noodle bows, tossed with a rich, quick tomato sauce.

Makes 4 servings.

- 1 pound bulk sausage
- 1 large onion, chopped (1 cup)
- 1 clove garlic, minced
- 1 can (1 pound) tomatoes
- 1 teaspoon leaf oregano, crumbled
- 1 teaspoon leaf basil, crumbled
- 1 teaspoon salt
- ⅛ teaspoon pepper
- 1 package (8 ounces) farfalle (egg-noodle bows)
- ½ cup grated Parmesan cheese

1. Flatten sausage meat into a large patty in a large skillet. Brown on one side; turn and brown on second side. Remove the sausage from the skillet and crumble onto paper towels.
2. Drain off all but 2 tablespoons of fat in skillet. Sauté onion and garlic in skillet until soft. Drain tomatoes; reserve liquid. Brown tomatoes in the same skillet for 5 minutes. (This is an Italian sauce trick that mellows the flavor of the tomatoes.)
3. Return crumbled sausage to skillet with liquid from canned tomatoes, oregano, basil, salt and pepper. Simmer, stirring occasionally, for 30 minutes.
4. Cook farfalle, following label directions, until done as you like. Drain and place on a large heated serving platter. Spoon the sauce over and top with the grated Parmesan cheese. Mix lightly at the table; serve immediately.

COD MEDITERRANEA

Around the Mediterranean, soup kettles often bubble with a hearty fish soup.

Makes 4 servings.

- 1 package (1 pound) frozen cod or pollock fillets
- 1 can condensed onion soup
- 1¼ cups water
- 1 bay leaf
- 1 cup cooked elbow macaroni
- 1 package (10 ounces) frozen Italian vegetables in sauce. (see Cook's Guide)
- 1 tablespoon butter or margarine

1. Allow frozen fish to stand at room temperature 20 minutes, then cut into 1-inch cubes.
2. Combine soup, water and bay leaf in a large saucepan; bring to boiling; add macaroni and cod; cover and simmer 4 minutes.
3. Break frozen vegetables into mixture; increase heat and bring to boiling, then stir; add butter or margarine; cover and lower heat to simmer.
4. Cook 3 minutes more, or until vegetables are tender. Serve in deep soup bowls with crusty Italian rolls.

France has long been noted for its "grande cuisine"—and with
BON APPETIT!
good reason. The recipes in this chapter are magnifique!

CRAB NEWBURG SOUFFLÉ

An asparagus and crab sauce layers under a classic mile-high cheese soufflé. The photograph is on page 77.

Bake at 350° for 45 minutes.
Makes 6 servings.

    1 small onion, chopped (¼ cup)
    ½ cup (1 stick) butter or margarine
    ½ cup all purpose flour
    1 teaspoon salt
       Dash white pepper
    2½ cups milk
    1 cup shredded Swiss cheese
       (4 ounces)
    ½ teaspoon dry mustard
    1 package (6 ounces) frozen crab
       meat, thawed
       OR: 1 can (7 ounces) tuna,
       drained and flaked
    1 package (10 ounces) frozen
       asparagus, cooked and cut
       into 1-inch pieces
    2 tablespoons dry Sherry
    4 eggs, separated

1. Sauté onion in butter or margarine in a large saucepan until soft; stir in flour, salt and pepper until mixture bubbles.
2. Stir in 2 cups of the milk and cook, stirring constantly, until sauce thickens and bubbles 1 minute.
3. Measure 1 cup of sauce into a medium-size bowl. Stir shredded cheese and dry mustard into sauce in saucepan; heat until cheese melts; remove from heat.
4. Fold crab meat, asparagus, remaining ½ cup milk and Sherry into sauce in bowl. Spoon into an 8-cup soufflé or straight-sided casserole, pushing pieces of crab and asparagus against side of dish.
5. Beat egg whites in a large bowl with electric mixer at high speed until they form soft peaks.
6. Beat egg yolks in a medium-size bowl with electric mixer at high speed; beat in cheese mixture until smooth.
7. Fold egg yolk mixture into beaten whites until well blended with a wooden or wire whip. Spoon over sauce in soufflé dish.
8. Bake in moderate oven (350°) 45 minutes, or until puffed and golden brown. Serve at once.
COOK'S TIP: To give your soufflé a top hat, cut a ring around soufflé mixture, 1-inch in from edge of dish,

with a table knife, just before baking. *Suggested Variation:* For SALMON NEWBURG SOUFFLÉ, substitute 1 can (8 ounces) salmon, drained and flaked for crab.

BOEUF NIÇOISE

Ripe olives, tarragon and a garlicky tomato sauce season beef to perfection. Shown with a bouquet of vegetables on page 78.

Makes 8 servings.

    1 eye round beef roast (about 4
       pounds)
    3 tablespoons olive or vegetable oil
    1 large onion, chopped (1 cup)
    2 cloves garlic, minced
    1 cup chopped celery
    2 large carrots, pared and chopped
    1 can (1 pound, 12 ounces) Italian
       tomatoes
    2 teaspoons salt
    ¼ teaspoon freshly ground pepper
    1 tablespoon chopped fresh
       tarragon
       OR: 1 teaspoon leaf tarragon,
       crumbled
    1 bunch leeks, trimmed and washed
    1 small yellow turnip, pared and
       cubed
    1 small cauliflower, separated into
       flowerets
    1 pound small white onions, peeled
    ½ cup pitted ripe olives, halved
       Bottled gravy coloring

1. Brown beef in oil in a large oval kettle; remove and reserve. Pour off all but 3 tablespoons pan drippings.
2. Sauté onion, garlic, celery and carrots in pan drippings until golden; place meat over mixture; add tomatoes and liquid, salt, pepper and tarragon; cover kettle.
3. Bring slowly to bubbling; lower heat; simmer 1 hour, 30 minutes; arrange leeks, turnip, cauliflower and onions in piles around meat; cover.
4. Simmer 40 minutes, or until meat and vegetables are tender when pierced with a two-tined fork. Arrange meat and vegetables in a heated oval casserole and keep warm.
5. Skim fat from surface of liquid in kettle; spoon into container of electric blender; cover; process on high until smooth; pour into saucepan. Heat to boiling; taste and season with salt and pepper, if needed; add olives and gravy coloring; spoon over meat.

COQUILLES ST. JACQUES

A subtle wine sauce enhances the flavor of scallops in this classic seafood recipe.

Broil 4 minutes.
Makes 4 servings.

    1 cup dry white wine
    ½ teaspoon salt
    1 pound fresh or frozen sea
       scallops, washed
    2 tablespoons finely chopped onion
    ¼ pound small mushrooms, sliced
    ¼ cup (½ stick) butter or margarine
    ¼ cup all purpose flour
    ½ cup heavy cream
    2 teaspoons lemon juice
    ⅓ cup grated Swiss cheese
    2 tablespoons chopped parsley
    ½ cup soft bread crumbs (1 slice)
    1 tablespoon melted butter or
       margarine

1. Bring wine to boiling in small saucepan; add salt and scallops; cover. Simmer until just tender, 5 minutes. Drain, reserving 1 cup liquid.
2. Sauté onion and mushrooms until soft in butter or margarine in a medium-size saucepan; remove from heat; stir in flour until smooth; gradually stir in reserved liquid. Cook, stirring constantly, till sauce thickens and bubbles 1 minute. Stir in cream and lemon juice. Bring to boiling; remove from heat. If sauce is too thick, add more cream or wine. Taste and add more salt or lemon juice, if necessary.
3. Add scallops, cheese and parsley to sauce; spoon into 4 buttered scallop shells or 1-cup casseroles, dividing.
4. Toss bread crumbs with melted butter or margarine; sprinkle around edges of shells.
5. Broil, 4 to 6 inches from heat, 4 minutes, or until crumbs are brown and sauce bubbles.

(Recipes continued on page 114)

☞

Crab Newburg Soufflé turns a cheese soufflé into something special with a crab and asparagus sauce layer. Tastes as good as it looks. Recipe is on this page.

Beaten egg whites
will stay fluffier
if you gently fold cheese
mixture in with a wooden or
wire whip, using a cutting-
down and lifting-over motion.

Boeuf Niçoise is simply pot roast seasoned with a French accent. Viva la différence!

Brown pot roast in hot oil in a heavy kettle, turning roast with two wooden spoons. Sauté vegetables, called mirepoix, until golden in pan drippings.

Spanish cooks like
to add a nutty taste
to rice in casseroles by
toasting the rice.
To toast rice: Heat
oil in a large, heavy
skillet; sprinkle raw, long-grain
rice over oil and cook, stirring
constantly, until rice is golden.

LAMB AND RICE VALENCIA

Skillet-toasted rice adds the special Spanish flavor to this colorful dish. Photo, page 80.

Bake at 350° for 1 hour.
Makes 6 servings.

- 1½ cups long grain rice
- 3 tablespoons olive or vegetable oil
- 1 pound small white onions, peeled and halved
- 3 pounds lamb riblets
- 4 cups chicken broth
- 2 teaspoons salt
- 1 teaspoon leaf thyme, crumbled
- ¼ teaspoon pepper
- 1 package (10 ounces) frozen peas
  Roast Peppers (recipe follows)

1. Sprinkle rice over heated oil in a large skillet; toast, stirring constantly, until rice turns a rich brown. Remove to a 12-cup shallow casserole with a slotted spoon.
2. Brown the cut edge of onions in same pan, adding more oil, if needed; place on rice in casserole.
3. Cut lamb between ribs into bite-size pieces; brown in same skillet, part at a time; remove with tongs and place over rice in casserole.
4. Stir chicken broth, salt, thyme and pepper into pan drippings; heat to boiling, stirring constantly; pour into casserole; cover.
5. Bake in moderate oven (350°) 45 minutes. Stir frozen peas into casserole; cover; bake 15 minutes longer, or until liquid is absorbed and rice is tender. Place ROASTED PEPPERS around casserole, just before serving.

ROAST PEPPERS: Makes 6 servings. Halve 2 large red and 2 large green peppers; seed and cut into strips. Brush with olive or vegetable oil. Arrange in a single layer on a large cookie sheet. Broil, 4 inches from heat, 10 minutes; turn; brush with oil; broil 10 minutes longer.

☞

Succulent pieces of lamb are teamed with rice and peas and garnished with roast peppers in Lamb and Rice Valencia. Recipe is on this page.

EGGPLANT SCALLOP

Two of the garden's best—eggplants and tomatoes—team in an easy casserole.

Makes 6 servings.

- 1 large onion, chopped (1 cup)
- 1 teaspoon curry powder
- 2 tablespoons vegetable oil
- 2 tablespoons sugar
- 2 teaspoons mixed Italian herbs, crumbled
- 2 teaspoons salt
- 1 envelope or teaspoon instant beef broth
- 1 tablespoon cider vinegar
- 1 teaspoon Worcestershire sauce
- ¼ cup water
- 1 large eggplant, pared and diced
- 4 large ripe tomatoes, diced
- 2 cups sliced celery
- ½ cup pitted sliced ripe olives
- 2 cups diced cooked ham or salami

1. Sauté onion with curry powder in oil just until onion is soft in a large skillet; remove from heat.
2. Stir in sugar, Italian herbs, salt, instant beef broth, vinegar, Worcestershire sauce, water, eggplant, tomatoes, celery and olives.
3. Cover; bring to boiling; simmer 15 minutes. Uncover and stir in ham or salami; simmer 10 minutes longer, or until eggplant and celery are tender.

PINTO BEANS

Hearty budget fare—and nutritious.

Makes 4 servings.

- 1 package (1 pound) dried pinto beans
- 5 cups water
- 1 medium-size onion, quartered
- 1 clove garlic, minced
- 1 teaspoon chili powder
- 2 teaspoons salt
- 1 ham hock
  OR: ½ pound salt pork

1. Soak pinto beans overnight in water to cover; drain.
2. Combine beans, water, onion, garlic, chili powder, salt and ham hock or salt pork in a large kettle.
3. Bring to boiling; lower heat; simmer over low heat 2 hours, 30 minutes; or until beans are very soft. Remove ham hock or salt pork; remove meat from bones and fat and return to beans before serving.

PAELLA

A classic chicken, seafood and rice dish that's not as complicated as it may seem.

Bake at 350° for 1 hour.
Makes 8 servings.

- 1 broiler-fryer, cut up (2½ to 3 pounds)
- 2 tablespoons all purpose flour
- ¼ cup olive or vegetable oil
- 1½ cups uncooked long grain rice
- 1 large onion, chopped (1 cup)
- 1 clove garlic, minced
- 1 small green pepper, chopped
- 1 pimiento, cut into thin strips
- 1 cup frozen peas (from a 1-pound bag)
- 4 tomatoes, peeled and sliced
- 1 bottle (8 ounces) clam juice
- 1½ cups water
- 1 teaspoon or envelope instant chicken broth
- ½ teaspoon salt
- ¼ teaspoon pepper
  Several strands saffron
- 2 cans (8 ounces each) minced clams (see Cook's Tip)
- 1 pound fresh or frozen shrimp, shelled and deveined

1. Coat chicken pieces with flour; brown in oil in a large skillet; place in a paella pan or 12-cup shallow casserole.
2. Sauté rice, onion, garlic, green pepper and pimiento in oil in same pan, stirring often, 10 minutes, or until rice is golden. Spoon over and around chicken in dish; top with peas and tomatoes.
3. Combine clam juice, water, instant chicken broth, salt, pepper and saffron in skillet and bring to boiling; pour over mixture in dish; cover.
4. Bake in moderate oven (350°) 30 minutes. Add clams and liquid and shrimp; cover; bake 30 minutes longer, or until chicken and rice are tender.
COOK'S TIP: If fresh steamer clams are available, buy 12 to 18 and use them in place of canned minced clams. To cook: Scrub shells well; place in large saucepan with 1 cup water; cover; bring to boiling; simmerr 3 to 5 minutes, or until shells open. Lift out with tongs. Strain broth through cheesecloth to remove any sand; measure (you should have 1 cup); substitute for bottled clam juice in Step 3. Use clams in shells in place of 2 cans minced clams in Step 4.

SPANISH

Spanish cooks know the secret of combining unexpected
BE ADVENTUROUS!
ingredients to create distinctive and delectable meals.

DEVILED CRAB BAKE

Zippy extras—dry mustard, lemon juice, red pepper seasoning and parsley—give zing to this partylike dish.

Bake at 375° for 20 minutes.
Makes 6 servings.

    1 tablespoon minced onion
    3 tablespoons butter or margarine
    3 tablespoons all purpose flour
 1½ teaspoons dry mustard
  ½ teaspoon salt
    2 cups milk
    2 tablespoons lemon juice
      Few drops liquid red pepper
        seasoning
    2 tablespoons chopped parsley
    2 cans (about 6¼ ounces each)
        crab meat
      OR:1 pound fresh crab meat
    4 hard-cooked eggs, shelled
    1 cup coarsely crumbled soda
        crackers (12 crackers)

1. Sauté onion in butter or margarine just until softened in a medium-size saucepan. Stir in flour, mustard and salt; cook, stirring constantly, until mixture bubbles. Stir in milk slowly; continue cooking and stirring until sauce thickens and bubbles 3 minutes.
2. Remove from heat; stir in lemon juice, red pepper seasoning and parsley.
3. Drain and flake crab meat, removing any bony tissue. Chop 3 eggs coarsely.
4. Stir crab meat, eggs and ½ cup cracker crumbs into sauce mixture. Spoon into buttered 6-cup shallow casserole and sprinkle remaining ½ cup crumbs over.
5. Bake in moderate oven (375°) 20 minutes, or until bubbly hot. Slice the remaining egg; arrange on top; garnish with additional parsley, if you wish.

CHILI BEANS AND SAUSAGE

For a spicier dish, use hot Italian sausages in this recipe.

Bake at 350° for 50 minutes.
Makes 6 servings.

    2 pounds mild or hot Italian
        sausages
    2 large onions, chopped (2 cups)
    2 cups diced tart apples
    3 cups tomato juice
    2 tablespoons brown sugar
    2 cloves garlic
    2 teaspoons salt
    2 teaspoons chili powder
  ¼ teaspoon freshly ground black
        pepper
    2 cans (1 pound each) red kidney
        beans, drained
      Dairy sour cream

1. Brown sausages in a 12-cup flame-proof casserole or a large skillet; remove and cut into 1-inch pieces. Pour off all but 3 tablespoons drippings;

sauté onion until limp. Add apples, tomato juice, brown sugar, garlic, salt, chili powder and pepper. Bring to boiling; add kidney beans and sliced sausages and mix well. (If a skillet is used, pour into a 12-cup casserole.)
2. Bake in moderate oven (350°) 50 minutes, or until bubbly hot. Serve with a dollop of sour cream.

BACALHAO À GOMES DE SÁ

Serve this dish as it comes from the oven—sizzling and lightly touched with brown.

Bake at 350° for 30 minutes.
Makes 4 servings.

    1 package (1 pound) boneless
        salted codfish
    4 cups boiling water
    2 tablespoons butter or margarine
    2 tablespoons olive or vegetable oil
    2 large onions, thinly sliced
    2 pounds new potatoes, boiled,
        cooled, peeled and sliced ¼-
        inch thick
  ¼ cup minced parsley
  ¼ teaspoon freshly ground pepper
    8 unpitted ripe olives
    1 hard-cooked egg, shelled and cut
        into wedges

1. Cover cod with cold water and soak overnight, changing the water several times in the beginning to remove excess salt. Next day, drain cod; rinse and place in a saucepan; cover with boiling water and simmer, uncovered, 12 to 15 minutes, or until tender. Drain, rinse, then flake, removing any bits of skin or bone; reserve.
2. Heat 1 tablespoon each of the butter or margarine and oil in a large heavy skillet over moderate heat; add onions and sauté, separating into rings, about 8 minutes, or until golden. Remove from skillet and reserve. Add remaining 1 tablespoon each of the butter and oil to skillet; add potatoes; sauté about 5 minutes.
3. Arrange half the potatoes in an 8-cup shallow casserole and sprinkle with some of the parsley and pepper. Add one-third of the sautéed onions, half the cod and another sprinkling of parsley and pepper. Top with remaining potatoes; sprinkle with the parsley and pepper; add another one-third of the onions, the remaining cod and sprinkle again with the parsley and pepper. Finally, top with remaining onions and sprinkle lightly with pepper. (Save a little of the parsley to sprinkle on the dish as it comes from the oven.)
4. Bake in moderate oven (350°) 30 minutes, or until sizzling and lightly browned.
5. Serve in the baking dish, garnished with minced parsley, olives and hard-cooked egg, if you wish.

EGGPLANT-HAM BAKE

An excellent leftover with a Spanish accent.

Bake at 350° for 30 minutes.
Makes 6 servings.

    1 medium-size onion, chopped
        (½ cup)
  ¼ cup chopped celery
  ¼ cup chopped green pepper
    1 clove garlic, minced
    3 tablespoons butter or margarine
    1 container (8 ounces) dairy sour
        cream
    1 teaspoon salt
    1 egg, slightly beaten
    2 tablespoons milk
  ⅛ teaspoon pepper
  ¾ cup fine dry bread crumbs
    1 medium-size eggplant, pared and
        cut into ½-inch slices
  ¼ cup vegetable oil
   12 thin slices cooked ham
    1 package (8 ounces) Muenster
        cheese, sliced

1. Sauté onion, celery, green pepper and garlic in butter or margarine just until tender in small skillet; put in small bowl; slowly stir in sour cream and ½ teaspoon of the salt.
2. Combine egg, milk, the remaining ½ teaspoon salt and pepper in a shallow dish; place bread crumbs on wax paper.
3. Dip eggplant in egg mixture, then in crumbs. Brown eggplant, a few pieces at a time, in oil in a large skillet, 3 minutes per side.
4. Line bottom of a 13x9x2-inch casserole with eggplant slices.
5. Spread half of sour cream mixture over eggplant; top with 6 ham slices and half of the cheese; repeat layers; cover pan with aluminum foil.
6. Bake in moderate oven (350°) 25 minutes, or until bubbly; uncover; bake another 5 minutes to brown top.

LAMB CHOPS CÓRDOBA

Lamb chops cook on a fluffy, fruit-and-nut pilaf. A touch of Spain at home.

Makes 4 servings.

    4 shoulder lamb chops
        (about 1½ pounds)
    1 tablespoon butter or margarine
    1 medium-size onion, chopped
        (½ cup)
    1 cup uncooked long grain rice
  ½ cup seedless green grapes
  ¼ cup chopped dried apricots
  ¼ cup roasted peanuts
    1 teaspoon salt
  ½ teaspoon ground ginger
  ¼ teaspoon ground cloves
  ¼ teaspoon pepper
  ⅛ teaspoon ground cardamom
    1 cup orange juice
    1 cup water

1. Trim fat from chops; melt butter or margarine in a large heavy skillet with tight-fitting cover; brown chops

on both sides; remove.

2. Sauté onion until tender in remaining fat in pan. Stir in rice, grapes, apricots, peanuts, salt, ginger, cloves, pepper, ground cardamom, orange juice and water. Arrange chops on top; cover.

3. Heat to boiling; reduce heat; simmer 40 minutes, or until chops and rice are tender and liquid is absorbed.

CALDEIRADA

This robust fish chowder is superbly adaptable—good with all kinds of fish. Here is a super economical version.

Makes 8 servings.

- **12 mussels or clams in the shell**
- **2 tablespoons olive or vegetable oil**
- **4 tablespoons butter or margarine**
- **1 large onion, chopped (1 cup)**
- **1 medium-size green pepper, halved, seeded and minced**
- **1 clove garlic, minced**
- **2 teaspoons salt**
  Freshly ground pepper
- **2 large ripe tomatoes, peeled, cored and coarsely chopped**
- **3 pounds fresh or frozen fish (1 pound each of 3 of the following: cod, scrod, mackerel or haddock, cut into 1½-inch chunks)**
- **¼ cup minced parsley**
- **1 cup dry white wine**
- **8 slices Italian bread, toasted**

1. Scrub mussels or clams under cool running water with a stiff brush; scrape the shells clean. Soak mussels in cool water 1 hour to remove grit.

2. Heat 1 tablespoon each of the oil and butter or margarine in a heavy kettle over moderate heat; add the onion, green pepper and garlic and sauté 8 minutes, or until golden. Remove and set aside. Mix ½ teaspoon salt and a pinch of pepper into tomatoes in a small bowl.

3. Add remaining 1 tablespoon oil and 1 more tablespoon butter or margarine to kettle; rinse mussels and arrange over bottom. Scatter one-third of the onion mixture on top, then one-third of the tomatoes. Top with half of the fish and sprinkle generously with some of the salt, pepper and minced parsley. Add another one-third each of onion mixture and tomatoes, top with the remaining fish, sprinkle with more salt, pepper and parsley. Finally, top with remaining onion mixture and tomatoes; sprinkle with parsley.

4. Pour in wine; bring mixture to a boil; reduce heat, cover and simmer 30 minutes. Dot with remaining 2 tablespoons butter or margarine; recover; simmer 10 minutes.

5. To serve, place toasted bread in soup plates; ladle fish on top, including plenty of broth.

BLACK BEAN SOUP

This soup is a variation of exotic Brazilian Feijoada, a soup-stew served as a main dish.

Makes 10 servings.

- **2 pounds dried black beans**
- **14 cups water**
- **½ pound pepperoni, cut into ½-inch slices**
- **3 large onions, sliced**
- **1 boneless smoked pork butt (about 2 pounds)**
- **2 cups dry red wine**
- **3 oranges, peeled and sectioned**
- **2 teaspoons salt**
- **¼ cup chopped parsley**

1. Combine beans with water in a large kettle. Bring to boiling and boil 2 minutes; cover. Remove from heat and let stand 1 hour.

2. Bring beans to boiling again; add pepperoni and onions; reduce heat; cover. Simmer 2 hours, stirring occasionally, or until beans are tender. Add pork and wine. Simmer 1 hour, or until meat is tender.

3. Remove meat and keep warm. With a slotted spoon, remove pieces of pepperoni and about 3 cups of whole beans. Purée remaining beans and soup in container of an electric blender, or press through a sieve. Return to kettle along with pepperoni and the whole beans.

4. Add sections from 2 of the oranges and the salt. Taste and add additional salt, if you wish. Bring to boiling; ladle into soup bowls. Garnish each serving with a section of reserved orange; sprinkle with parsley.

5. Slice pork butt thinly and pass it around on a separate plate to eat with mustard and whole wheat bread.
COOK'S TIP: This soup freezes well; freeze soup and meat separately.

CASTILLIAN MEATBALLS

Apple-flavored meatballs simmer in a tomato-wine sauce.

Makes 8 servings.

- **2 pounds ground lean beef**
- **2 large apples, peeled and shredded**
- **2 eggs, lightly beaten**
- **1 large onion, chopped (1 cup)**
- **2 teaspoons salt**
- **½ teaspoon pepper**
- **2 tablespoons vegetable oil**
- **1½ cups dry red wine**
- **1½ cups water**
- **2 cans (6 ounces each) tomato paste**
- **2 teaspoons leaf basil, crumbled**
- **½ teaspoon leaf rosemary, crumbled**
- **2 packages (10 ounces each) frozen lima beans**

1. Combine beef, apples, eggs, onion, salt and pepper in a large bowl; mix

lightly. Shape into 1-inch meatballs.

2. Heat oil in a large skillet; brown meatballs, half at a time; remove and reserve. Stir wine, water, tomato paste, basil and rosemary into drippings in pan. Add meatballs and lima beans; bring to boiling; cover; simmer 15 minutes, or until meatballs and lima beans are tender.

SPICY LAMB-STUFFED SQUASH

Lamb is tossed with rice and seasoned with mint, parsley, cinnamon, currants and piñon nuts.

Bake at 400° for 25 minutes, then at 350° for 30 minutes.
Makes 6 servings.

- **3 medium-size acorn squash, halved and seeded**
- **1 pound ground lean lamb**
- **1 tablespoon olive or vegetable oil**
- **1 tablespoon butter or margarine**
- **1 medium-size onion, chopped (½ cup)**
- **2 tablespoons minced parsley**
- **2 tablespoons minced fresh mint OR: 2 teaspoons mint flakes**
- **⅓ cup dried currants or raisins**
- **2 tablespoons piñon (pine) nuts**
- **1 tablespoon cider vinegar**
- **1½ teaspoons salt**
- **¼ teaspoon pepper**
- **¼ teaspoon leaf rosemary, crumbled**
- **⅛ teaspoon ground cinnamon Pinch ground nutmeg**
- **1½ cups cooked rice**
- **1 can (8 ounces) tomato sauce**
- **¼ cup (½ stick) butter or margarine, melted**

1. Cut a thin slice off the bottom of each squash half. Place squash halves, hollow-sides up, in a 13x9x2-inch baking pan; add ¼ inch water; cover dish with aluminum foil.

2. Bake in hot oven (400°) 25 minutes, or until squash are tender.

3. Brown lamb in oil and butter or margarine in a large heavy skillet. Add onions; sauté until soft, about 5 minutes. Add parsley, mint, currants or raisins, nuts, vinegar, salt, pepper, rosemary, cinnamon and nutmeg; cover skillet. Simmer 10 minutes, or until currants or raisins are plump. Add rice and stir to blend; cover; simmer 10 minutes. Stir in tomato sauce and simmer, uncovered, 10 minutes, stirring occasionally.

4. Drain squash halves on paper towels; brush lightly with melted butter or margarine; mound meat filling into hollows. Arrange in baking pan.

5. Bake in moderate oven (350°) 30 minutes, or until stuffing and squash are heated through.
COOK'S TIP: Squash can be prepared and stuffed several hours ahead of time; refrigerate until about 45 minutes before serving.

SPANISH EGGPLANT BAKE

Eggplant bakes in a richly seasoned tomato sauce and cheese filling.

Bake at 375° for 45 minutes.
Makes 8 servings.

- 2 **large eggplants, sliced ½-inch thick but not pared**
- 2 **teaspoons salt**
- ¼ **cup olive or vegetable oil**
- ⅔ **cup grated Parmesan cheese Tomato Sauce**
- 3 **medium-size onions, chopped (1½ cups)**
- 1 **clove garlic, crushed**
- 2 **tablespoons olive or vegetable oil**
- 4 **medium-size ripe tomatoes, peeled, cored and coarsely chopped**
- 1 **tablespoon dried mint flakes**
- 2 **tablespoons minced parsley**
- 2 **teaspoons sugar**
- 1 **teaspoon salt**
- ¼ **teaspoon pepper**
- ¼ **teaspoon leaf rosemary, crumbled**
- 1 **can (8 ounces) tomato sauce Cheese Filling**
- 1 **container (1 pound) cream-style cottage cheese**
- 1 **egg**
- 2 **tablespoons grated Parmesan cheese**
- ¼ **teaspoon salt**
- ⅛ **teaspoon pepper**
- ⅛ **teaspoon leaf rosemary, crumbled**
- ⅛ **teaspoon ground mace**

1. Sprinkle both sides of the eggplant slices with the 2 teaspoons salt; place slices between several thicknesses of paper towels; weigh down with a plate and let stand 1 hour.
2. Meanwhile, make Tomato Sauce: Sauté onions and garlic in oil in a large heavy skillet over moderate heat about 8 minutes, or until limp and golden. Add tomatoes, mint, parsley, sugar, salt, pepper and rosemary; heat uncovered, stirring constantly, until tomatoes begin to bubble. Cover, reduce heat to low and simmer 1 hour; stir in tomato sauce and simmer, uncovered, 15 minutes longer.
3. Prepare Cheese Filling while tomato sauce simmers: Mix together cottage cheese, egg, grated Parmesan, salt, pepper, rosemary and mace; refrigerate until needed.
4. Brush both sides of each eggplant slice lightly with oil; place slices on broiler pan, slide pan under the broiler and brown the slices quickly on each side.
5. To assemble, spoon half the Tomato Sauce over the bottom of a 13x9x2-inch casserole. Sprinkle generously with grated Parmesan, then arrange half the browned eggplant slices on top. Spread with cheese filling, sprinkle with grated Parmesan, arrange the remaining eggplant slices on top, sprinkle with grated Parmesan and cover with remaining Tomato Sauce and one last sprinkling of grated Parmesan.
6. Bake in moderate oven (375°) 45 minutes, or until bubbling and brown; remove from oven; let stand 15 minutes before cutting into serving-size squares.

CLASSIC ARROZ CON POLLO

A fast version of the classic Spanish dish.

Bake at 375° for 20 minutes.
Makes 4 servings.

- 1 **barbecued chicken, about 2½ pounds (from deli section of supermarket)**
- 1 **package (about 7 ounces) chicken flavored rice mix**
- 3 **tablespoons butter or margarine Dash saffron powder**
- 1 **can (4 ounces) green chili peppers, seeded and diced**

1. Cut the chicken into serving-size pieces with poultry shears.
2. Sauté chicken flavored rice mix in butter or margarine 3 minutes in an 8-cup flameproof casserole or a medium-size skillet.
3. Add saffron powder and water called for on the rice mix label. Heat to bubbling. If a skillet is used, transfer rice mixture to an 8-cup casserole; arrange chicken and green chilies on rice; cover.
4. Bake in moderate oven (375°) 20 minutes, or until liquid is absorbed. Garnish with diced pimiento and halved ripe olives, if you wish.

PUCHERO

Argentine beef stew with corn-on-the-cob chunks and two kinds of potatoes.

Makes 8 servings.

- 1 **fresh brisket (about 3 pounds)**
- ½ **pound pepperoni (1 sausage)**
- 1 **teaspoon salt**
- ¼ **teaspoon pepper**
- 1 **clove garlic, chopped**
- 1 **medium-size onion, chopped (½ cup)**
- ½ **cup chopped celery**
- 2 **sprigs parsley**
- 4 **cups boiling water**
- 1 **yellow turnip, pared and cut into cubes**
- 3 **medium-size carrots, pared and cut into 2-inch pieces**
- 4 **sweet potatoes or yams, pared and cut into quarters**
- 2 **large white potatoes, pared and cut into quarters**
- 4 **medium-size ears of corn, cut into 2-inch pieces**
- 2 **tablespoons all purpose flour**
- ¼ **cup water**

1. Cut beef into 1½-inch pieces, trimming fat; reserve. Slice sausage.
2. Heat a kettle or Dutch oven. Melt the fat trimmings to make 2 tablespoons drippings. Brown the beef pieces on all sides, a few at a time, removing pieces as they brown. Add sausage, salt, pepper, garlic, onion and celery; sauté until vegetables are almost tender. Return beef; add parsley and boiling water. Bring to boiling; lower heat; cover. Simmer 1 hour, 30 minutes, or until meat is almost tender.
3. Add turnip, carrots, sweet potatoes and white potatoes; simmer 50 minutes longer, or until meats and vegetables are tender. Add corn; simmer 10 minutes longer.
4. Remove meats and vegetables to a large serving platter. Skim fat from liquid in pan, if necessary. Blend flour and water in a cup. Stir into boiling liquid in pan. Cook, stirring constantly, until sauce thickens and bubbles 3 minutes. Serve over stew.

BASQUE POTATOES

Bacon-flavored potato slices with eggs make an omelet with a Spanish touch.

Makes 6 servings.

- 4 **large Idaho potatoes**
- 6 **slices bacon**
- 1 **medium-size onion, chopped (½ cup)**
- ¼ **cup chopped parsley**
- 4 **eggs**
- ¼ **teaspoon paprika**
- 1 **teaspoon salt**
- ¼ **teaspoon pepper**

1. Pare potatoes and cut in half crosswise. Cook in a large saucepan with boiling salted water 20 minutes, or until potatoes are tender but not crumbly. Drain and cut crosswise into ⅛-inch slices.
2. Cook bacon over moderate heat until crisp in a large skillet. Drain on paper towels and crumble; reserve. Pour off all but ¼ cup bacon fat from pan. Add onion and sauté over moderate heat until tender.
3. Add parsley and potato slices. Shake pan back and forth until potato slices lie flat. Cook over moderate heat 20 minutes, or until potatoes are golden brown on the bottom. Loosen potatoes by sliding a spatula around the edge of skillet and as far under the potatoes as possible.
4. Place a large cookie sheet over skillet and, grasping cookie sheet and skillet together firmly, turn over. Slide potatoes back into skillet, brown side up. Cook over moderate heat 2 to 3 minutes to brown the bottom.
5. Beat eggs, paprika, salt and pepper until mixed in a medium-size bowl. Pour over potatoes and sprinkle reserved bacon over top. Cover skillet; cook 5 minutes, or until set.

CUSTARD-FILLED SQUASH

Thyme-flavored, cottage-and-mozzarella-cheese custard bakes in squash boats.

Bake at 350° for 30 minutes.
Makes 4 servings.

- **4 medium-size zucchini or summer squash**
- **1 container (8 ounces) cream-style cottage cheese**
- **1 cup shredded mozzarella cheese (4 ounces)**
- **2 eggs**
- **½ teaspoon leaf thyme, crumbled**
- **½ teaspoon salt**
- **¼ teaspoon pepper**
- **½ cup buttered soft bread crumbs**

1. Halve zucchini or summer squash lengthwise; parboil in boiling salted water to cover in a large saucepan 5 minutes; drain and carefully scoop out seeds.
2. Mix cottage cheese and mozzarella cheese, eggs, thyme, salt and pepper in a medium-size bowl, then spoon into the squash halves. (Do not mound.)
3. Bake in moderate oven (350°) 25 minutes, or until custard is set. Sprinkle with bread crumbs; bake 5 minutes longer, or until crumbs are toasty brown. Garnish each with a sweet pickle slice, if you wish.

ARROZ CON CERDO

This "something different" dish of pork, rice and peanuts is easy to make.

Bake at 350° for 1 hour.
Makes 8 servings.

- **8 slices bacon, diced**
- **2 pounds boneless lean pork shoulder, cubed**
- **1 large onion, chopped (1 cup)**
- **1 clove garlic, minced**
- **2 cups uncooked long grain rice**
- **5 envelopes or teaspoons instant chicken broth**
- **¼ teaspoon crushed saffron**
- **6 cups water**
- **1 package (10 ounces) frozen peas, cooked, drained and buttered**
- **¼ cup chopped peanuts**
- **1 pimiento, diced**

1. Cook bacon until almost crisp in a large skillet; drain on paper towels. Remove and reserve.
2. Pour all pan drippings into a cup. Brown pork slowly, a little at a time, in same skillet; remove and reserve.
3. Return 2 tablespoons bacon drippings to pan; add onion and garlic; sauté until soft; push to one side. Add rice and sauté, stirring constantly, until golden. Stir in instant chicken broth, saffron and water; bring to boiling.
4. Pour mixture into a 12-cup casserole; top with browned pork; cover.

5. Bake in moderate oven (350°) 1 hour, or until liquid is absorbed and rice is tender; fluff up with a fork. Sprinkle reserved bacon in a ring in center; spoon cooked peas around edge. Sprinkle chopped peanuts and diced pimiento over top.

COOK'S TIP: Saffron, a typical Spanish seasoning, is expensive, but very little goes a long way to give rice a rich, golden color and an unusual flavor.

SPEEDY PAELLA

A streamlined version of the Catalonian original.

Makes 4 servings.

- **2 tablespoons olive or vegetable oil**
- **½ cup frozen chopped onion**
- **1 package (1 pound, 6 ounces) frozen fried chicken breasts**
- **1 package (6 ounces) chicken flavored rice mix (not precooked)**
- **1 can (24 ounces) steamed clams in shells**
- **1 bag (1 pound) frozen peas**
- **2 whole pimientos, sliced**

1. Heat oil in a large skillet; sauté onion until soft. Add the chicken breasts; sauté on one side for 2 minutes.
2. Add rice mix with seasoning to skillet. Measure liquid from clams into a 2-cup measure; add water if necessary to equal liquid called for on rice mix label. Reserve clams.
3. Add clam liquid to rice; stir gently to mix; add peas. Bring to boiling; lower heat; cover. Simmer 20 minutes.
4. Add clams and pimientos; simmer 5 minutes longer. Serve paella directly from the skillet.

MEATBALL CHOWDER

Beef and pork balls simmer in onion-rich bean and tomato soup.

Makes 6 servings.

- **¾ pound ground round or chuck**
- **¾ pound ground pork**
- **1 egg**
- **2 teaspoons dried mint leaves, crumbled**
- **1½ teaspoons salt**
- **⅛ teaspoon pepper**
- **4 cups water**
- **1 envelope onion soup mix**
- **1 can (about 1 pound) stewed tomatoes**
- **1 can (about 1 pound) red kidney beans**
- **¼ cup chopped parsley**

1. Mix ground beef and pork with egg, mint leaves, salt and pepper in a bowl; shape into tiny balls.
2. Bring water to boiling in a kettle; stir in onion soup mix; cover; simmer

10 minutes.
3. Place meatballs in soup; cover; simmer 15 minutes. Stir in tomatoes and beans and liquid; bring just to boiling; stir in parsley.
4. Ladle into soup bowls. Serve with chowder crackers, if you wish.

LAMB STUFFED CABBAGE

Ground cooked lamb plus crisp bacon go into the savory filling, which steams inside big green cabbage leaves.

Makes 6 servings.

- **1 large cabbage (about 3 pounds)**
- **4 cups ground cooked lamb**
- **8 slices cooked crisp bacon, crumbled**
- **¼ cup soda cracker crumbs**
- **1 medium-size onion, chopped (½ cup)**
- **1 small clove garlic, minced**
- **1 cup tomato juice**
- **2 eggs, lightly beaten**
- **½ teaspoon salt**
- **⅛ teaspoon pepper**
- **3 tablespoons butter or margarine**
- **1 vegetable bouillon cube**
- **1 cup hot water**
- **1 tablespoon all purpose flour**
- **2 tablespoons water**

1. Cut core out of cabbage with a sharp knife. Pull off and discard any coarse outer leaves, then carefully remove 18 whole leaves, one at a time. (Save any remaining cabbage for another meal.)
2. Steam leaves, covered, in a small amount of boiling salted water in a large skillet 5 minutes, or until limp; drain.
3. Combine lamb, bacon, cracker crumbs, onion, garlic, tomato juice, eggs, salt and pepper in a large bowl; mix lightly with a fork.
4. Lay cabbage leaves flat; place 2 to 3 tablespoons meat mixture in middle of each. Fold thick end up over filling, then fold both sides toward middle. Roll up, jelly-roll fashion, to cover filling completely; fasten with one or two wooden picks.
5. Brown rolls, a few at a time, in butter or margarine in a large skillet. Pile all rolls back into pan.
6. Dissolve bouillon cube in the 1 cup hot water in a 1-cup measure; pour over rolls; cover. Steam 20 minutes, or until cabbage is tender. Remove to heated serving platter; keep hot while making gravy.
7. Pour drippings from pan into 1-cup measure; add water, if necessary, to make 1 cup; return to pan. Blend flour with the 2 tablespoons water until smooth in a cup; stir into liquid in pan. Cook over low heat, stirring constantly, until gravy thickens and bubbles 3 minutes. Taste and season with salt and pepper; spoon over cabbage rolls.

Chinese cooking
is easy and fun!
And our recipes,
like Chinese
Chicken and Shrimp,
don't call for
exotic ingredients
or special equipment.

EAST MEETS WEST

The secret is
in the slicing and
quick cooking.
Try it tonight!

Slice vegetables and meats thinly and to a uniform size and shape for successful Oriental cooking. Be sure your knife is razor sharp and vegetables are fresh. Cut mushrooms crosswise, holding them by stems. Cut carrots and celery in long, diagonal slices.

MONGOLIAN HOT POT

All the food's prepared before mealtime in this meal-in-a-dish, so it's ideal for carefree entertaining or a family supper.

Makes 6 servings.

- 1½ pounds frozen turkey breast fillets, thawed
- ½ pound green beans
- 1 bunch green onions
- ½ pound fresh spinach
- ½ pound fresh mushrooms
- 1 medium-size zucchini
- 1 medium-size yellow squash
- 2 cans condensed chicken broth
- 2½ cups water
- 1 package (8 ounces) frozen shelled deveined raw shrimp, thawed
- Mustard Sauce (recipe follows)
- Duck sauce or ham glaze
- Teriyaki sauce or soy sauce
- Hot rice

1. Cut turkey fillets into 1-inch squares; tip green beans and cut into 2-inch pieces; trim green onions and cut into 3-inch pieces; wash and trim spinach; cut mushrooms, crosswise, into thin slices; tip and slice zucchini and yellow squash. (This can be done ahead, if you wish; wrap food separately in plastic wrap and refrigerate until serving time.)
2. At serving time, pour chicken broth and water into a Mongolian hot pot or electric wok; heat to simmering, following manufacturer's directions. Arrange prepared vegetables with turkey and shrimp in rows on a large flat tray. Spoon MUSTARD SAUCE, duck sauce or ham glaze and teriyaki or soy sauce into individual bowls.
3. Each guest spears assorted food onto a fondue fork or bamboo skewer and cooks it in bubbling broth 3 minutes, or until vegetables are crisply tender. Serve with sauces over rice.
4. When all food has been cooked, ladle remaining broth into tiny cups and pass to guests.

MUSTARD SAUCE

Makes about ½ cup.

- ¼ cup dry mustard
- ¼ cup cold water
- ¼ cup honey

Combine dry mustard and cold water in a cup until smooth; stir in honey until well blended. Refrigerate.

Sweet and Sour Pork is stir-fried to perfection with a medley of crunchy fresh vegetables in a tangy sauce. Recipe is on this page.

HAM ICEBERG STIR-FRY

Cooked turkey or chicken can be substituted for the ham in this recipe.

Makes 4 servings.

- 1 head iceberg lettuce
- 1 medium-size onion, sliced
- 1 clove garlic, crushed
- 2 tablespoons peanut or vegetable oil
- 6 medium-size carrots, pared and thinly sliced
- 1 envelope or teaspoon instant chicken broth
- ⅔ cup water
- ½ teaspoon leaf basil, crumbled
- 2 tablespoons lemon juice
- 1 teaspoon cornstarch
- 2 cups diced cooked ham

1. Core, rinse and drain lettuce completely; shred; refrigerate in plastic bag or plastic crisper.
2. Sauté onion and garlic in oil until soft in a wok or large skillet. Add carrots and sauté until shiny; stir in instant chicken broth, water and basil; cover pan; steam 5 minutes.
3. Combine lemon juice and cornstarch in a cup until smooth. Stir into skillet until sauce thickens and bubbles 3 minutes. Add ham and shredded lettuce and toss to coat lettuce evenly. Serve immediately with Chinese fried noodles, if you wish.

SWEET AND SOUR PORK

You've loved it in Chinese restaurants, now serve it at home. Shown on page 92.

Makes 6 servings.

- 2 pounds lean pork shoulder, cubed
- 1 egg white
- ¼ cup cornstarch
- ¼ cup peanut or vegetable oil
- 1 clove garlic, sliced
- 3 slices fresh ginger root
  - OR: 3 slices candied or preserved ginger, well washed
- 1 large onion, sliced
- 1 hot or sweet red pepper, sliced and seeded
- 1 hot or sweet green pepper, sliced and seeded
- 1 can (8½ ounces) pineapple chunks in syrup
- 1 jar (8 ounces) sweet pickles
- ½ cup cider vinegar
- ½ cup water
- ¼ cup soy sauce
- ¼ cup dry Sherry
- 1 teaspoon monosodium glutamate (optional)
- ½ cup sugar
- 3 tablespoons cornstarch
- ½ cup cold water

1. Dip pork shoulder cubes into egg white in a pie plate to coat evenly; roll in the ¼ cup cornstarch on wax paper to coat evenly.
2. Heat oil with garlic and ginger in a wok or large skillet; add pork and

brown on all sides; cover wok or skillet; lower heat. Cook 10 minutes; remove pork with a slotted spoon to paper towels and keep warm.
3. Sauté onion and peppers in pan drippings until crisply tender; pour in pineapple syrup, juice from pickles, cider vinegar, water, soy sauce, Sherry and monosodium glutamate, if used; bring to boiling; simmer 3 minutes.
4. Combine sugar, remaining cornstarch and cold water in a small bowl; stir into bubbling liquid in pan. Cook, stirring constantly, until sauce thickens and bubbles 3 minutes; add pork, pineapple chunks and mixed pickles and cook 3 minutes, or until heated through. Serve with green onion fans, radish roses and white turnip pinwheels, if you wish.

CHINESE CHICKEN AND SHRIMP

A wok, skillet or electric frypan can be used to stir-fry dinner in minutes. Vary the vegetables, seafood or meat for many delectable dinners. Photo is on page 90.

Makes 6 servings.

- 2 whole chicken breasts, split (about 12 ounces each)
- 1 pound shelled fresh or frozen shrimp
- 4 large carrots
- 4 stalks celery
- ½ pound fresh mushrooms
- 1 bunch green onions
- 4 tablespoons peanut or vegetable oil
- 1 clove garlic, halved
- ½ pound Chinese snow peas
  - OR: 1 package (6 ounces) frozen Chinese snow peas
- ½ cup chicken broth
- 1 tablespoon cornstarch
- 2 tablespoons dry Sherry
- 1 tablespoon finely chopped fresh ginger
- Chinese noodles or vermicelli

1. Remove chicken from bone; cut into 1-inch pieces. Cut shrimp in half, lengthwise. Slice carrots, celery and mushrooms, following directions on page 91. Cut green onions into 2-inch pieces.
2. Heat 2 tablespoons of the oil with garlic in a wok, large skillet or an electric frypan. Stir-fry chicken and shrimp 2 minutes, or until chicken is golden; push to one side.
3. Add remaining 2 tablespoons oil; add carrots, celery, mushrooms, green onions and snow peas; stir-fry until vegetables are coated with oil.
4. Pour chicken broth into pan; cover; steam 5 minutes, or until vegetables are crisply tender.
5. Combine cornstarch, Sherry and ginger in a cup; stir into pan. Cook, stirring constantly, until sauce thickens and bubbles 2 minutes. Serve over Chinese noodles or vermicelli.

KUNG PAO BEEF

The Chinese do not eat the whole pepper pods, but leave them in the wok for the flavor they add. A hot and hearty dish.

Makes 6 servings.

    1 pound flank steak
    1 tablespoon cornstarch
    2 tablespoons egg white
    1 tablespoon peanut or vegetable
      oil
    1 tablespoon soy sauce
    2 green onions
    5 cloves garlic
    4 thin slices fresh ginger root
      OR: 4 thin slices preserved or
      candied ginger, well washed
   20 dried red pepper pods
      OR: 1 tablespoon crushed red
      pepper
    ½ cup dry-roasted peanuts
    2 tablespoons dry white wine
    2 tablespoons soy sauce
    2 tablespoons cider vinegar
   1½ teaspoons sugar
    1 teaspoon salt
    ¼ teaspoon monosodium
      glutamate (optional)
    2 teaspoons cornstarch
    1 tablespoon water
    2 cups peanut or vegetable oil
    2 teaspoons sesame oil (optional)
      Hot fluffy rice

1. Cut flank steak in half, lengthwise. Cut meat across the grain into slices ⅛-inch thick, using cleaver or heavy knife; place in a large bowl. Add the 1 tablespoon cornstarch, egg white, the 1 tablespoon oil and the 1 tablespoon soy sauce. Stir in one direction until meat is thoroughly coated. Place on a platter large enough to hold remaining ingredients; refrigerate.
2. Cut green onions into 1½-inch pieces. Peel garlic; smash. Arrange green onions, garlic, sliced ginger, pepper pods and peanuts in separate piles on platter with meat.
3. Combine wine, the 2 tablespoons soy sauce, vinegar, sugar, salt and monosodium glutamate, if using, in a small bowl. Combine the 2 teaspoons cornstarch with water in a cup.
4. Heat the 2 cups oil in a wok or large skillet just until a piece of meat bubbles when dropped in (about 280°). Add rest of meat; cook 1 minute, or just until steak strips separate and lose most of their red color; remove to a bowl with a slotted spoon. Carefully pour hot oil into a glass or ceramic bowl; cool. Oil may be reused. (This technique, known as "passing through," serves the purpose of separating the pieces of meat at this lower temperature. When the meat is cooked at the higher stir-fry temperature, it will remain separated.)
5. Measure 2 tablespoons oil from the hot drained oil into wok or skillet; place over medium-high heat. Add pepper pods or crushed pepper; stir-fry until pods are very dark to add an almost burnt flavor. Rapidly stir in ginger, wine-soy mixture, cornstarch mixture, onions, garlic and meat. Stir-fry 2 or 3 minutes, or until mixture is hot. Stir in sesame oil, if used; sprinkle with peanuts. Serve over rice.

CHICKEN WITH WALNUTS

Walnuts with a special sugar glaze give a pleasant contrast to stir-fried chicken.

Makes 4 servings.

    2 whole chicken breasts
    2 thin slices fresh ginger root,
      minced
      OR: 2 thin slices preserved or
      candied ginger, well washed
    1 clove garlic, minced
    1 tablespoon cornstarch
    1 tablespoon Sherry
    1 tablespoon soy sauce
    1 tablespoon water
    ½ teaspoon salt
    3 tablespoons peanut or vegetable
      oil
    1 cup sliced celery
    1 can (5 ounces) water chestnuts,
      sliced
    1 tablespoon soy sauce
    ½ cup chicken stock
    1 cup Glazed Walnuts (recipe
      follows)
      OR: 1 cup walnuts

1. Bone chicken breasts with a sharp knife; remove skin. Cut each breast half into thin strips.
2. Mix ginger, garlic, cornstarch, Sherry, 1 tablespoon soy sauce, water and salt in a medium-size bowl. Add chicken strips; toss to coat well; let stand 15 minutes.
3. Heat half the oil in a large skillet or wok. Add chicken, a handful at a time, and stir-fry until it starts to brown, about 3 minutes; remove.
4. Heat remaining oil; add celery and water chestnuts; stir-fry 2 minutes. Sprinkle with 1 tablespoon soy sauce; stir in stock; heat quickly; cover.
5. Simmer over medium heat until vegetables are crisply tender, about 2 minutes.
6. Add reserved chicken; stir in just to reheat and blend flavors. Top with GLAZED WALNUTS and serve immediately with hot rice.
COOK'S TIP: This dish is also delicious cold. Top with walnuts just before serving, to retain crispness.

GLAZED WALNUTS

Makes 1½ cups.

   1½ cups walnuts
    1 cup water
    ½ cup sugar
      Dash ground anise (optional)
    ½ cup peanut or vegetable oil

1. Place walnuts in a small bowl. Bring water to boiling; pour over walnuts; let stand 2 minutes; drain.
2. Add sugar and anise, if used; toss to coat. Place walnuts on a greased cookie sheet; let dry overnight.
3. Heat oil in a medium-size skillet or wok; fry walnuts until golden, being careful not to burn them. Drain on paper towels.
COOK'S TIP: These walnuts are delicious warm or cold, sprinkled over main dishes or desserts.

MANDARIN BAKED CHICKEN

A soy Sherry sauce glazes tender chicken quarters and acorn squash rings.

Bake at 350° for 1 hour.
Makes 4 servings.

    ¼ cup water
    ¼ cup soy sauce
    ¼ cup dry Sherry
    ¼ cup corn syrup
    2 teaspoons seasoned salt
    1 broiler-fryer, quartered
      (about 3 pounds)
    1 acorn squash, cut into rings and
      seeded

1. Combine water, soy sauce, Sherry, corn syrup and seasoned salt in a small bowl.
2. Arrange chicken, skin-side up, on the rack of broiler pan or in a shallow baking pan; arrange squash rings around chicken. Brush generously with part of the soy Sherry sauce.
3. Bake in moderate oven (350°), basting with the remaining sauce every 20 minutes, for 1 hour, or until the chicken and squash are tender and deep golden brown. Place on a heated serving platter.

SHRIMP ORIENTAL

Enjoy a Chinese restaurant favorite at home.

Makes 4 servings.

    1 package (10 ounces) frozen fried
      rice with pork
    1 package (10 ounces) frozen
      broccoli spears
    ½ cup water
    ¼ cup white cooking wine
    3 tablespoons soy sauce
    2 teaspoons cornstarch
    1 envelope or teaspoon instant
      chicken broth
    1 teaspoon sugar
    1 large clove garlic, crushed
    ¼ teaspoon ground ginger
    1 tablespoon peanut oil
    1 package (10 ounces) frozen
      Chinese style vegetables
    1 package (8 ounces) frozen shrimp

1. Prepare rice, following package directions. Pour boiling water over broccoli spears; let stand 2 minutes and drain well.
2. Mix water, wine, soy sauce, cornstarch, instant chicken broth, sugar,

garlic and ginger in a 1-cup measure. Heat oil in an electric wok or electric frypan until hot. Add broccoli and Chinese vegetables and stir-fry 2 minutes. Push to one side; quickly sauté shrimp 3 minutes. Stir in soy mixture and cook, stirring, until mixture thickens and bubbles. Reduce heat and simmer 3 minutes, or until broccoli spears are crisply tender. Stir in rice and heat to boiling; serve.

VEGETABLE-TUNA PILAF

Zucchini and brown rice make a healthful supper dish that's ready in an hour.

Makes 6 servings.

    2 cans (6 ½ ounces each) tuna in
        vegetable oil
    1 medium-size onion, chopped
        (½ cup)
    1 cup uncooked brown rice
    1 can condensed chicken broth
 1¼ cups water
    ¼ teaspoon leaf thyme, crumbled
    ¼ teaspoon pepper
    1 cup sliced carrots
    2 medium-size zucchini, sliced
    ¼ cup hulled sunflower seeds
        (optional)

1. Drain oil from 1 can tuna into a wok or a large skillet. Heat oil; add onion and rice; cook, stirring frequently, until onion is tender. Add broth, water, thyme and pepper.
2. Cover and cook over medium heat 30 minutes. Add carrots, cover and cook 15 minutes.
3. Add zucchini, sunflower seeds, if used, and tuna. Cook 5 minutes longer, or until heated through.

CHOW MEIN CASSEROLE

This Oriental dinner-in-a-dish has all the flavor of the original.

Bake at 350° for 15 minutes.
Makes 4 servings.

    1 pound boneless chicken breasts
    2 tablespoons vegetable oil
    3 tablespoons soy sauce
    1 envelope or teaspoon instant
        chicken broth
    1 cup water
    1 divider pack (28 ounces)
        mushroom chow mein
    2 cups cooked rice
    1 can (3 ounces) chow mein noodles

1. Cut chicken into ¼-inch strips.
2. Heat oil in a medium-size skillet for 30 seconds. Add the chicken. Stir-fry quickly until chicken turns white, about 5 minutes.
3. Stir in soy sauce, instant chicken broth, water and can of sauce from chow mein.
4. Drain and rinse can of vegetables; stir into the chicken mixture; heat to bubbly hot.

5. Layer half the cooked rice in buttered 8-cup casserole; add half the hot chicken mixture; repeat the layering; sprinkle the top with chow-mein noodles.
6. Bake in moderate oven (350°) 15 minutes, or until the mixture is bubbly-hot. Serve with soy sauce.

CANTONESE TUNA PACKETS

Stir-fry supper in just minutes.

Makes 4 servings.

    2 cans (6½ ounces each) tuna in
        vegetable oil
    2 tablespoons soy sauce
    2 tablespoons Sherry
    ⅛ teaspoon ground ginger
    ⅛ teaspoon pepper
    1 bunch green onions, sliced
    1 red pepper, halved, seeded and
        cut into strips
    1 package (6 ounces) frozen
        Chinese snow peas thawed
    1 can (5 ounces) water chestnuts,
        drained and sliced
      Cashews

1. Drain oil from tuna into a wok or large skillet; break tuna into chunks.
2. Combine tuna, soy sauce, Sherry, ginger and pepper in a small bowl.
3. Heat wok or skillet; stir-fry green onions, red pepper and snow peas 3 minutes; stir in tuna mixture and water chestnuts; cover and cook 3 minutes, or until hot. Sprinkle with cashews. Serve over hot rice.

CRAB PILAF

Cooking the rice the day before actually improves the flavor of this dish.

Makes 4 servings.

    1 can (6¼ ounces) crab meat
    6 tablespoons vegetable oil
    1 small onion, sliced
    ½ cup diced celery
    1 package (10 ounces) frozen mixed
        vegetables, thawed
    3 cups cooked rice
    ¼ cup salted peanuts

1. Drain crab meat; flake and remove bony tissue, if any.
2. Heat 4 tablespoons of the vegetable oil in a large wok or skillet; stir in onion, celery and mixed vegetables. Sauté, stirring several times, 5 minutes, or until vegetables are crisply tender. Remove and reserve.
3. Stir remaining 2 tablespoons of oil and cooked rice into same pan; cook, stirring often, over medium heat 5 minutes, or just until rice grains separate and turn creamy.
4. Stir in crab meat, sautéed vegetables and salted peanuts. Heat, stirring once or twice, just until hot. Spoon into heated bowl; serve with soy sauce to drizzle over, if you wish.

LEMON CHICKEN

Succulent bite-sized pieces of chicken in a delightful fresh lemon sauce.

Roast at 400° for 50-60 minutes.
Makes 4 servings.

    1 whole broiler-fryer (about 3
        pounds)
    ⅓ cup water
    3 tablespoons sugar
 1½ tablespoons soy sauce
    2 to 3 large lemons
    3 tablespoons peanut or vegetable
        oil
    ⅓ cup shredded fresh ginger
        OR: ⅓ cup preserved or candied
        ginger, well washed
    ⅓ cup shredded red or green
        pepper
    ⅓ cup shredded canned bamboo
        shoots
    4 Chinese dried mushrooms,
        soaked in hot water 30 minutes
        OR: 4 large fresh or canned
        mushrooms, drained
    ¼ cup sugar
    2 teaspoons salt
    ¼ teaspoon monosodium
        glutamate (optional)
 1¼ cups chicken broth
    2 tablespoons cornstarch

1. Wipe chicken dry with paper towels; place in a large bowl. Heat water, the 3 tablespoons sugar and soy sauce in a small saucepan until hot; pour over chicken. Let chicken stand, turning often, 15 minutes, then rub mixture into skin of chicken. Shake off excess moisture. Place, breast-side down, on rack in a small shallow roasting pan.
2. Roast chicken in hot oven (400°) 20 minutes; turn breast-side up; brush with oil. Roast, brushing several times with fat in pan, 30 to 40 minutes longer, or until skin is crisp and richly browned and juices run clear.
3. While chicken roasts, prepare sauce: Grate rind from 1 lemon; peel the thin yellow rind (no white) from 1 lemon, then cut into julienne strips. Squeeze enough juice to make ½ cup.
4. Heat oil in a large saucepan; add lemon peel strips, ginger, pepper, bamboo shoots and mushrooms; stir-fry 2 minutes; stir in ¼ cup sugar, salt and msg, if used. Add 1 cup of the chicken broth; bring to boiling. Mix remaining broth with cornstarch in a small cup; stir into boiling sauce; boil 1 minute. Stir in lemon juice and grated rind. Remove from heat.
5. Remove chicken to cutting board; cut off wings at joints; remove and disjoint legs and thighs. Remove backbone from chicken with poultry shears; split breast lengthwise and cut each half into 3 pieces. Cut backbone into 3 or 4 pieces. Arrange chicken on heated deep platter; pour sauce over. Garnish with watercress.
COOK'S TIP: Have all ingredients for sauce ready before you begin.

BEEF CHOP SUEY

Purely American in origin, but with a satisfying Oriental touch.

Broil for 10 minutes.
Makes 6 servings.

- 1 pound lean sirloin tip
- 1 tablespoon dry Sherry
- 2 tablespoons soy sauce
- 2 tablespoons peanut or vegetable oil
- ½ cup thinly sliced carrots
- ½ cup thinly sliced celery
- ½ cup thinly sliced onion
- 1 cup sliced fresh mushrooms
- 1 teaspoon sugar
- ½ teaspoon salt
- ¼ cup water
- 1 can (1 pound) bean sprouts, drained
- 1 tablespoon cornstarch
- 1 tomato, cut into wedges
  Hot cooked rice

1. Marinate meat in Sherry and 1 tablespoon of the soy sauce 10 minutes; broil, 4 inches from heat, 5 minutes on each side; cool; cut into very thin slices.
2. Heat oil in a wok or large skillet over high heat; add carrots, celery, onion and mushrooms. Cook and stir-fry 2 minutes. Add remaining 1 tablespoon soy sauce, sugar and salt; mix.
3. Add water; lower heat to medium. Cover; cook 2 minutes.
4. Add bean sprouts and sliced beef; mix well. Combine cornstarch and 2 tablespoons cold water; gradually stir into skillet. Cook, stirring constantly, until mixture bubbles 3 minutes.
5. Add tomato wedges; cook 1 minute longer. Serve at once with hot cooked rice.

CHINESE VEGETABLE BOWL

A beef and vegetable dish with flavor, color and crunch.

Makes 4 servings.

- ¼ cup peanut or vegetable oil
- 1 Bermuda onion, thin sliced
- 2 cups thinly sliced celery
- 1 can (6 ounces) sliced mushrooms
- 1 package (6 ounces) frozen Chinese pea pods
  OR: 1 package (9 ounces) frozen Italian green beans
- 2 cups coarsely chopped Chinese cabbage
- 2 cups sliced cooked beef
- 1 can (5 ounces) water chestnuts, drained and sliced

1. Heat oil in large wok or skillet; sauté onion lightly 2 to 3 minutes. Add celery and liquid from mushrooms; cover; steam 5 minutes.
2. Stir in Chinese pea pods or green beans, Chinese cabbage, beef, water chestnuts and mushrooms. Cover; steam 5 minutes longer, or just until crisply tender. Pass soy sauce.

PEKING PORK

Roast pork and Chinese style vegetables make a winning combination.

Broil for 10 minutes.
Makes 4 servings.

- 1 clove garlic, peeled
- 1 teaspoon or envelope instant chicken broth
- 2 tablespoons sugar
- ½ cup water
- ¼ cup soy sauce
- 12 thin slices roast pork
- 4 cups hot cooked rice
- 1 package (10 ounces) frozen Chinese style vegetables, cooked (see Cook's Guide)

1. Combine garlic, instant chicken broth, sugar, water and soy sauce in small saucepan; heat to boiling; simmer 5 minutes to blend flavors; remove garlic.
2. Place pork slices in single layer on broiler rack; brush with sauce.
3. Broil 4 inches from heat, brushing several times with sauce, 5 minutes on each side, or until crisp and brown.
4. Spread hot rice in bottom of a heated 6-cup casserole; arrange pork slices on top; spoon Chinese vegetables around edge; garnish with sliced green onion, if you wish.

CHINESE LAMB SKILLET

Fresh bean sprouts, Chinese snow peas, lotus root or water chestnuts also may be added.

Makes 4 servings.

- 2 tablespoons peanut oil
- 4 shoulder lamb chops, about ¾-inch thick
- 1 medium-size onion, sliced
- ⅓ cup diced green pepper
- ⅓ cup diced celery
- 1 can (5 ounces) sliced bamboo shoots
- 1 can (1 pound) bean sprouts
- 1 tablespoon cornstarch
- ½ teaspoon salt
- ¼ teaspoon pepper
- 2 tablespoons soy sauce
- 1 medium-size tomato, cut in wedges

1. Preheat an electric wok or electric frypan to 360°. Pour in oil; add lamb chops. Cook until lamb is brown on both sides; remove and reserve.
2. Add onion, green pepper and celery to pan; stir-fry 2 minutes. Drain liquid from bamboo shoots and bean sprouts into pan; add reserved lamb. Cover and simmer at 200° 30 minutes, or until lamb is tender.
3. Add bamboo shoots and bean sprouts. Combine cornstarch, salt, pepper and soy sauce in a cup; stir into bubbling liquid in pan. Add tomato wedges. Cover and cook 5 minutes, or until sauce thickens. Serve with Chinese noodles, if you wish.

SHRIMP IMPERIAL

Shrimp and vegetables go into the wok or skillet to cook the Far East way.

Makes 4 servings.

- 3 tablespoons peanut oil
- 1 Bermuda onion, thin sliced and separated into rings
- 2 cups thinly sliced celery
- 1 pound fresh shrimp, shelled and deveined
  OR: 1 package (12 ounces) frozen shelled deveined raw shrimp, thawed
- ½ pound Chinese snow peas
  OR: 1 package (6 ounces) frozen Chinese snow peas, thawed
- 1 pound fresh spinach, washed and stemmed
- 1 can (5 ounces) water chestnuts, drained and sliced
- ⅓ cup soy sauce
- 1 tablespoon sugar
- 1 envelope or teaspoon instant vegetable broth
- ½ cup hot water
  Hot cooked rice

1. Heat peanut oil in a wok or large skillet. Add onion rings and sliced celery; sauté lightly. Push to one side of pan.
2. Add shrimp and sauté, turning often, 5 minutes; push to one side. Place snow peas, spinach and water-chestnuts in pan.
3. Mix soy sauce, sugar, instant vegetable broth and hot water in a cup. Pour into pan; cover.
4. Bring to boiling; lower heat and simmer 2 minutes, or just until the spinach wilts and shrimp are tender. Serve with hot cooked rice.

ORIENTAL TUNA STIR-FRY

A San Francisco favorite.

Makes 4 servings.

- 2 cups thinly sliced broccoli
- 2 cups thinly sliced zucchini
- 2 cups thinly sliced cauliflower
- 4 green onions, cut into 2-inch pieces
- 2 tablespoons butter or margarine
- 2 tablespoons peanut or vegetable oil
  Rind and juice of ½ lemon
- 2 tablespoons soy sauce
- 1 can (7 ounces) tuna, drained and chunked
- 4 cups cooked rice

1. Toss broccoli, zucchini, cauliflower and green onions in hot butter or margarine and oil in a wok or large skillet over medium-high heat.
2. Stir-fry 5 minutes, or until crisply tender; add lemon rind, juice and soy sauce and cook 2 minutes. Add tuna chunks and stir just to warm tuna.
3. Spoon over rice in serving bowl.

(Recipes continued on page 122.)

FLUFFY LIGHT DUMPLINGS

Always have stew or fricassee bubbling hot when dropping dumplings in and never peek while dumplings steam.

Bake at 375° for 20 minutes.
Makes 8 dumplings.

- 1½ **cups all purpose flour**
- 2 **teaspoons baking powder**
- ¾ **teaspoon salt**
- 3 **tablespoons vegetable shortening**
- ¾ **cup milk**

1. Sift flour, baking powder and salt into a medium-size bowl; cut in shortening with pastry blender until crumbly. Stir in milk, just until moist.
2. Drop dough by tablespoons onto hot meat or chicken and vegetables; cover casserole or kettle.
3. Bake in moderate oven (375°) or bubble on top of range 20 minutes (do not remove cover), or until light.

PARSLEY DUMPLINGS: Stir ⅓ cup chopped parsley into flour-shortning mixture, before adding milk.

CARAWAY DUMPLINGS: Stir 1 teaspoon crushed caraway seeds into sifted dry ingredients.

HUNGARIAN DUMPLINGS: Brown 1 cup bread cubes in 1 tablespoon butter or margarine in a large skillet until golden. Fold into dumpling dough, after adding milk.

MAIN DISH PASTRY

Here's the perfect amount of pastry to top your favorite casserole.

Bake at 400° for 15 minutes.
Makes enough topping for 1 casserole.

- 1½ **cups all purpose flour**
- ¾ **teaspoon salt**
- ⅓ **cup vegetable shortening**
- 3 **tablespoons ice cold water**

1. Mix flour and salt together in a medium-size bowl; cut in shortening with a pastry blender until mixture is crumbly.
2. Sprinkle cold water over and toss with a fork until pastry clings together and leaves side of bowl; wrap in wax paper and shape into a ball.
3. Roll out dough on a lightly floured pastry cloth or board to size of top of casserole plus 1 inch; cut slits near center for steam to escape.
4. Place pastry on hot casserole, turning edge under and securing pastry to edges with the tines of a dinner fork.
5. Bake in hot oven (400°) 15 minutes, or until golden brown.

CRISSCROSS TOP: Roll out pastry to the size of top of casserole, if rectangular or square, or to a square

the size of the diameter of a round casserole. Cut pastry into 1-inch strips. Lay half the pastry strips evenly across a piece of wax paper. Fold alternate strips halfway back; lay first cross strip over center; bring folded strips back over it. Continue, alternating folded-back strips each time a cross strip is added. Invert lattice pastry onto top of hot casserole; trim ends and secure pastry strips to edge with tines of a dinner fork and bake.

PARMESAN PASTRY: Stir ¼ cup grated Parmesan cheese into flour mixture before cutting in shortening.

GOLDEN GLOW PASTRY: Brush pastry on casserole with a mixture of beaten egg and 1 teaspoon cold water. Cut pastry trims into pretty designs. Arrange on top of pastry; brush with egg mixture. Sprinkle with sesame seeds or poppy seeds and bake.

CHEDDAR CHEESE PINWHEELS

Refrigerated rolls and biscuits make quick and easy toppers for casseroles.

Bake at 375° - 400° for 10-15 minutes.
Makes enough topping for 1 casserole.

- 1 **package (8 ounces) refrigerated crescent rolls**
- 1 **cup shredded Cheddar cheese (4 ounces)**

1. Open refrigerated rolls, following package directions; separate into 4 rectangles of dough.
2. Sprinkle each rectangle with ¼ cup shredded cheese; roll up, starting at short end. Cut each roll into 4 slices. Arrange pinwheels on hot casserole; bake extras on a cookie sheet.
3. Bake in moderate oven (375°) or hot oven (400°) 10 to 15 minutes, or until rolls are golden.

SESAME SEED TWISTS: Open 1 package (8 ounces) refrigerated biscuits; separate into individual biscuits. Shape each biscuit into a 4-inch twist; roll in sesame seeds on wax paper. Arrange as spokes in a wheel on top of hot casserole.

BUTTERFLAKE CHIPS: Open 1 package (8 ounces) refrigerated butterflake rolls and separate into 24 parts. Dip into melted butter or margarine, then dry onion soup mix. Arrange on top of hot casserole.

BISCUIT PETALS: Open 1 package (8 ounces) refrigerated buttermilk biscuits; separate into 10 biscuits. Cut biscuits into ovals with a round cookie cutter. Sprinkle half with paprika and the other half with curry powder. Alternate ovals on top of hot casserole.

FLAKY BUTTERMILK BISCUITS

Always place biscuits on hot casserole mixture and bake until golden at temperature given in casserole recipe.

Bake at 375° - 400° for 15 - 20 minutes.
Makes 12 biscuits.

- 2 **cups all purpose flour**
- 2 **teaspoons baking powder**
- 1 **teaspoon salt**
- ¼ **teaspoon baking soda**
- ¼ **cup vegetable shortening**
- ¾ **cup buttermilk**

1. Sift flour, baking powder, salt and baking soda into a large bowl; cut in shortening with a pastry blender until crumbly.
2. Stir in buttermilk with a fork, just until blended. Turn dough out onto a lightly floured pastry cloth or board; knead gently for 30 seconds.
3. Roll out dough to a ¾-inch thickness; cut with a 2-inch round cutter, rerolling and cutting out trims. Arrange biscuits on hot casserole, placing any extra ones on a small cookie sheet.
4. Bake in moderate oven (375°) or hot oven (400°) 15 to 20 minutes, or until biscuits are golden.

POPPY SEED BISCUITS: Brush cut out biscuits with milk; sprinkle generously with poppy seeds before baking.

SWISS CHEESE BISCUITS: Stir 1 cup shredded Swiss cheese into flour-shortening mixture before adding buttermilk.

HERB DROP BISCUITS: Stir 1 teaspoon crumbled mixed Italian herbs into sifted dry ingredients and increase buttermilk to 1 cup. Drop by tablespoons onto bubbling casserole.

ONION BISCUITS: Stir ¼ cup sliced green onions or 1 small onion, chopped, into flour-shortening mixture, before adding buttermilk.

HOT WATER PASTRY

Makes enough for one 8-inch deep pie.

- 4 **cups all purpose flour**
- 1 **teaspoon salt**
- 1 **cup lard or vegetable shortening**
- ⅔ **cup water**

1. Combine flour and salt in a large bowl. Heat lard or vegetable shortening and water to boiling in a small saucepan.
2. Pour hot liquid over flour and stir with a fork until well blended. Turn out onto a lightly floured pastry cloth or board; knead 3 minutes, or until smooth; cover with a damp paper towel. Allow to rest at room temperature 30 minutes.

MELTON MOWBRAY PIE

English pub pies are a treat too good to keep on the other side of the Atlantic. This one combines pork and veal in a rich gelatin broth. Photo, page 54.

Bake at 350° for 2 hours.
Makes 8 servings.

Hot Water Pastry (recipe, page 97)
- 1 can condensed chicken broth
- ¾ cup water
- 1 large onion, chopped (1 cup)
- 2 carrots, pared and sliced
- 4 sprigs parsley
- 1 bay leaf
- 1 teaspoon whole peppercorns
- 2 pounds boneless pork shoulder
- 1 pound boneless veal shoulder
- 1 tablespoon salt
- 1 teaspoon leaf sage, crumbled
- ½ teaspoon pepper
- 1 tablespoon anchovy paste
- 1 egg
- 1 tablespoon milk
- 1 envelope unflavored gelatin

1. Prepare HOT WATER PASTRY and allow to rest.
2. Combine chicken broth, water, onion, carrots, parsley, bay leaf and peppercorns in a medium-size saucepan; bring to boiling; reduce heat; simmer 15 minutes; strain into a 2-cup measure.
3. Cut pork and veal shoulders into ½-inch pieces; combine in a large bowl with 1 cup strained liquid, salt, sage, pepper and anchovy paste until well blended.
4. Butter and flour an 8-inch spring-form pan. Roll out three-quarters HOT WATER PASTRY to a 14-inch round on a lightly floured pastry cloth or board. Fit pastry gently into spring-form pan, pressing pastry against bottom and side.
5. Spoon meat mixture into prepared pan. Roll out remaining pastry to a 9-inch round; cut a 1-inch hole in center. Place pastry over meat mixture; turn pastry edge over; flute edge. Reroll pastry trims into a 12-inch strip; cut a ¾-inch wide piece; wrap in a tight circle, to make a "rose." Cut remaining pastry into leaf shapes. Place "rose" and leaves on pie.
6. Beat egg and milk with a fork in a cup; brush over top of pie, "rose" and leaves.
7. Bake in moderate oven (350°) 1 hour, 30 minutes; brush again with egg mixture; bake 30 minutes longer, covering "rose" with foil if it is getting too dark, or until pastry is golden brown. Cool in pan on wire rack 30 minutes.
8. Pour remaining strained liquid into a small saucepan; sprinkle gelatin over; heat, stirring constantly, until gelatin dissolves. Remove pastry center and rose from pie with tip of knife; pour in hot gelatin, tilting pan from side to side to help distribute liquid;

return pastry center and rose to pie.
9. Cool on wire rack 2 hours, then chill 6 hours, or overnight, to firm-up pie filling.
10. Run a long thin knife around edge of pie. Loosen side of spring-form pan. Cut pie into wedges.

CRISSCROSS CHICKEN PIE

Chicken in curry-sparked sauce nestles under a lattice pastry.

Bake at 400° for 20 minutes,
then at 350° for 25 minutes.
Makes 6 servings.

- 1 broiler-fryer, cut up (about 3 pounds)
- 3 cups water
  Handful celery tops
- 1 teaspoon salt
- 6 peppercorns
  Curry-Cream Sauce (recipe follows)
- 1 package (10 ounces) frozen peas, cooked and drained
- 1 pimiento, chopped
- 2 cups all purpose flour
- 1 teaspoon salt
- ⅓ cup vegetable shortening
- ⅔ cup milk

1. Simmer chicken with water, celery tops, 1 teaspoon salt and peppercorns in kettle 45 minutes, or until tender. Remove from broth and let cool until easy to handle.
2. Strain broth into a 4-cup measure; add water, if needed, to make 3 cups. Make CURRY-CREAM SAUCE.
3. Slip skin from chicken, then remove meat from bones. (It comes off easily if still warm.) Cut meat into bite-size pieces; toss with peas, pimiento and 2 cups of the CURRY-CREAM SAUCE in a medium-size bowl. (Keep remaining sauce warm.)
4. Sift flour and 1 teaspoon salt into medium-size bowl; cut in shortening until mixture is crumbly, using pastry blender or two knives; stir in milk with a fork just until dough holds together.
5. Turn out onto a lightly floured pastry cloth or board; knead dough lightly 5 or 6 times. Roll out two-thirds of dough to a 16x12-inch rectangle; fit dough into a 10x6x2-inch casserole. Spoon chicken mixture into shell.
6. Roll out remaining pastry to a 12x8-inch rectangle; cut into 9 strips with knife or pastry wheel. Lay 5 strips lengthwise over filling. Halve remaining 4 strips; weave across long strips to make a crisscross top. Trim overhang to 1 inch; fold under; flute.
7. Bake in hot oven (400°) 20 minutes; reduce heat to moderate (350°). Bake 25 minutes longer, or until golden. Serve with remaining hot CURRY-CREAM SAUCE.

CURRY-CREAM SAUCE: Makes

about 4½ cups. Melt ⅓ cup (¾ stick) butter or margarine over low heat in medium-size saucepan. Stir in ⅓ cup all purpose flour, 1 teaspoon salt, 1 teaspoon curry powder and ⅛ teaspoon pepper. Cook, stirring constantly, just until mixture bubbles. Stir in 3 cups chicken broth slowly; continue cooking and stirring until sauce thickens and bubbles 3 minutes. Stir in 1 tall can (1⅔) cups) evaporated milk; heat slowly.

STEAK-AND-KIDNEY PIE

It's been a favorite for years.

Bake at 400° for 10 minutes,
then at 300° for 2 hours, 50 minutes.
Makes 8 servings.

- 1 beef kidney (about ¾ pound)
- 1 round steak (about 2 pounds)
- 1½ pounds small white onions, peeled and halved
- ¼ pound mushrooms, sliced
  OR: 1 can (3 or 4 ounces) sliced mushrooms
- 1 medium-size carrot, pared and grated
- ¼ cup chopped parsley
- 1 envelope (about 1 ounce) brown gravy mix
- 2 teaspoons salt
- 1 teaspoon leaf thyme, crumbled
- ¼ teaspoon pepper
- ¼ teaspoon ground allspice
  Meat Pie Pastry (recipe follows)
- ½ cup hot water
- 1 teaspoon Worcestershire sauce
- 1 egg
- 1 tablespoon milk

1. Soak kidney overnight in lightly salted water to cover; drain. Cut into ½-inch-thick slices; cut out tubes and white membrane. (Scissors do a neat, quick job.) Dice meat; place in large bowl.
2. Cut steak into ½-inch cubes; place in bowl with kidney; add onions, mushrooms, carrot and parsley; sprinkle with gravy mix, salt, thyme, pepper and allspice. Toss to mix well.
3. Make MEAT PIE PASTRY. Roll out two-thirds of dough on a lightly floured pastry cloth or board to a circle 3 inches larger than an 8-cup shallow casserole; fit into dish; trim overhang to ½ inch. Spoon meat mixture into dish.
4. Mix hot water and Worcestershire sauce in a 1-cup measure; pour over meats and vegetables.
5. Roll out remaining pastry to a circle 2 inches larger than dish. Cut out a 2-inch circle from center to let steam escape; cover pie. Trim overhang to 1 inch; turn under, flush with rim; flute.
6. Beat egg slightly with milk in a cup; brush part over top crust of pie.
7. Roll out pastry trimmings ¼-inch thick; cut into fancy shapes with truf-

fle cutters or sharp knife. Arrange cutouts on top of pie; brush with egg mixture.

8. Bake in hot oven (400°) 10 minutes; reduce oven heat to slow (300°). Bake 2 hours, 20 minutes; brush again with egg mixture. Bake 30 minutes longer, or until meat is tender. Let stand about 10 minutes to cool. Garnish with a sprig of parsley and serve with a platter of sliced carrots and Brussels sprouts tossed in butter or margarine and sprinkled with ground nutmeg, if you wish.

MEAT PIE PASTRY: Makes enough for the bottom and top crusts of an 8-cup shallow casserole. Combine 3 cups all purpose flour and 2 teaspoons salt in a medium-size bowl until well blended; cut in 1 cup vegetable shortening with pastry blender or 2 knives until mixture is crumbly. Sprinkle ½ cup cold water over, 2 tablespoons at a time, mixing lightly with a fork just until pastry holds together and leaves side of bowl clean. Shape lightly into a ball with wax paper.

DEVILED EGGS INDIENNE

Rich curried cheese sauce accents deviled eggs for a meatless entrée.

Makes 4 servings.

- 8 hard-cooked eggs, shelled
- ¼ cup mayonnaise or salad dressing
- 1 teaspoon salt
- ½ teaspoon dry mustard
- ¼ teaspoon pepper
- 2 teaspoons chopped pimiento
- 1 package (6 ounces) shredded process Gruyere cheese
- 1 package (10 ounces) frozen peas
- 1 envelope or teaspoon instant chicken broth
- 1 cup boiling water
- ¼ cup (½ stick) butter or margarine
- 1 medium-size onion, chopped (½ cup)
- ¼ cup all purpose flour
- 1½ teaspoons curry powder
- ¼ teaspoon ground ginger
- 1 cup milk
- 4 cups hot cooked rice

1. Halve eggs lengthwise; remove yolks and press through coarse sieve into small bowl; blend in mayonnaise or salad dressing, ½ teaspoon of the salt, dry mustard, ⅛ teaspoon of the pepper, chopped pimiento and ¼ cup of the shredded cheese; pile into egg white halves.
2. Cook peas, following label directions; drain and reserve. Dissolve instant chicken broth in boiling water.
3. Melt butter or margarine in a medium-size saucepan; sauté onion until tender. Stir in flour, remaining ½ teaspoon salt, remaining ⅛ teaspoon pepper, curry powder and gin-

ger. Cook, stirring constantly, just until bubbly. Stir in dissolved chicken broth and milk; continue cooking and stirring until sauce thickens and bubbles 3 minutes. Remove from heat; stir in remaining cheese until melted; add peas and blend well.

4. Spoon hot cooked rice into heated serving dish; spoon sauce over; arrange eggs around edge of dish. Garnish with pimiento strips and serve with a salad of cucumber slices in plain yogurt or dill vinaigrette dressing, if you wish.

ASPARAGUS PINWHEEL PIE

As fragrant and fresh as spring, and a delightful luncheon dish.

Bake at 425° for 15 minutes.
Makes 6 servings.

- 1 package piecrust mix
- 1 bunch asparagus (about 2 pounds)
- 4 hard-cooked eggs, shelled
- 3 tablespoons butter or margarine
- 3 tablespoons all purpose flour
- ¼ teaspoon mixed salad herbs, crumbled
  Dash ground nutmeg
- 1 cup milk
- 1 envelope instant chicken broth

1. Prepare piecrust mix, following label directions. Roll dough out to a 12-inch round on a lightly floured pastry cloth or board; fit into a 9-inch pie plate. Trim overhang to ½ inch; turn under, flush with rim; flute to make a stand-up edge. Prick shell all over with a fork.
2. Bake in hot oven (425°) 15 minutes, or until golden.
3. While pie shell bakes, break tough woody ends from asparagus; wash stalks well. If scales are large or sandy, cut off with a sharp knife; wash stalks again. Cut tips of 16 of the stalks into 4-inch lengths; tie in bundle; then stand in deep saucepan. Cut all remaining asparagus into 1-inch pieces; place around stalks in pan. Pour in enough boiling water to cover asparagus pieces; cover.
4. Cook 15 minutes, or just until tender; drain well.
5. Slice one egg, crosswise; set aside; dice remaining eggs.
6. Melt butter or margarine in a medium-size saucepan; stir in flour, mixed salad herbs and nutmeg; cook, stirring constantly, just until bubbly. Stir in milk and instant chicken broth; continue cooking and stirring until sauce thickens and bubbles 3 minutes. Fold in asparagus pieces and diced eggs. Spoon into pastry shell.
7. Cut string from asparagus spears; arrange, tip ends out, on top; place egg slices, overlapping, in center. To serve, cut pie into wedges; lift out with a wide spatula.

AUSTRALIAN BEEF PLATTER

There'll be enough beef and gravy left over to make a casserole or hot sandwiches.

Bake at 325° for 1 hour, 40 minutes.
Makes 4 servings, plus leftovers.

- 4 medium-size parsnips
- 4 medium-size onions
- 4 medium-size potatoes
- 4 medium-size carrots
- 1 large acorn squash
- 5 pounds boneless beef rump, chuck or round
  Instant unseasoned meat tenderizer
- 2 tablespoons vegetable oil
  Melbourne Gravy (recipe follows)

1. Pare parsnips; halve lengthwise, then cut crosswise into 3-inch chunks. Peel onions. Pare potatoes and cut each in half. Scrape carrots and cut diagonally into 2-inch chunks. Quarter squash; scoop out seeds and membrane, but do not pare.
2. Parboil parsnips and onions together, and potatoes, carrots and squash together, in lightly salted boiling water in two kettles, 15 minutes, Drain, reserving 3 cups of the potato-carrot-squash liquid.
3. Moisten roast and sprinkle with meat tenderizer, following label directions. Place on rack in a large shallow roasting pan. If using a meat thermometer, insert bulb into center of roast.
4. Arrange vegetables in separate piles around meat; brush vegetables lightly all over with vegetable oil; sprinkle with pepper, if you wish.
5. Roast in slow oven (325°), allowing about 20 minutes per pound for rare (thermometer should register 140°), or 25 minutes per pound for medium (thermometer should register 150°). During roasting, turn vegetables and baste once or twice with drippings in pan. Vegetables and roast should be done at the same time.
6. Remove roast to a heated serving platter; lift out vegetables with a slotted spoon and arrange in separate piles around roast. Keep hot while making gravy.

MELBOURNE GRAVY: Makes 3 cups. Remove rack from roasting pan. Tip pan and let fat rise in one corner; skim off all fat into a cup, leaving juices in pan. Return 4 tablespoons fat to pan; blend in 4 tablespoons all purpose flour. Cook, stirring constantly, just until mixture bubbles. Slowly stir in reserved 3 cups potato-carrot-squash liquid. Continue cooking and stirring, scraping baked-on juices from bottom and sides of pan, until gravy thickens and bubbles 1 minute. Season to taste with salt and pepper, if needed. Darken with a few drops bottled gravy coloring.

SHEPHERD'S PIE

Wonderful for a cold winter evening!

Bake at 375° for 30 minutes.
Makes 4 servings.

- 1 **medium-size onion, chopped (½ cup)**
- 2 **tablespoons butter or margarine**
- 2 **cups ground cooked beef or lamb**
- 1 **can (10½ ounces) beef gravy**
- 2 **tablespoons Worcestershire sauce**
- 1 **teaspoon salt**
- ¼ **teaspoon pepper**
- 4 **cups hot mashed potatoes**
- 1 **egg, slightly beaten**
- 1 **can (1 pound) whole baby carrots**
- 1 **tablespoon butter or margarine**
- 1 **teaspoon grated lemon rind (optional)**

1. Sauté onion in the 2 tablespoons butter or margarine in a medium-size saucepan until soft; stir in meat, gravy, Worcestershire sauce, salt and pepper. Spoon meat mixture into a greased 10-cup casserole.
2. Spread hot mashed potatoes evenly over meat; score with a fork; brush with egg.
3. Bake in moderate oven (375°) 30 minutes, or until golden and bubbly.
4. Drain liquid from carrots into a medium-size saucepan; bring to boiling. Add carrots; lower heat; simmer 10 minutes, or until hot; drain. Add the 1 tablespoon butter or margarine and lemon rind, if used; toss to coat carrots. Wreathe casserole with buttered carrots, before serving.

CREAMY HAM PUFF

Leftover ham bakes with broccoli and cheese sauce beneath a cream-puff topping.

Bake at 350° for 35 minutes.
Makes 4 servings.

- ½ **bunch broccoli (about ¾ pound)**
- 2 **envelopes (about 1 ounce each) white sauce mix**
  Water or milk
- 1 **cup shredded Cheddar cheese (4 ounces)**
- 1 **tablespoon prepared mustard**
- 1 **cup chopped cooked ham**
- 1 **large tomato, sliced**
- ½ **cup water**
- ¼ **cup (½ stick) butter or margarine**
- ½ **teaspoon salt**
- ½ **cup all purpose flour**
- 2 **eggs**

1. Wash and trim broccoli; cut stalks and flowerets into bite-size pieces. Cook in boiling salted water in a medium-size saucepan 10 minutes, or just until crisply tender; drain.
2. While broccoli cooks, make white sauce with water or milk, following label directions; add cheese and mustard. Stir in ham.
3. Layer broccoli and ham mixture in a 6-cup casserole, beginning and ending with broccoli. Arrange tomato slices on top.
4. Bring water, butter or margarine and salt to boiling in a small saucepan. Add flour all at once. Stir with a wooden spoon until mixture forms a thick, smooth ball that leaves side of pan, about 1 minute. Remove from heat; cool slightly.
5. Break in eggs one at a time, beating well after each addition. Spoon mixture onto tomato slices in baking dish.
6. Bake in moderate oven (350°) 35 minutes, or until topping is puffed and brown and ham mixture is bubbly hot. Serve with a spinach and orange salad, topped with a few coarsely chopped walnuts, if you wish.

BEEF 'N' CABBAGE PIE

Shakespeare himself tells of the Englishman's delight for salty beef with hearty cabbage.

Bake at 400° for 30 minutes.
Makes 6 servings.

- 2 **cups all purpose flour**
- 1 **tablespoon baking powder**
- 1 **teaspoon salt**
- ¼ **cup vegetable shortening**
- 1 **tablespoon prepared hot mustard**
- ¾ **cup milk**
- 1 **can (12 ounces) corned beef**
- 2 **tablespoons instant minced onion**
- 4 **cups shredded cabbage**
- 2 **tablespoons butter or margarine**
  Horseradish Sauce (recipe follows)

1. Sift flour, baking powder and salt into a medium-size bowl. Cut shortening and mustard into flour with a pastry blender until mixture is crumbly. Blend in milk to make a soft dough.
2. Turn out onto a lightly floured pastry cloth or board and knead gently for 30 seconds. Roll out to a 9-inch circle.
3. Mash corned beef with fork in a medium-size bowl; blend in instant onion. Sauté cabbage in butter or margarine in a large skillet until tender, about 2 minutes.
4. Press corned beef mixture into bottom of a 9-inch pie pan. Cover with sautéed cabbage. Place pastry on top; trim excess; cut vents in pastry to allow steam to escape.
5. Bake in hot oven (400°) 30 minutes, or until pastry is golden brown. Cut into wedges and serve with HORSERADISH SAUCE and a canned pear and leaf lettuce salad.

HORSERADISH SAUCE: Makes 1 cup. Combine ½ cup mayonnaise or salad dressing, ½ cup milk and 2 tablespoons prepared horseradish in a small saucepan. Heat, stirring constantly, until sauce thickens and bubbles. Serve warm over pie.

SOUTHDOWN LIVER

Southdown sheep once roamed the hills of Sussex and Hampshire counties in England. This recipe glorfies lamb liver.

Makes 6 servings.

- 6 **slices bacon, cut into 1-inch pieces**
- 18 **small white onions, peeled**
- 1 **pound lamb liver, sliced**
- 3 **tablespoons all purpose flour**
- 1 **teaspoon salt**
- ¼ **teaspoon pepper**
- 1 **can (1 pound) stewed tomatoes**
- ¼ **cup water**
- 1 **package (10 ounces) frozen green peas and celery**

1. Sauté bacon until crisp in a kettle or Dutch oven; remove and set aside. Pour off all drippings into a measuring cup, then measure 3 tablespoons and return to kettle. Add onions; sauté until golden; lift out with a slotted spoon; reserve.
2. Cut liver into 1-inch-wide strips; shake with flour, salt and pepper in a plastic bag to coat well.
3. Brown liver quickly in same kettle, adding more bacon drippings, if needed; stir in tomatoes, water and onions; bring to boiling; cover.
4. Simmer 30 minutes, or until liver and onions are tender.
5. While liver cooks, cook peas and celery, following label directions.
6. Spoon liver mixture into a heated serving bowl; spoon peas and celery in a ring on top; garnish with bacon. Serve with mashed potatoes and a tossed green salad, if you wish.

MULLIGATAWNY SOUP

From the days of the British in India comes this hearty chicken and vegetable soup. Vary the amount of curry powder you add to suit your own taste.

Makes 6 servings.

- 6 **envelopes or teaspoons instant chicken broth**
- 6 **cups boiling water**
- 3 **medium-size carrots, pared and sliced**
- 2 **stalks celery, sliced**
- 3 **cups diced cooked chicken**
- 1 **large onion, chopped (1 cup)**
- ¼ **cup (½ stick) butter or margarine**
- 1 **apple, pared, quartered, cored and chopped**
- 3 **to 6 teaspoons curry powder**
- 1 **teaspoon salt**
- ¼ **cup all purpose flour**
- 1 **tablespoon lemon juice**
- 2 **cups hot cooked rice**
- ¼ **cup chopped parsley**
- 6 **lemon slices**

1. Dissolve 1 teaspoon of the instant chicken broth in 1 cup boiling water in a medium-size saucepan. Stir in carrots and celery; cook over medium heat 20 minutes, or until tender. Add

chicken; heat until hot; keep warm.
2. Sauté onion until soft in butter or margarine in Dutch oven; stir in apple, curry powder to taste and salt; sauté 5 minutes longer, or until apple is soft; add flour. Gradually stir in remaining instant chicken broth and water; bring to boiling; cover; simmer 15 minutes.
3. Add vegetables and chicken with stock; bring just to boiling. Stir in lemon juice.
4. Ladle into soup plates or bowls. Pass hot cooked rice, chopped parsley and lemon slices for garnish, and serve with crusty bread, if you wish.

ISLE OF JERSEY BEEF PIE

Meat pie with a French influence, brimming with vegetables and the mellow flavor of dry red wine.

Bake at 375° for 25 minutes.
Makes 8 servings.

- 1 package hot-roll mix
- ½ cup sliced celery
- ⅓ cup sliced carrots
- 1 tablespoon vegetable oil
- 3 tablespoons catsup
- 1 can condensed onion soup
- ½ cup dry red wine
- ½ teaspoon leaf tarragon, crumbled
- 1 bay leaf
  Dash ground cloves
- 1 package (10 ounces) frozen cut green beans
- ¼ cup all purpose flour
- ⅓ cup water
- 1 can (2 ounces) anchovy fillets, chopped
- ½ cup stuffed green olives
- 8 slices cooked beef
- 1 egg, slightly beaten

1. Prepare roll mix, following label directions; let rise 45 minutes.
2. Meanwhile, sauté celery and carrots in oil in a large skillet 10 minutes. Stir in catsup; cook, stirring constantly, 1 minute. Add condensed onion soup, wine, tarragon, bay leaf, cloves and green beans. Cover; simmer 5 minutes. Remove bay leaf. Combine flour and water in a small bowl; blend until smooth. Pour into skillet; cook, stirring constantly, until sauce thickens and bubbles 3 minutes. Stir in anchovies and olives.
3. Pour half of sauce into a 13x9x2-inch casserole. Arrange beef slices in dish. Top with remaining sauce.
4. Turn dough out onto lightly floured board. Knead a few times. Roll to a 15x10-inch rectangle. Place on beef mixture; trim overhang to 1 inch; turn under and flute edges. Cut several slits in center for steam to escape. Brush with egg.
5. Bake in moderate oven (375°) 25 minutes, or until pastry is golden. Serve with a romaine salad garnished with pimiento, if you wish.

COUNTRY STYLE PORK PIE

Mashed potatoes make an unusual "crust" for this thrifty dish. A marvelous way to use up leftover pork.

Bake at 400° for 15 minutes.
Makes 4 servings.

- 1 small cabbage (about 1 pound)
- ¼ cup (½ stick) butter or margarine
- 1 teaspoon salt
- ¼ teaspoon pepper
- 4 cups prepared instant mashed potatoes
- 1 cup diced cooked pork
- 1 can (10½ ounces) brown gravy with onions
- 4 hard-cooked eggs, shelled and diced
- ¼ cup chopped parsley

1. Trim cabbage and shred (you will have about 5 cups). Cook in lightly salted water in a large saucepan 5 minutes, or just until crisply tender; drain well. Toss with 2 tablespoons of the butter or margarine, salt and pepper, until butter melts and cabbage is evenly coated.
2. Fold prepared potatoes into cabbage. Spoon over the bottom and sides of a buttered 8-cup shallow casserole.
3. Melt remaining 2 tablespoons butter or margarine in a small skillet; sauté pork 1 minute; add gravy; bring to boiling; remove from heat. Carefully mix in eggs and parsley. Spoon into potato-lined dish.
4. Bake in hot oven (400°) 15 minutes, or until bubbly hot. Serve with a carrot slaw garnished with candied ginger pieces, if you wish.

TOMATO CHEESE TART

A savory pie that's high in protein but low in cost.

Bake at 425° for 10 minutes,
then at 325° for 20 minutes
Makes 4 servings.

- ½ package piecrust mix
- 1 cup shredded Cheddar cheese (4 ounces)
- 2 packages (6 ounces each) shredded process Gruyère cheese
- 3 ripe medium-size tomatoes
- 1 teaspoon salt
- ⅛ teaspoon pepper
- 1 teaspoon leaf basil, crumbled
- 1 teaspoon leaf oregano, crumbled
- ½ cup chopped green onions
- 2 tablespoons butter or margarine
- 2 tablespoons soft bread crumbs

1. Prepare piecrust mix, following label directions and adding ½ cup of the Cheddar cheese. Roll out to a 12-inch round on lightly floured pastry cloth or board; fit into a 9-inch pie plate. Trim overhang to ½ inch; turn under; flute to make stand-up edge. Prick with fork.

2. Bake in hot oven (425°) 10 minutes, or until golden; cool.
3. Spoon remaining Cheddar cheese and Gruyère into piecrust. Slice tomatoes into thin wedges. Arrange, slightly overlapping, in circular pattern over the cheese. Sprinkle with salt, pepper, basil and oregano.
4. Sauté green onions in butter or margarine until tender in a small skillet. Spoon into the center of pie; sprinkle with bread crumbs.
5. Bake in moderate oven (325°) 20 minutes, or until tomatoes are tender. *Suggested Variations:* This tart is also delicious when made with other kinds of cheese. Mix bread crumb topping with grated Parmesan cheese for an additional flavor boost.

SOMERSET CASSEROLE

Cheddar cheese was once known as Somerset cheese.

Bake at 350° for 30 minutes.
Makes 6 servings.

- 1 package (8 ounces) elbow macaroni
- 1 small onion, grated
- 3 tablespoons butter or margarine
- 2 tablespoons all purpose flour
- 1 teaspoon dry mustard
  Dash pepper
- 2 cups milk
- 1 package (8 ounces) sliced Cheddar cheese
- 2 cups cubed cooked ham
  Cherry tomatoes

1. Cook macaroni, following label directions; drain and keep hot.
2. While macaroni cooks, sauté onion until soft in 2 tablespoons of the butter or margarine in a medium-size skillet. Stir in flour, mustard and pepper; cook, stirring constantly, just until bubbly.
3. Stir in milk; continue cooking and stirring until sauce thickens and bubbles 3 minutes. Cut up half of the cheese slices; add to sauce, stirring until cheese is melted. Cut remaining cheese slices into 6 strips each.
4. Combine drained macaroni and ham in a buttered 8-cup shallow casserole; pour cheese sauce over; arrange cheese strips, spoke-fashion, on top.
5. Bake in moderate oven (350°) 30 minutes, or until bubbly.
6. While casserole bakes, sauté cherry tomatoes in remaining 1 tablespoon butter or margarine in a medium-size skillet 3 minutes, or just until skins start to pop; mound on baked casserole just before serving. Serve with pickled onions and beets for a typical British side dish.
COOK'S TIP: To keep macaroni hot, place over simmering water in kettle in which it was cooked; for extended periods, cover top with foil.

NORTH SEA SHRIMP AU GRATIN

A dish from the sea, made in minutes.

Bake at 350° for 20 minutes.
Makes 4 servings.

- 1 package (5½ ounces) noodles with sour cream sauce (see Cook's Guide)
  Milk
  Butter or margarine
- 1 package (1 pound) frozen shelled deveined raw shrimp
  OR: 2 cans (6½ ounces each) tuna, drained and flaked
- 1 can (3 or 4 ounces) sliced mushrooms, drained
- 1 container (8 ounces) cream-style cottage cheese
- ½ teaspoon dillweed
- 3 tablespoons fine dry bread crumbs
- 1 tablespoon butter or margarine, softened

1. Prepare noodles with milk and butter or margarine in a medium size saucepan, following label directions.
2. Cook shrimp in a medium-size saucepan, following label directions; drain and chop. Add shrimp or tuna to noodle mixture.
3. Stir in mushrooms, cottage cheese and dillweed. Spoon into a 6-cup casserole.
4. Combine bread crumbs and butter or margarine in a small bowl. Sprinkle over casserole.
5. Bake in moderate oven (350°) 20 minutes, or until casserole is bubbly.

CORNED BEEF LOAF

In Britain, beef is cured in saltpeter brine; our corned beef is an overseas approximation.

Bake at 425° for 30 minutes.
Makes 6 servings.

- 4 cups diced cooked corned beef
- 1 medium-size onion, peeled
- 2 medium-size potatoes, cooked, peeled and diced
- 2 eggs, slightly beaten
- ⅛ teaspoon pepper
- ½ cup milk
- 2 cups all purpose flour
- 1 teaspoon salt
- ⅓ cup vegetable shortening
- ⅔ cup milk
  Mustard Sauce (recipe follows)

1. Put corned beef and onion through food chopper, using coarse blade. Mix with potatoes, eggs, pepper and ½ cup milk in large bowl; reserve.
2. Sift flour and salt into medium-size bowl; cut in shortening with pastry blender until mixture is crumbly; blend in ⅔ cup milk with fork just until flour is moist and dough is the consistency of biscuit dough.
3. Turn dough out onto lightly floured pastry cloth or board; knead gently 5 or 6 times; roll out to a 12x10-inch rectangle.
4. Spoon meat mixture into a 9x4-inch loaf shape in center of pastry; fold pastry up over loaf; seal edges. Place, seam-side down, on greased cookie sheet; cut several slits in top of pastry to allow steam to escape.
5. Bake in hot oven (425°) 30 minutes, or until pastry is golden brown. Serve with MUSTARD SAUCE.

MUSTARD SAUCE: Makes about ¾ cup. Blend ½ cup mayonnaise or salad dressing, ¼ cup dairy sour cream, 1 tablespoon prepared mustard and ¼ teaspoon Worcestershire sauce in a 1-cup measure.

DAIRY BAKE

Two cheeses—cottage and Cheddar—combine with sour cream and egg for a hearty macaroni dish.

Bake at 350° for 45 minutes.
Makes 6 servings.

- 1 package (8 ounces) elbow macaroni
- 1 container (1 pound) cream-style cottage cheese
- 2 cups shredded Cheddar cheese (8 ounces)
- ¾ cup dairy sour cream (from an 8-ounce container)
- 1 egg, slightly beaten
- 2 teaspoons grated onion
- 1 teaspoon salt
- ⅛ teaspoon pepper
- 1 package (10 ounces) frozen Brussels sprouts

1. Cook macaroni, following label directions; drain.
2. Combine cottage and Cheddar cheeses, sour cream, egg, onion, salt and pepper in a large bowl; mix until blended; fold in macaroni. Spoon mixture into a 10-cup casserole.
3. Bake in moderate oven (350°) 45 minutes, or until bubbly.
4. Prepare Brussels sprouts according to package directions. Place around edge of baked macaroni and cheese.

OVEN-BAKED IRISH STEW

This stew has all the flavor of the longer-cooking variety, yet it's ready in less than an hour.

Bake at 400° for 45 minutes.
Makes 6 servings.

- 6 shoulder lamb chops (about 2 pounds)
- 1 package (1 pound, 8 ounces) frozen stew vegetables
- 1 can condensed chicken broth
- 1 teaspoon onion salt
- 1 tablespoon chopped fresh mint
  OR: 1 teaspoon leaf marjoram, crumbled

1. Trim excess fat from chops. Melt several pieces in a large skillet for 2 tablespoons fat; discard the rest.
2. Brown chops, 3 at a time, in fat in skillet; remove and reserve. Brown stew vegetables in fat remaining in pan. Stir in chicken broth, onion salt and mint or marjoram. Heat to boiling, stirring often.
3. Arrange browned chops down the center of an 8-cup shallow casserole; spoon vegetables and liquid around chops; cover dish.
4. Bake in hot oven (400°) 45 minutes, or until chops are fork-tender. Garnish with fresh mint, if you wish.
COOK'S TIP: If you like gravy, sprinkle 2 tablespoons all purpose flour over browned vegetables; stir lightly before adding broth.

BRITISH CREAM SOUP

Brussels sprouts and bacon make a hearty winter soup team.

Makes 6 servings.

- 2 packages (10 ounces each) frozen Brussels sprouts
- ½ pound sliced bacon, diced
- 3 medium-size onions, sliced
- 4½ cups chicken broth
  OR: 4 envelopes or teaspoons instant chicken broth and 4½ cups hot water
- 1 bay leaf
- 1 clove garlic
- 2 teaspoons salt
- ½ teaspoon leaf marjoram, crumbled
- ½ teaspoon pepper
  Dash ground cloves
- 1½ cups heavy cream
- ¼ cup dry Sherry
  Chopped parsley

1. Cook Brussels sprouts in a medium-size saucepan, following package directions; drain.
2. Sauté bacon and onions over low heat in a large saucepan for 10 minutes. Drain bacon drippings. Add Brussels sprouts, broth, bay leaf, garlic, salt, marjoram, pepper and cloves; cover. Cook 20 minutes.
3. Cool mixture; process, part at a time, in an electric blender or food processor; return to saucepan.
4. Add cream and Sherry to saucepan. Heat slowly over low heat, stirring several times. Garnish with parsley.

ISLE OF WIGHT LIVER

Lotte Laurence treats her guests to this liver dish, made with peppers from her garden.

Makes 4 servings.

- 1 pound beef or calf's liver, cut into serving-size pieces
- 3 tablespoons all purpose flour
- 1 teaspoon salt
- ¼ teaspoon freshly ground pepper

2 tablespoons butter or margarine
2 tablespoons vegetable oil
1 large onion, chopped (1 cup)
2 red peppers, halved, seeded and chopped
2 teaspoons paprika
1 cup chicken broth
1 container (8 ounces) dairy sour cream or plain yogurt

1. Coat liver on all sides with flour, salt and pepper. Melt butter or margarine with oil in a medium-size skillet; brown liver 2 minutes on each side; remove and reserve.
2. Sauté onion and peppers in drippings left in skillet until soft, about 3 minutes; stir in paprika; cook 1 minute; stir in chicken broth, stirring up browned bits from bottom of pan; simmer 3 minutes.
3. Stir ½ cup liquid from pan into sour cream in a small bowl; return to skillet; return liver; simmer just until heated through, about 1 minute. Serve with rice and a spinach salad.

DEEP-DISH CHICKEN PIE

The British way to use up leftover chicken or turkey—under a crust.

Bake at 425° for 30 minutes.
Makes 6 servings.

6 medium-size potatoes, pared and quartered
6 medium-size carrots, pared and quartered
1 small onion, chopped (¼ cup)
¼ cup chopped green pepper
2 tablespoons butter or margarine
1 can condensed cream of chicken soup
3 cups cooked chicken or turkey
    Biscuit Wedges (recipe follows)

1. Cook potatoes and carrots in boiling salted water in a large saucepan for 15 minutes, or until tender; drain; save 1 cup of the cooking liquid.
2. Sauté onion and green pepper in butter or margarine until soft in a medium-size saucepan; stir in chicken soup and reserved liquid.
3. Spoon vegetables and chicken into an 8-cup casserole; pour sauce over.
4. Bake in hot oven (425°) 15 minutes while making BISCUIT WEDGES; arrange biscuits on top of hot mixture; bake 15 minutes longer, or until biscuits are golden.
BISCUIT WEDGES: Makes 6 wedges. Sift 1½ cups all purpose flour, 2 teaspoons baking powder and ½ teaspoon salt into a medium-size bowl; cut in ¼ cup (½ stick) butter or margarine; add ½ cup milk all at once; stir just until blended. Turn dough out onto a lightly floured pastry cloth or board; knead lightly ½ minute; roll out to a 7-inch round and cut into 6 wedges; brush tops lightly with milk and sprinkle with poppy seeds or sesame seeds.

DEVILED TUNA

So easy to make, the kids can fix it.

Bake at 350° for 20 minutes.
Makes 4 servings.

1 can condensed cream of mushroom soup
1 teaspoon dry mustard
½ cup milk
1 tablespoon lemon juice
1 can (7 ounces) tuna, drained and flaked
¾ cup coarsely crumbled saltines
4 hard-cooked eggs, shelled
    Parsley

1. Combine soup, dry mustard and milk in a small saucepan; heat, stirring constantly, until sauce bubbles.
2. Remove from heat; stir in lemon juice, tuna and ½ cup cracker crumbs.
3. Chop eggs coarsely; stir into tuna mixture. Pour into buttered 4-cup shallow casserole or 9-inch pie plate; sprinkle remaining ¼ cup cracker crumbs over top.
4. Bake in moderate oven (350°) 20 minutes, or until crumbs are golden. Garnish with parsley before serving.

BOILED BEEF DINNER

A ribsticking beef and vegetable dinner that gets a meal together in one pot.

Makes 6 servings

1 lean boneless chuck roast (3 to 4 pounds)
1 tablespoon salt
2 peppercorns
1 bay leaf
6 cups water
6 small potatoes, scrubbed
6 small white onions, peeled
6 medium-size carrots, pared and quartered
1 medium-size cabbage (about 2 pounds)

1. Place meat in large kettle; add salt, peppercorns, bay leaf and water. Cover; bring to boiling; simmer 1 hour, 30 minutes.
2. Cut off a band of skin around middle of each potato; place potatoes, onions and carrots around meat in kettle; simmer 1 hour longer, or until meat is tender.
3. Cut cabbage into 6 wedges; arrange on top of meat and vegetables; cover. Cook 15 minutes longer, or until cabbage is tender.
4. Remove cabbage with slotted spoon and place at one side of a large serving platter; place meat in center and carrots at other side. Place onions and potatoes in separate serving bowls.
5. Skim any fat from broth; spoon broth over vegetables.
COOK'S TIP: If you prefer, you can chill all the broth and use it to make soup for another meal.

COLCANNON SOUP

Potatoes and cabbage simmer with knackwurst for a hearty soup.

Makes 6 servings.

2 tablespoons butter or margarine
1 medium-size onion, sliced
4 cups chicken broth
2 cups sliced celery with leaves
4 medium-size potatoes, pared and diced
4 sprigs parsley
4 cups coarsely chopped cabbage
1 package (1 pound) knackwurst, sliced
1 cup light cream
1 tablespoon lemon juice
2 teaspoons salt
¼ teaspoon bottled red pepper seasoning
¼ teaspoon dillweed
1 tablespoon chopped chives

1. Melt butter or margarine in a large saucepan. Add onion and sauté until tender. Add chicken broth, celery, half of the potatoes and parsley. Cover and simmer 30 minutes. Cool.
2. Pour, part at a time, into container of electric blender; cover and process at high speed until smooth.
3. Return puree to pan. Add remaining potatoes, cabbage, knackwurst, light cream, lemon juice, salt, red pepper seasoning, dillweed and chives. Simmer, covered, 20 minutes, or until potatoes are tender.

BEACON ROAD CASSEROLE

From Yorkshire, England, comes Maria Polachowska's recipe for sausages in a sweet and savory sauce.

Bake at 350° for 1 hour.
Makes 4 servings.

1 pound breakfast sausage links
1 large onion, peeled and sliced
2 tablespoons raisins
2 tablespoons chopped almonds
4 large tomatoes, peeled and sliced
4 bananas, peeled
1¼ cups water
¼ cup firmly packed brown sugar
1 teaspoon salt
¼ teaspoon pepper

1. Prick sausages with a fork; place in greased 8-cup casserole.
2. Cover sausages with onion slices; sprinkle with ⅓ of the raisins and almonds. Cover with tomatoes; sprinkle with another ⅓ raisins and almonds.
3. Slice bananas lengthwise and arrange on top of tomato slices.
4. Mix water, sugar, salt and pepper in a small bowl; pour over bananas. Sprinkle remaining raisins and almonds over all; cover casserole.
5. Bake in moderate oven (350°) 1 hour, or until sausages, tomatoes and bananas are tender and mixture bubbles. Serve with crusty rye bread.

(Continued from page 16.)

LOUISIANA JAMBALAYA

Rich from the fields of southwestern Louisiana is the backbone of this one-dish dinner.

Makes 8 servings.

- 1 broiler-fryer (about 2½ pounds)
- 2 cups water
- 1 tablespoon salt
- ¼ teaspoon pepper
- 1 bay leaf
- 2 large onions, chopped (2 cups)
- 1 large clove garlic, crushed
- ¼ cup (½ stick) butter or margarine
- 2 cups cubed cooked ham
- 1 can (1 pound, 12 ounces) tomatoes
- 1 large green pepper, halved, seeded and chopped
- 1 teaspoon leaf thyme, crumbled
- ¼ teaspoon cayenne pepper
- 1 cup long grain rice

1. Place chicken in a large kettle or Dutch oven; add water, salt, pepper and bay leaf; bring to boiling; reduce heat; cover.
2. Simmer 45 minutes, or until chicken is tender; remove chicken from broth; reserve. When cool enough to handle, remove meat from bones; cut into cubes; reserve.
3. Pour broth into a 2-cup measure; remove bay leaf; add water, if necessary, to make 2 cups; reserve.
4. Sauté onion and garlic in butter or margarine until soft in same kettle; add ham, tomatoes, green pepper, thyme, cayenne and reserved chicken and broth. Bring to boiling; stir in rice; reduce heat; cover. Simmer, following rice label directions for cooking, until rice is tender.
5. Serve in large bowls. Sprinkle with chopped parsley and serve with crusty French bread, if you wish.

PARSLEY DUMPLING FRICASEE

Parsley adds color and flavor to the dumplings in this old fashioned dish.

Makes 6 servings.

- 1 stewing chicken, cut up (about 5 pounds)
- 4 cups water
- 1 large onion, sliced
- 1 cup chopped celery and leaves
- 1 medium-size carrot, scraped and sliced
- 2 teaspoons salt
- ¼ teaspoon pepper
- ½ cup cold water
- ⅓ cup all purpose flour
  Parsley Dumplings *(recipe page 97)*

1. Combine chicken, the 4 cups water, onion, celery and leaves, carrot, salt and pepper in a large kettle or Dutch oven with a tight-fitting cover. Cover; heat to boiling; simmer 1½ to 2 hours, or until chicken is tender.
2. Remove chicken from broth; cool lightly; slip off skin, if you wish. Strain and measure broth; add water, if needed, to make 5 cups. Press vegetables through strainer into broth; return to kettle; heat to boiling.
3. Stir the ½ cup cold water into flour in cup to make a smooth paste; stir into hot broth. Cook, stirring constantly, until gravy thickens and boils 1 minute. Season with salt and pepper to taste, if needed.
4. Return chicken to gravy in kettle; heat slowly to boiling while stirring up PARSLEY DUMPLINGS.
5. Drop batter in 12 mounds on top of steaming chicken. Cook, covered, 30 mintues. (No peeking, they won't be puffy and light.)
6. Arrange chicken and dumplings on a heated serving platter; pass gravy in separate bowl.

CAPE COD MACARONI BAKE

Oven-baked cod with macaroni bubbles in a sharp Cheddar cheese sauce.

Bake at 450° for 20 minutes,
then at 350° for 30 minutes.
Makes 4 servings.

- 1 package (1 pound) frozen cod or haddock fillets
  Salt and pepper
  Juice of ½ lemon
- 1 tablespoon butter or margarine
- 1½ cups uncooked macaroni
- ¼ cup (½ stick) butter or margarine
- 1 small onion, chopped (¼ cup)
- ¼ cup all purpose flour
- 1 teaspoon salt
- ¼ teaspoon pepper
- 2 cups milk
- 2 cups shredded Cheddar cheese (8 ounces)
- ½ cup sliced stuffed olives

1. Place frozen fish on a piece of aluminum foil; season with salt and pepper; drizzle with lemon juice and dot with the 1 tablespoon butter or margarine. Wrap foil securely and place on a cookie sheet.
2. Bake in very hot oven (450°) 20 minutes. Remove fish from foil; break into chunks.
3. Cook macaroni in boiling salted water in a large saucepan until tender, about 6 minutes; drain.
4. Melt the ¼ cup butter or margarine in saucepan; sauté onion until soft. Blend in flour, salt and pepper; add milk and cook, stirring constantly, until sauce thickens and bubbles 3 minutes. Add cheese, reserving ¾ cup for top. Stir sauce until cheese melts. Stir in macaroni; fold in fish and olives. Pour into an 8-cup casserole. Top with reserved Cheddar cheese.
5. Bake in moderate oven (350°) 30 minutes, or until mixture bubbles.

TEX-MEX BEAN POT

No barbecue along the Rio Grande is official without a bubbling pot of beans.

Bake at 325° for 3 hours.
Makes 8 servings.

- 1 package (1 pound) dried pinto, red kidney, Great Northern or lima beans
- 5 cups water
- 2 teaspoons salt
- 1 pound hot Italian sausages, skinned and cut into 1-inch pieces
- 1 Spanish onion, chopped
- 2 large green peppers, halved, seeded and cut into 1-inch pieces
- 1 can (1 pound) tomatoes
- 1 teaspoon leaf oregano, crumbled
- ½ teaspoon cumin seeds, crushed
- ½ teaspoon pepper

1. Pick over beans and rinse under running water. Combine beans and water in a large kettle. Bring to boiling; cover kettle; boil 2 minutes; remove from heat; let stand 1 hour. Return kettle to heat; bring to boiling; add salt; lower heat; simmer 1 hour, or until beans are firm but tender.
2. Brown sausage in a large skillet; remove with a slotted spoon. Sauté onion and green pepper until soft in pan drippings; stir in tomatoes, oregano, cumin and pepper; heat until bubbling.
3. Drain beans, reserving liquid. Combine beans, green pepper mixture and browned sausage in a 12-cup bean pot or casserole. Add enough reserved liquid to cover beans; cover bean pot.
4. Bake in slow oven (325°) 2 hours, 30 minutes, adding reserved liquid, if needed, to prevent beans from drying. Remove cover; bake 30 minutes longer, or until beans are tender.

MACARONI FAVORITE

Everyone will want seconds of this creamy rich pasta dish.

Bake at 350° for 30 minutes.
Makes 4 servings.

- 1 package (7 ounces) elbow macaroni (see Cook's Guide)
- 1 small onion, grated
- 2 tablespoons butter or margarine
- 2 tablespoons all purpose flour
- 1½ teaspoons dry mustard
- 1 teaspoon salt
- ¼ teaspoon pepper
- 1 teaspoon Worcestershire sauce
- 1¾ cups milk
- 1 package (8 ounces) sliced Cheddar cheese
- 1 can (3 or 4 ounces) sliced mushrooms
- 2 pimientos, diced
- 1 tomato cut into wedges
  Melted butter or margarine

1. Cook macaroni in boiling salted

water in a large saucepan, following package directions; drain.

2. Sauté onion lightly in butter or margarine in a medium-size saucepan; stir in flour, mustard, salt, pepper and Worcestershire sauce. Cook, stirring constantly, until mixture bubbles; stir in milk slowly. Continue cooking and stirring until sauce thickens and bubbles 3 minutes. Stir in half the cheese until it melts.

3. Combine drained macaroni, mushrooms and liquid and pimientos in buttered shallow casserole; pour cheese sauce over.

4. Arrange tomato wedges on top of macaroni. Cut remaining cheese slices in strips; arrange around tomatoes.

5. Bake in moderate oven (350°) 20 minutes; brush tomatoes with melted butter or margarine. Bake 10 minutes longer, or until cheese melts and filling bubbles.

TACOS

Tacos are folded tortilla shells filled with well-seasoned ground beef, chicken or beans, then topped with chopped lettuce and tomatoes. Shredded cheese and a little hot pepper sauce are also sprinkled on the tacos.

Makes 12 tacos.

- 1 **medium-size onion, chopped (½ cup)**
- 1 **clove garlic, minced**
- 2 **tablespoons vegetable oil**
- 1 **pound ground round or chuck**
- 1 **large tomato, peeled and chopped (1 cup)**
- 1 **teaspoon leaf oregano, crumbled**
- 1 **teaspoon salt**
- ⅛ **teaspoon pepper**
  Vegetable oil for frying
- 1 **package (9 ounces) frozen tortillas (12 per package)**
- 1 **small head lettuce, shredded (about 2 cups)**
- 2 **cups Cheddar cheese, shredded (8 ounces)**
- 3 **medium-size tomatoes, peeled and chopped**
  Bottled hot pepper sauce

1. Make beef filling: Sauté onion and garlic in the 2 tablespoons oil until soft in a large skillet, about 5 minutes; add ground beef; cook until brown. Add tomato, oregano, salt and pepper; cook, stirring frequently, 10 minutes, or until thick.

2. Make fried tacos: Heat about 1 inch of oil in an electric frypan or a large skillet to 370° on a deep-fat thermometer. Drop tortillas into oil, 1 at a time. Using 2 forks, fold tortilla into a U shape. Hold tortilla folded and fry until it keeps its shape and is lightly browned and crisp, about 3 minutes. Drain on paper towels.

3. Stuff 3 tablespoons beef filling, lettuce, cheese and tomatoes into each taco. Garnish with onion rings, if you wish. Pass bottled hot pepper sauce.

GOLDEN CORN PUDDING

From the cornfields of Iowa comes this delicious ham and custard recipe.

Bake at 350° for 50 minutes.
Makes 4 servings.

- 2 **cups corn kernels (cut from 3 or 4 ears uncooked corn) OR: 1 can (12 or 16 ounces) whole kernel corn, drained**
- 2 **cups diced cooked ham**
- 2 **tablespoons chopped pimiento**
- 1 **tablespoon chopped parsley**
- 1 **tablespoon grated onion**
- 1 **tablespoon sugar**
- 1 **teaspoon salt**
  Dash pepper
- 2 **eggs**
- 1½ **cups scalded milk**
- 1 **tablespoon butter or margarine**

1. Combine corn, ham, pimiento, parsley, onion, sugar, salt and pepper in a buttered 6-cup shallow casserole. Beat eggs slightly in a 4-cup measure; slowly stir in scalded milk, then butter or margarine.

2. Pour over corn in casserole; stir just to blend. Place dish in a shallow pan on oven shelf; pour boiling water into pan to a depth of 1-inch.

3. Bake in moderate oven (350°) 50 minutes, or until center is almost set but still soft; remove from water at once let rest 10 minutes.

COOK'S TIP: To cut kernels from fresh corn, husk corn and remove silks. Holding ear upright on a cutting board covered with foil or wax paper, or in a shallow dish, slice downward, 2 or 3 rows at a time; with sharp knife. Try not to cut too deeply into hulls. Hold cob over measuring cup, press out remaining pulp and milk with back of knife. Spoon kernels into a 2-cup measure; repeat until you have enough for your recipe.

BOSTON COD PIE

The Sacred Cod is enshrined in Boston, state capitol of Massachusetts.

Bake at 400° for 30 minutes.
Makes 6 servings.

- 1 **package (1 pound) frozen cod or pollock fillets**
- 1 **cup water**
- ¼ **teaspoon salt**
- 1 **bay leaf**
- 1 **small onion, chopped (¼ cup)**
- 2 **tablespoons chopped celery**
- ¼ **cup (½ stick) butter or margarine**
- ¼ **cup all purpose flour**
- 2 **cups light cream or milk**
- ¼ **teaspoon dry mustard**
- ¼ **cup chopped walnuts**
- 1 **tablespoon dry vermouth**
- 1 **tablespoon chopped pimiento**
- 1 **package piecrust mix**

1. Place frozen fish, water, salt and bay leaf in a large skillet; cover. Bring to boiling; reduce heat and simmer 6

minutes. Remove fish from liquid, drain and flake.

2. Sauté onion and celery in butter or margarine until soft; stir in flour and cook over low heat 1 minute. Add cream or milk and dry mustard; continue cooking and stirring over low heat until mixture thickens and bubbles 3 minutes. Remove from heat and stir in nuts, vermouth, chopped pimiento and flaked fish.

3. Prepare piecrust mix, following label directions; roll out half to an 11-inch round on a lightly floured pastry cloth or board; line an 8-inch pie plate with pastry. Pour fish mixture into pie plate. Roll remaining pastry to a 10-inch round. Cover pie plate with top crust; trim, then seal edges tightly and flute. Cut steam vents in top of pie.

4. Bake in hot oven (400°) 30 minutes, or until pastry is golden. Let stand 10 minutes before cutting.

ZUCCHINI LATKES

Eleanor Schwartz makes this colorful new variation of potato pancakes with zucchini from her garden.

Bake at 375° for 10 minutes.
Makes 4 servings.

- 2 **medium-size zucchini, trimmed and coarsely grated (about 2 cups)**
- 1 **medium-size onion, chopped (½ cup)**
- 4 **eggs, slightly beaten**
- 1 **cup matzoh meal or dry bread crumbs**
- 1 **teaspoon salt**
  Dash pepper
- 3 **tablespoons vegetable oil**
- 1 **package (8 ounces) mozzarella cheese, sliced**
- 1 **large tomato, sliced**
- ¼ **cup grated Parmesan cheese**

1. Mix zucchini, onion, eggs, matzoh meal or bread crumbs, salt and pepper in a medium-size bowl; cover bowl and refrigerate 1 hour.

2. Heat oil, half at a time, in a large skillet over medium heat. Stir zucchini mixture; drop by rounded tablespoons, a few at a time, into skillet; flatten with a spatula. Cook 1 or 2 minutes on each side, or until light brown. Remove and place on a heated plate; keep warm. Repeat with remaining zucchini and oil.

3. Overlap zucchini latkes, tomato slices and mozzarella cheese in a 6-cup shallow casserole, beginning with latkes and ending with cheese; sprinkle with Parmesan cheese.

4. Bake in moderate oven (375°) 15 minutes, or until cheese melts and tomato and latkes are heated through.

COOK'S TIP: Other cheeses, such as mild, but not too sharp Cheddar, Bel Paese and Swiss, are also delicious with ZUCCHINI LATKES.

RIVEL CHOWDER

From the Amish country comes a hearty deviled ham soup, loaded with tender miniature dumplings.

Makes 8 servings.

    4 medium-size potatoes, pared
        and sliced
    1 large onion, sliced
   3½ cups water
   1¾ teaspoons salt
    ⅛ teaspoon white pepper
    1 egg
    1 cup all purpose flour
    1 can (4 ounces) deviled ham
    4 cups milk

1. Combine potatoes, onion, water, 1¼ teaspoons of the salt and pepper in a large heavy saucepan or Dutch oven; cover. Simmer 15 minutes, or until potatoes are tender.
2. To make rivels (tiny dumplings): Beat egg in a medium-size bowl; add remaining ½ teaspoon salt and flour; mix well to form a soft dough.
3. Stir ham and milk into chowder; heat just until bubbly; cover, then simmer 2 minutes.
4. Rub a small amount of rivel dough between palms of hands, over kettle of simmering chowder, allowing tiny pieces of dough to drop into soup. Repeat with remaining dough. Simmer 5 minutes, or until rivels are tender and soup is thick.
5. Ladle into soup bowls. Serve with hot muffins and a cucumber salad, if you wish.

TABOR CITY 'TATER BAKE

In America's "Yam Capital," Tabor City, North Carolina, "tater" means sweet potato.

Bake at 325° for 3 hours.
Makes 6 servings.

    1 pound bulk sausage
    1 medium-size onion, finely
        chopped (½ cup)
    1 stalk celery, minced
    1 teaspoon leaf sage, crumbled
    1 teaspoon leaf thyme, crumbled
    1 teaspoon celery salt
    1 teaspoon salt
    ⅛ teaspoon pepper
    4 large yams or sweet potatoes
    1 tablespoon bacon drippings
   1½ cups soft bread crumbs (3 slices)
    2 tablespoons melted butter or
        margarine

1. Brown sausage lightly in a large skillet over moderately high heat, breaking up with a fork. Add onion and celery; reduce heat to moderate and sauté 8 to 10 minutes until limp. Mix in sage, thyme, celery salt, salt and pepper; while preparing potatoes.
2. Peel yams, then grate coarsely. Place yams in a large mixing bowl; add mixture, bacon drippings; toss

well. Spoon mixture into an 8-cup casserole, packing down lightly (it will cook down). Cover dish.
3. Bake in slow oven (325°) 2 hours, stirring mixture up from bottom now and then, until yams are tender but not mushy.
4. Toss together crumbs and melted butter or margarine in a small bowl; sprinkle on top and toss again; arrange on top of casserole and bake, uncovered, 1 hour longer.

CHUCK WAGON POT ROAST

Chili dumplings add the crowning touch to he-man slices of beef in a zesty gravy.

Makes 8 servings

    1 boneless chuck roast
        (about 3 pounds)
    1 large onion, chopped (1 cup)
    1 clove garlic, minced
    1 can (8 ounces) tomato sauce
    ¼ cup firmly packed brown sugar
    3 tablespoons cider vinegar
    1 tablespoon prepared mustard
    1 tablespoon Worcestershire sauce
    2 teaspoons salt
    ¼ teaspoon pepper
    1 package (1 pound) frozen peas
        and carrots
      Chili Dumplings (recipe follows)

1. Brown beef in its own fat in a Dutch oven or large kettle; remove and reserve. Drain off all but 2 tablespoons fat.
2. Sauté onion and garlic in pan drippings until soft; stir in tomato sauce, brown sugar, vinegar, mustard, Worcestershire sauce, salt and pepper. Bring to boiling; return beef to pan; cover; lower heat.
3. Simmer, turning meat once or twice, 2 hours, or until beef is tender; remove beef to carving board; cut into ¼-inch slices; place in a heated 10-cup casserole and keep warm.
4. Add frozen peas and carrots to liquid in kettle; bring to boiling; drop CHILI DUMPLINGS into boiling liquid by rounded tablespoons; cover pan. Steam 30 minutes, or until dumplings are puffy and light. (No peeking, or the dumplings won't puff up.)
5. Ladle gravy and vegetables over sliced beef in casserole; top with dumplings and serve immediately.

CHILI DUMPLINGS

Makes 8 servings
    ⅔ cup milk
    2 tablespoons vegetable oil
    ¾ cup all purpose flour
    ½ cup yellow cornmeal
    1 teaspoon chili powder
    1 teaspoon salt

Combine milk and oil in a medium-size bowl; stir in flour, cornmeal, chili powder and salt, until dough is moist.

BUTTERNUT SQUASH PUFF

New England cooks have a special way to serve winter squash.

Bake at 400° for 50 minutes,
then at 375° for 1 hour.
Makes 6 servings.

    1 butternut squash
    2 tablespoons butter or margarine
    3 eggs, separated
    2 teaspoons grated onion
    2 teaspoons lemon juice
    ¼ cup all purpose flour
    ½ pound ground cooked ham
    ¼ teaspoon salt
    ½ teaspoon leaf thyme, crumbled
    ¼ cup chopped parsley

1. Cut butternut squash in half and scoop out seeds. Place, cut side down, in a shallow baking pan and add 1 inch of water.
2. Bake in hot oven (400°) 50 minutes, or until squash is tender when pierced with a two-tined fork. Remove squash from water; scoop out pulp to make 2 cups mashed squash.
3. Mix butter or margarine, egg yolks, onion, lemon juice and flour in a medium-size bowl. Stir in ham, salt, thyme, parsley and reserved squash pulp. Beat egg whites until stiff but not dry in a small bowl; fold into squash mixture with a wire whip. Pour into a greased 8-cup soufflé dish.
4. Bake in moderate oven (375°) 1 hour, or until the tip of a knife inserted in center of puff comes out clean. Serve immediately.

MEATBALLS HAWAIIAN

Sweet-sour sauce adds the flavor of the islands to everyday ground beef.

Makes 4 servings.

    1 pound ground beef
    ½ teaspoon salt
    ¼ teaspoon ground ginger
    1 egg
    1 teaspoon water
    ¼ cup all purpose flour
    3 tablespoons vegetable oil
    1 can (about 14 ounces) pineapple
        chunks in syrup
    ¼ cup firmly packed brown sugar
    2 tablespoons cornstarch
    ¼ cup cider vinegar
    1 tablespoon soy sauce
    2 green peppers, halved, seeded
        and cut into strips
      Hot cooked noodles

1. Mix ground beef with salt and ginger in a medium-size bowl; shape into 16 balls. Beat egg slightly with water in a pie plate; dip balls into egg mixture, then into flour, to coat well.
2. Brown in oil in a large skillet; remove with slotted spoon; reserve.
3. Drain syrup from pineapple into a 1-cup measure; add water to make

106

1 cup; stir into drippings in pan. Mix brown sugar, cornstarch, vinegar and soy sauce in 1-cup measure; stir into pineapple juice mixture. Cook, stirring constantly, until sauce thickens and bubbles 3 minutes.

4. Arrange meatballs, pineapple chunks and pepper strips in pan; stir each gently to coat with sauce; cover. Simmer 10 minutes, or until meatballs are cooked through. Serve with hot cooked noodles.

GARDEN PEPPER PIE

Corn meal adds a unique flavor to the crust.

Bake at 375° for 40 minutes.
Makes 6 servings.

Crust
- ¾ cup all purpose flour
- ½ cup yellow corn meal
- 1½ teaspoons baking powder
- ½ teaspoon salt
- 4 tablespoons vegetable shortening
- ⅓ cup milk

Filling
- 2 medium-size sweet red peppers
- 2 medium-size green peppers
- 1 large onion, chopped (1 cup)
- ¼ cup (½ stick) butter or margarine
- 3 tablespoons all purpose flour
- 1 teaspoon salt
- 1 teaspoon leaf oregano, crumbled
- 2 eggs
- ¾ cup milk
- 1 cup shredded Monterey Jack cheese or sharp Cheddar (4 ounces)

1. Make crust: Combine flour, cornmeal, baking powder and salt in a medium-size bowl; cut in shortening with pastry blender until mixture is crumbly. Stir in milk with a fork just until dough clings together and leaves side of bowl clean.
2. Press evenly over bottom and side of a 10-inch pie plate or 6-cup shallow casserole; sprinkle cheese over bottom.
3. Make filling: Wash peppers; cut out stems, seeds and membrane; cut peppers into 1-inch squares. Parboil in small amount of salted boiling water in a medium-size saucepan 5 minutes; drain well.
4. Sauté onion in butter or margarine in same saucepan; stir in drained peppers. Sprinkle with flour, salt and oregano; toss lightly to mix; spoon into crust-lined dish.
5. Beat eggs slightly with milk in a 2-cup measure; pour over vegetable mixture. Sprinkle with cheese.
6. Bake in moderate oven (375°) 40 minutes, or until top is golden and custard is set but soft in center. Let stand 10 to 15 minutes; cut into wedges.

Suggested Variation: For PEPPERONI PIE, add 1 cup sliced pepperoni to vegetables in Step 4.

MULBERRY STREET ZUCCHINI

Serve this stuffed zucchini dish with hot noodles tossed with melted butter and toasted slivered almonds.

Bake at 350° for 30 minutes.
Makes 6 servings.

- 6 small zucchini (about 2 pounds)
- 1 pound ground beef
- 1 small onion, chopped (¼ cup)
- 1 tablespoon vegetable oil
- 1 tablespoon chopped pimiento
- 1 egg, lightly beaten
- 1½ teaspoons salt
- ⅛ teaspoon pepper
- 1 cup soft bread crumbs (2 slices)
- ⅓ cup grated Parmesan cheese

1. Trim ends from zucchini but leave whole; parboil in boiling salted water 10 minutes; drain. Cut in half, lengthwise; scoop out centers, being careful not to break shells. Place in a 10-cup shallow casserole. Chop scooped-out centers; drain. Reserve.
2. Shape ground beef into a large patty in a skillet; brown with onion in oil 5 minutes on each side, then break up into small chunks.
3. Stir in chopped zucchini, pimiento, egg, salt, pepper and bread crumbs. Spoon into zucchini shells, dividing evenly; sprinkle with cheese.
4. Bake in moderate oven (350°) 30 minutes, or until golden brown.
COOK'S TIP: If zucchini shells roll in casserole, slice off a thin piece from the rounded side.

CREAMY MACARONI

Wisconsin cooks love to surprise the family with a bubbling dish on a brisk winter's day.

Bake at 350° for 30 minutes.
Makes 4 servings.

- 1 package (7 ounces) macaroni (see Cook's Guide)
- 1 small onion, grated
- 2 tablespoons butter or margarine
- 2 tablespoons all purpose flour
- 1 teaspoon Worcestershire sauce
- ½ teaspoon salt
- 2½ cups milk
- 2 cups shredded Cheddar cheese (8 ounces)
- 1 cup soft bread crumbs (2 slices)
- 2 tablespoons butter or margarine, melted
- Buttered green beans

1. Stir macaroni into a large saucepan of boiling salted water; cook, stirring often, 10 minutes, or just until tender; drain. Spoon macaroni into an 8-cup shallow casserole.
2. Sauté onion in 2 tablespoons butter or margarine 1 minute; blend in flour, Worcestershire sauce and salt; cook, stirring constantly, just until bubbly.
3. Stir in milk; cook, stirring constantly, until the sauce thickens and bubbles 3 minutes; stir in cheese until melted. Pour over macaroni; mix.
4. Combine bread crumbs and 2 tablespoons butter or margarine in a small bowl; sprinkle on top of the macaroni and cheese.
5. Bake in moderate oven (350°) for 30 minutes, or until the center is bubbly hot and the crumbs are toasty-golden. Spoon green beans around.

BARBECUED POT ROAST

Cornmeal puffs steam fluffy and light in the tomato-rich sauce after the meat is done.

Makes 6 servings.

- 1 round, rump or boneless chuck roast (about 4 pounds)
- 1 large onion, chopped (1 cup)
- 1 clove garlic, minced
- 1 can (1 pound) tomatoes
- ¼ cup firmly packed brown sugar
- 2 teaspoons salt
- 1 teaspoon mixed Italian herbs, crumbled
- ¼ teaspoon pepper
- 3 tablespoons cider vinegar
- 1 tablespoon prepared mustard
- 1 tablespoon Worcestershire sauce
- 3 tablespoons all purpose flour
- Golden Dumplings (recipe follows)

1. Brown beef in its own fat in a Dutch oven or in an electric frypan over medium heat; remove.
2. Sauté onion and garlic until soft in same pan; stir in tomatoes, brown sugar, salt, Italian herbs, pepper, vinegar, mustard and the Worcestershire sauce. Return meat to pan; bring to boiling; cover.
3. Simmer, turning meat once or twice, 2 hours, 30 minutes, or until very tender. Remove meat to a heated serving platter; keep hot while making gravy and GOLDEN DUMPLINGS.
4. Pour liquid into a 4-cup measure; let stand about 1 minute, or until fat rises to top. Skim off fat; measure 3 tablespoonfuls back into pan. Add water, if necessary, to the liquid to make 3 cups.
5. Blend flour into fat in pan; cook, stirring constantly, just until bubbly. Stir in the 3 cups liquid; continue cooking, stirring constantly, until gravy thickens and bubbles 3 minutes.
6. Mix GOLDEN DUMPLINGS. Drop batter in 6 mounds into bubbling hot gravy; cover. Cook, without peeking, 30 minutes.

GOLDEN DUMPLINGS: Makes 6 dumplings. Combine ¾ cup sifted all purpose flour, 2 teaspoons baking powder, 1 teaspoon salt and ½ cup cornmeal in a medium-size bowl. Combine ⅔ cup milk and 2 tablespoons vegetable oil; stir into dry ingredients just until mixture is moist.

FIERY CHILI CON CARNE

For those who like their food hot, this is an ideal choice.

Makes 8 servings.

8 medium-size onions, chopped (4 cups)
2 cloves garlic, minced
4 to 6 teaspoons chili powder
2 tablespoons bacon drippings
2 pounds ground beef
2 teaspoons salt
3 cups water
3 cans (about 1 pound each) red kidney beans
2 teaspoons ground cumin

1. Sauté onions and garlic with chili powder in bacon drippings just until onions are soft in a large heavy skillet; remove with a slotted spoon and set aside.
2. Shape ground beef into a large patty in same pan; brown 5 minutes on each side, then break up into chunks. Stir in sautéed onion mixture, salt and water; simmer 45 minutes.
3. Stir in kidney beans and liquid and cumin; simmer 1 hour.
4. Spoon into soup bowls; serve with buttered hard rolls or corn bread.

CHICKEN ROYALE

Southern cooks love to combine ham with chicken for an aristocratic taste.

Makes 6 servings.

3 whole chicken breasts (2½ to 3 pounds), split
2 cups water
1 slice of onion
Handful of celery tops
1 teaspoon salt
4 peppercorns
1 package (8 ounces) noodles
1 can (7 ounces) pork luncheon meat
2 tablespoons butter or margarine
1 package (9 ounces) frozen Italian green beans, cooked and drained
1 can (about 11 ounces) chicken gravy

1. Combine chicken breasts, water, onion slice, celery tops, salt and peppercorns in large saucepan. Simmer, covered, 20 minutes, or until chicken is tender.
2. While chicken simmers, cook noodles in boiling salted water, following label directions; drain; place in 8-cup shallow casserole.
3. Cut pork luncheon meat into 12 sticks; sauté in butter or margarine in large skillet; arrange in clusters on top of noodles; spoon beans around edge of casserole. (Keep casserole warm in heated oven while browning chicken and heating gravy.)
4. Drain chicken breasts. (Strain broth and save for soup.) Brown chicken quickly in same pan, adding

more butter or margarine, if needed; place on noodles with Italian beans.
5. Stir chicken gravy into skillet; heat to boiling; pour over chicken.

BEEF-MACARONI LOAF

Warm up a chilly winter evening with this savory dish for your family.

Bake at 350° for 1 hour.
Makes 6 to 8 servings.

Macaroni Layers
1 package (8 ounces) elbow macaroni
2 tablespoons butter or margarine
2 tablespoons all purpose flour
1 teaspoon salt
¼ teaspoon pepper
1 egg
2 cups milk
½ cup grated Parmesan cheese
Meat Layer
1 small onion, chopped (¼ cup)
1 tablespoon butter or margarine
1½ pounds ground beef
1 egg
1 can condensed tomato soup
1 teaspoon salt
¼ teaspoon pepper
Sauce
1 can (8 ounces) tomato sauce
1 teaspoon sugar
¼ teaspoon leaf basil, crumbled

1. Grease a 9x5x3-inch loaf pan; line bottom and ends with a double-thick strip of aluminum foil, leaving a 1-inch overhang; grease foil.
2. Make Macaroni Layers: Cook macaroni, following label directions; drain; return to kettle. Stir in butter or margarine; sprinkle flour, salt and pepper over; toss to mix well.
3. Beat egg; stir in milk; pour over macaroni mixture. Cook over medium heat, stirring constantly, until thickened; remove from heat. Stir in Parmesan cheese.
4. Make Meat Layer: Sauté onion in butter or margarine until soft; add ground beef and brown, breaking meat up with a fork as it cooks.
5. Beat egg; stir in ½ can of tomato soup, salt and pepper; stir into cooked meat mixture.
6. Spoon half the macaroni mixture in an even layer in prepared pan; top with all of the meat mixture, then remaining macaroni mixture.
7. Bake in moderate oven (350°) 1 hour, or until firm and brown on top.
8. Make sauce: While loaf bakes, heat tomato sauce with remaining ½ can of tomato soup, sugar and basil to boiling in a small saucepan; simmer 2 to 3 minutes to blend flavors.
9. Cool loaf in pan 10 minutes; loosen from sides with knife, then lift up ends of foil and set loaf on a heated serving platter; slide out foil. Frame platter and top loaf with steamed green and red pepper rings, if you wish. Slice loaf; serve sauce to spoon over.

CREOLE FISH SOUP

Try this fast, frugal and filling chowder on a blustery day.

Makes 4 servings.

½ cup frozen chopped onion
½ cup sliced celery
1 to 3 teaspoons chili powder
1 tablespoon olive or vegetable oil
2 cans (8 ounces each) tomato sauce
1 cup water
1 teaspoon salt
¼ teaspoon Worcestershire sauce
1 package (12 ounces) frozen cod or haddock
2 cups hot cooked rice
2 tablespoons chopped parsley

1. Sauté onion, celery and chili powder lightly in oil in a large saucepan until soft; stir in tomato sauce, water, salt and Worcestershire sauce; bring to boiling.
2. Add frozen fish in one piece; simmer, separating fish with a fork as it thaws, 15 minutes, or until fish flakes easily.
3. Spoon into chowder bowls; top each with a mound of rice mixed with chopped parsley.

NAPA VALLEY BEEF STEW

Hearty California Burgundy gives special character to beef.

Bake at 450° for 20 minutes.
Makes 6 servings.

1½ pounds boneless beef stew meat, cubed
2 tablespoons all purpose flour
1 tablespoon vegetable oil
1 medium-size onion, chopped (½ cup)
1 clove garlic, minced
2 cups water
2 envelopes or teaspoons instant beef broth
½ teaspoon salt
¼ teaspoon pepper
1 bay leaf
1 teaspoon leaf basil, crumbled
1 teaspoon leaf oregano, crumbled
½ teaspoon leaf thyme, crumbled
1 cup sliced carrots
1 can (4 ounces) sliced mushrooms
½ cup red Burgundy
¼ cup chopped parsley
Mushroom Biscuits (recipe follows)

1. Toss beef in flour in a plastic bag to coat evenly. Brown beef in hot oil in a large skillet. Push meat to one side; add onion and garlic; sauté until tender. Stir in water, instant beef broth, salt, pepper, bay leaf, basil, oregano and thyme.
2. Cover and simmer 1 hour. Add carrots and mushrooms; simmer 30 minutes. Stir in Burgundy and parsley. Pour into a 10-cup shallow

casserole. Top with MUSHROOM BISCUITS.

3. Bake in a very hot oven (450°) 20 minutes, or until biscuits are golden.

MUSHROOM BISCUITS

2 cups all purpose flour
1 tablespoon baking powder
½ teaspoon salt
1 envelope (1¼ ounces) beef mushroom soup mix
¼ cup vegetable shortening
¾ cup milk

1. Stir together flour, baking powder, salt and soup mix in a medium-size bowl with wire whip. Cut in shortening with pastry blender until mixture is crumbly. Blend in milk to make a soft dough.

2. Turn out onto lightly floured pastry cloth or board and knead gently for 30 seconds. Roll out to 1-inch thickness; cut with a 2-inch round cutter. Place on hot casserole.

CAJUN MAQUECHOU

A Cajun classic, chicken braised with corn, tomatoes, sweet green pepper and onions.

Makes 4 servings.

1 broiler-fryer, cut up (2½ pounds)
3 teaspoons salt
¼ teaspoon pepper
⅛ teaspoon cayenne pepper
½ cup all purpose flour
¼ cup vegetable oil
2 tablespoons bacon drippings
½ large green pepper, cored, seeded and diced
1 large onion, chopped (1 cup)
1 clove garlic, crushed
1 package (10 ounces) frozen whole kernel corn
1 bay leaf
1 teaspoon leaf thyme, crumbled
2 large tomatoes, peeled, cored and coarsely chopped
4 cups cooked rice

1. Rub chicken pieces thoroughly with 1½ teaspoons of the salt mixed with ⅛ teaspoon of the pepper and the cayenne. Toss chicken in flour in a plastic bag.

2. Heat vegetable oil in a large heavy kettle and brown chicken on all sides; drain chicken on paper towels. Drain all oil from kettle, wipe bottom with paper towels, then add 2 tablespoons bacon drippings. When hot, add green pepper, onion, garlic, corn, bay leaf and thyme and stir-fry over moderately high heat 10 to 12 minutes or until lightly browned. Stir in tomatoes and their juice, the remaining 1½ teaspoons salt and ⅛ teaspoon pepper.

3. Arrange chicken pieces on top; lower heat; cover kettle; simmer 45 minutes. Uncover and simmer 15 minutes longer.

4. To serve, mound rice on a large round platter, top with the cooked vegetables, then arrange chicken pieces on vegetables.

HARVEST CHOWDER

Chowder is a traditional American soup you fix in minutes.

Makes 4 servings.

8 strips bacon, cut in 1-inch pieces
½ cup frozen chopped onion
1 clove garlic, minced
1 teaspoon leaf basil, crumbled
1 package (10 ounces) frozen whole kernel corn
1 package (10 ounces) frozen peas and carrots
1 bag (1 pound) frozen Southern-style hash browns
1 can (13¾ ounces) chicken broth
1 teaspoon salt
¼ teaspoon pepper
1 tall can evaporated milk
1½ cups water
2 tablespoons chopped parsley

1. Cook bacon until crisp in a large saucepan. Remove bacon and pour off all but 2 tablespoons fat; add onion, garlic and basil to saucepan.

2. Cook until onion is tender. Add corn, peas and carrots, hash browns, broth, salt and pepper.

3. Bring to a boil; cover saucepan and reduce heat to simmer. Cook 10 minutes, or until vegetables are tender. Stir evaporated milk and water into chowder. Cook, stirring, until soup heats. Add parsley and bacon; sprinkle with Parmesan cheese.

BRISKET DINNER

Beef, four vegetables and rich gravy team in this thrifty dinner.

Makes 6 servings.

1 fresh beef brisket (about 3 pounds)
1 cup water
2 envelopes instant beef broth OR: 2 beef bouillon cubes
1 clove garlic, minced
1 bay leaf
1 medium-size onion, peeled
8 whole cloves
12 small white onions, peeled
6 medium-size carrots, pared and cut in 2-inch pieces
6 medium-size parsnips, pared and cut in 2-inch pieces
2 teaspoons salt
¼ teaspoon pepper
6 large mushrooms
3 tablespoons all purpose flour

1. Brown beef in its own fat in a Dutch oven over medium heat or in an electric frypan; stir in water, instant beef broth or cubes, garlic and bay leaf. Stud onion with cloves; drop into pan; cover.

2. Simmer, turning meat once, 1½ hours. Place small onions, carrots and parsnips around meat, basting with pan liquid to coat; sprinkle with salt and pepper; cover again.

3. Simmer 45 minutes; add mushrooms. Simmer 15 minutes longer, or until vegetables are tender.

4. Remove meat to a heated serving platter; place the vegetables around, discarding onion with cloves and bay leaf; keep hot while making gravy.

5. Pour liquid into a 4-cup measure; let stand about a minute, or until fat rises to top. Skim off fat, then measure 3 tablespoons of fat back into pan. Add water, if needed, to liquid to make 3 cups.

6. Blend flour into fat in pan; cook, stirring constantly, just until bubbly. Stir in the 3 cups liquid; continue cooking, stirring constantly, until gravy thickens and bubbles 3 minutes.

7. Carve meat ¼-inch thick. Serve with gravy and cooked vegetables.

CHILI ENCHILADAS

Along the Rio Grande, Mexican dishes are hot and delicious. You may want to use less chili powder in this recipe.

Bake at 350° for 30 minutes.
Makes 8 servings.

Filling
1 pound frankfurters, sliced thin
1 medium-size onion, chopped (½ cup)
1 clove garlic, minced
1 tablespoon vegetable oil
1 to 3 teaspoons chili powder
¼ teaspoon salt
1 can (8 ounces) tomato sauce
1 can (about 1 pound) red kidney beans, drained
Tortillas
1 can (10 ounces) tortillas
Topping
2 cans (8 ounces each) tomato sauce
1 cup chili sauce
2 large onions, chopped (2 cups)
1 cup shredded Cheddar cheese

1. Make filling: Sauté frankfurters, onion and garlic in vegetable oil in medium-size skillet 5 minutes, or just until onion is soft. Stir in chili powder and cook 2 minutes; add salt, tomato sauce and beans. Simmer 15 minutes.

2. Prepare tortillas: Heat griddle over low heat. Grill tortillas, one at a time, 1 minute; turn; grill 1 minute longer. As each is baked, spread with scant ¼ cup filling; roll up and place, seam-side down, in double row in buttered 13x9x2-inch casserole.

3. Make topping: Combine tomato sauce, chili sauce and onions in a small saucepan; simmer 15 minutes, or until slightly thick. Spoon over filled tortillas; sprinkle with cheese.

4. Bake in moderate oven (350°) 20 minutes, or until bubbly.

ALL AMERICAN CLASSICS

(Continued from page 76.)

CHICKEN CHARTRES

Delicately flavored with herbs and young vegetables, a simple, one-dish dinner.

Bake at 325° for 1 hour, 15 minutes.
Makes 4 servings.

    1 broiler-fryer (about 3 pounds)
 1½ teaspoons salt
    ¼ teaspoon pepper
  16 small white onions
  12 small red new potatoes
    3 tablespoons butter or margarine
    3 tablespoons vegetable oil
    ½ cup boiling water
    1 envelope or teaspoon instant
        chicken broth
    1 teaspoon leaf basil, crumbled
    1 tablespoon chopped parsley

1. Sprinkle chicken cavity with ½ teaspoon of salt and the pepper. Peel onions. Scrub potatoes; pare a band around the center of each.
2. Melt butter or margarine with vegetable oil in a large heavy flameproof casserole or Dutch oven. Add chicken; brown on all sides.
3. Combine boiling water and instant chicken broth in a 1-cup measure, stirring until dissolved; add to casserole with chicken.
4. Place onions and potatoes around chicken; sprinkle with basil and remaining 1 teaspoon salt; cover.
5. Bake in slow oven (325°), basting once or twice with juices, 1 hour, 15 minutes, or until chicken and vegetables are tender. Sprinkle with parsley.

VEAL LOAF GARNI

A gourmet veal loaf, surrounded by broiled tomatoes and mashed potato ribbons.

Bake at 350° for 1 hour, 15 minutes.
Broil for 10 to 12 minutes.
Makes 4 servings.

 1½ pounds ground veal
    2 cups grated raw carrots
    1 container (8 ounces) dairy sour
        cream
    1 small onion, chopped (¼ cup)
    1 can (3 to 4 ounces) chopped
        mushrooms
    ½ cup fine dry bread crumbs
    1 teaspoon salt
    ¼ teaspoon pepper
        Grilled Tomatoes (recipe follows)
    3 cups hot seasoned mashed
        potatoes

1. Combine veal, carrots, sour cream, onion, mushrooms, bread crumbs, salt and pepper in a large bowl; mix lightly with a fork.
2. Spoon mixture into a 9x5x3-inch loaf pan; invert onto shallow baking pan; carefully remove loaf pan. Score top of loaf lightly.
3. Bake in moderate oven (350°) 1 hour, 15 minutes, or until top is a rich golden brown.
4. Place baked loaf on sizzle platter or broiler-proof platter; edge with GRILLED TOMATOES and mashed potatoes piped through a pastry bag fitted with a star tip.
5. Broil, 4 inches from heat, 10 to 12 minutes, or until tomatoes are bubbly and potatoes are lightly browned. Sprinkle tomatoes with finely chopped parsley, if you wish.

GRILLED TOMATOES: Makes 4 servings. Cut out stems from 4 large ripe tomatoes; halve each tomato, crosswise. Brush cut sides generously with melted butter or margarine, or bottled Italian salad dressing.

BEEF JARDINIÉRE

Rich dumplings double the beef flavor in this meat and vegetable ragoût..

Makes 4 servings.

 1½ pounds lean beef chuck or
        shank, cubed
    1 can (1 pound) tomatoes
    1 cup water
    1 teaspoon sugar
    1 teaspoon salt
    1 bay leaf
    ½ teaspoon leaf thyme, crumbled
    ¼ teaspoon pepper
        Marrow Dumplings (recipe
        follows)
    4 medium-size carrots, scraped
        and cut into 3-inch lengths
    1 can (1 pound) green peas

1. Brown beef quickly in a few melted fat trimmings in a large skillet.
2. Stir in tomatoes, water, sugar, salt, bay leaf, leaf thyme and pepper. Cover; simmer 1 hour, just until tender.
3. While stew cooks, make and chill MARROW DUMPLINGS.
4. Add carrots to hot stew; cook 25 minutes, or until tender. Remove bay leaf. Stir in peas and liquid; arrange MARROW DUMPLINGS on top; cover; cook 5 minutes longer.

MARROW DUMPLINGS

        Beef marrow from a 3- to 4-inch
        beef marrow bone (½ cup
        mashed)
    1 egg
    1 cup soft bread crumbs (2 slices)
    1 tablespoon chopped parsley
    ½ teaspoon salt
    ⅛ teaspoon pepper

1. Cut out marrow from bone with a sharp thin-bladed knife; mash and place in small bowl. Stir in egg, bread crumbs, parsley, salt and pepper until well blended
2. Form lightly into marble-size balls. Set in a shallow pan; chill at least 1 hour. (Dumplings hold their shape better when chilled before cooking.)

SOUFFLÉD CHICKEN

Leftover chicken bubbles under a puffy soufflé mixture.

Bake at 375° for 40 minutes.
Makes 6 servings.

    1 can condensed cream of shrimp
        soup
    1 cup milk
    2 cups diced cooked chicken or
        turkey
    3 tablespoons butter or margarine
    ¼ cup all purpose flour
    ¾ cup milk
    4 eggs, separated
    ¼ teaspoon cream of tartar
    1 teaspoon salt
        Few drops bottled red pepper
        seasoning

1. Blend soup with the 1 cup milk. Combine with chicken in an 8-cup soufflé or a straight-sided casserole.
2. Melt butter or margarine in a small saucepan. Blend in flour; cook, stirring constantly, until mixture bubbles. Stir in the ¾ cup milk; continue cooking and stirring until mixture thickens and bubbles 3 minutes; cool.
3. Beat egg whites with cream of tartar just until stiff peaks form in a medium-size bowl. Beat yolks with salt and red pepper seasoning in a large bowl. Beat in the sauce.
4. Fold whites, into yolk mixture until well combined. Spoon soufflé mixture over chicken in dish.
5. Bake in moderate oven (375°) 40 minutes, or until puffed and browned. Serve with green bean salad, if you wish.

BOEUF PROVENÇALE

A flavorful make-ahead casserole from the province famous for its wines, cuisine and song.

Bake at 350° for 30 minutes.
Makes 8 servings.

    2 pounds ground round or chuck
    1 clove garlic, minced
    2 envelopes or teaspoons instant
        onion broth
    ½ cup vegetable oil
    1 eggplant, (about 1½ to 2 pounds)
        All purpose flour
    2 cans (1 pound each) tomatoes
    2 envelopes (1½ ounces each)
        Sloppy Joe seasoning mix
    1 teaspoon leaf basil, crumbled
    2 large zucchini, cut into ½-inch
        slices

1. Mix beef, garlic and instant onion broth lightly; divide and shape mixture into 8 patties.
2. Heat 1 tablespoon of the oil in a large skillet. Brown patties about 2 minutes on each side. Remove.
3. Meanwhile, wash eggplant and cut into ½-inch slices. Spread flour on piece of wax paper. Dip eggplant in flour to coat well. Add 2 tablespoons

of the oil to same skillet. Sauté eggplant, a few slices at a time, adding oil as needed; remove slices as they brown; keep warm.

4. Add tomatoes, seasoning mix and basil to skillet; heat to boiling, stirring.

5. Reserve 8 slices eggplant; place remaining slices with half the sauce and half the zucchini in a 12-cup shallow casserole. Arrange reserved eggplant slices alternately with beef patties over the bottom layer in casserole. Top with remaining zucchini and sauce.

6. Bake in moderate oven (350°) 30 minutes, or until bubbly.

CHICKEN À LA VÉRONIQUE

Véronique means "with grapes," and this gives chicken pot pie the French touch.

Bake at 450° for 15 minutes.
Makes 6 servings.

  1 **medium-size onion, chopped (½ cup)**
  3 **tablespoons butter or margarine**
  3 **cups chopped cooked chicken**
  1 **can condensed cream of chicken soup**
  1 **container (8 ounces) dairy sour cream**
1½ **cups green grapes, halved**
1½ **teaspoons salt**
  ¼ **teaspoon ground nutmeg**
  ¼ **teaspoon pepper**
     Crisscross Pastry (recipe follows)

1. Sauté onion in butter or margarine in a large saucepan until tender. Stir in chicken, soup, sour cream, grapes, salt, nutmeg and pepper.

2. Spoon into a 7 x 11-inch casserole. Place CRISS-CROSS PASTRY on top in a lattice design.

3. Bake in very hot oven (450°) 15 minutes, or until lightly browned.

CRISSCROSS PASTRY

Makes pastry top for one pie.

1½ **cups all purpose flour**
  ¼ **cup cornmeal**
  2 **teaspoons baking powder**
  ½ **teaspoon salt**
  ¼ **cup vegetable shortening**
  1 **egg**
  ⅓ **cup milk**

1. Stir together flour, cornmeal, baking powder and salt in a medium-size bowl with a wire whip. Cut in shortening with a pastry blender until crumbly.

2. Combine egg and milk in a 1-cup measure. Stir into dry ingredients to make a soft dough. Turn out onto lightly floured pastry cloth or board and knead gently 30 seconds. Roll out to a 9 x 11-inch rectangle. Cut into ½-inch strips.

LAMB PERU

Lima beans complement the hearty flavor of lamb.

Bake at 325° for 3 hours.
Makes 6 servings.

  1 **pound (2 cups) large dried lima beans**
  4 **cups water**
  2 **teaspoons salt**
  1 **cup grated raw carrots**
  4 **slices bacon**
  2 **cups cubed roast lamb**
  2 **tablespoons vegetable oil**
  1 **large onion, chopped (1 cup)**
  1 **clove garlic, minced**
  1 **can (about 1 pound) tomatoes**
  ¼ **cup light molasses**

1. Cover lima beans with water in a large kettle; heat to boiling; cover; cook 2 minutes. Remove from heat; let stand 30 minutes.

2. Reheat beans to boiling; add salt, grated carrots and bacon. (Do not cut slices.) Cover; cook 45 minutes, or until skins of beans burst when you blow on a few in a spoon.

3. While beans cook, brown lamb lightly in oil in a large skillet. Push to one side of pan and sauté onion and garlic lightly; stir in tomatoes and molasses; cover; simmer 15 minutes.

4. Remove bacon from beans; reserve. Stir lamb mixture into beans; pour into a 12-cup casserole. Cover.

5. Bake in slow oven (325°) 2 hours; remove cover; crisscross reserved strips of bacon on top of casserole. Bake 1 hour, or until beans are tender.

BREAST OF VEAL SAUCISSE

Stuffed with sausage and carrots, this inexpensive meat is braised, then sauced.

Makes 8 servings.

  1 **boned breast of veal (about 3 pounds)**
  ¾ **teaspoon salt**
  ⅛ **teaspoon pepper**
  2 **tablespoons chopped parsley**
  ½ **teaspoon leaf basil, crumbled**
  ½ **pound bulk sausage (from a 1-pound package)**
  1 **cup grated carrots**
  1 **tablespoon butter or margarine**
  ½ **cup sliced celery**
  1 **medium-size onion, sliced**
  1 **can (14 ounces) chicken broth
     Water**
  3 **tablespoons all purpose flour**

1. Spread breast of veal flat on a cutting board. (It should measure about 15×8 inches.) Sprinkle with salt, pepper, parsley and basil. Combine sausage meat with grated carrots in a small bowl; spread evenly over surface of veal, pressing firmly. Roll up veal from short end, jelly-roll fashion. Tie crosswise with heavy string at 1½-inch intervals.

2. Brown meat in butter or margarine in Dutch oven; add celery, onion and chicken broth; simmer, covered, 2 hours, or until meat is tender. Remove meat to a carving board.

3. Strain pan juices through a sieve; press vegetables through; pour into a 2-cup measure; add water if necessary to make 1¾ cups. Return to pan.

4. Combine flour and 6 tablespoons water in a 1-cup measure; blend until smooth. Pour into juices in Dutch oven. Cook, stirring constantly, until sauce thickens and bubbles 3 minutes.

5. Remove string from veal; cut into thin slices; serve with vegetable sauce and hot buttered noodles, if you wish.

QUICHE LORRAINE

The French original—a marvelously mellow pie made with cheese, eggs, bacon and onion.

Bake at 425° for 5 minutes,
then at 400° for 30 minutes.
Makes 6 servings.

  ½ **package piecrust mix**
  6 **slices bacon**
  1 **medium-size onion, chopped (½ cup)**
  2 **cups shredded Swiss cheese (8 ounces)**
  4 **eggs**
  2 **cups milk**
  1 **teaspoon salt**
  ¼ **teaspoon ground nutmeg**
  ⅛ **teaspoon pepper**

1. Prepare piecrust mix, following label directions, or make your own single-crust pastry recipe. Roll out to a 12-inch round on a lightly floured pastry board; fit into a 9-inch pie plate or fluted quiche dish. Trim overhang to ½ inch; turn under, flush with rim; flute to make a stand-up edge. Prick shell all over with fork. (If using a fluted quiche dish, level pastry even with rim.)

2. Bake in hot oven (425°) 5 minutes; remove to rack; cool slightly. Reduce oven temperature to 400°.

3. Cook bacon in small skillet until crisp; drain off all but 1 tablespoon fat; crumble bacon; reserve.

4. Sauté onion in bacon fat until soft. Sprinkle cheese in layer in pastry shell; add bacon and onion.

5. Beat eggs slightly in a medium-size bowl; beat in milk, salt, nutmeg and pepper; pour into shell.

6. Bake in hot oven (400°) 30 minutes, or until center is almost set but soft. (Do not overbake; custard will set as it cools.) Let stand 15 minutes. Garnish with additional bacon curls and serve with sliced tomatoes, if you wish.

COOK'S TIP: For an especially crisp crust, drain sautéed onion and bacon on paper towel before placing in pastry shell.

HAM AND CHEESE FONDUE

Layers of French bread, ham and cheese bake in a soufflé dish. Serve with a tossed salad.

Bake at 350° for 1 hour.
Makes 6 servings.

- 3 cups cubed French bread (about ½ loaf)
- 3 cups cubed cooked ham
- ½ pound Cheddar cheese, cut into 1-inch cubes
- 3 tablespoons all purpose flour
- 1 tablespoon dry mustard
- 3 tablespoons melted butter or margarine
- 4 eggs
- 3 cups milk
  Few drops bottled red pepper seasoning

1. Make a layer of one third of the bread, ham and cheese cubes in a buttered 8-cup soufflé dish.
2. Mix flour and mustard in a cup; sprinkle about 1 tablespoon over layer; drizzle 1 tablespoon melted butter or margarine over. Repeat with remaining bread, ham, cheese, flour mixture and butter or margarine to make 2 more layers.
3. Beat eggs with milk and red pepper seasoning until foamy in a medium-size bowl; pour over layers in soufflé dish. Cover; chill at least 4 hours, or overnight. Uncover before baking.
4. Bake in moderate oven (350°) 1 hour, or until puffed and golden. Serve at once.

AVOCADO SOUFFLÉ

A silky green soufflé, served with a delicate Swiss cheese sauce.

Bake at 350° for 45 minutes.
Makes 6 servings.

- 6 eggs
- 1 large ripe avocado
- ¼ cup (½ stick) butter or margarine
- ¼ cup all purpose flour
- ½ teaspoon salt
  Few drops bottled red pepper seasoning
- 1 teaspoon minced onion
- 1 cup milk
  Fondue Sauce (recipe follows)

1. Separate eggs, putting whites into a medium-size bowl, yolks into a large bowl.
2. Peel, pit and mash avocado by pressing through a sieve into a small bowl with a wooden spoon.
3. Melt butter or margarine in a medium-size saucepan; blend in flour, salt, red pepper seasoning and onion. Cook, stirring constantly, until mixture bubbles; stir in milk. Cook over low heat, stirring constantly, until sauce thickens and bubbles 1 minute; remove from heat. Blend in avocado; cool.

4. Beat egg whites just until they form soft peaks in a medium-size bowl.
5. Beat egg yolks well in large bowl; slowly stir in cooled avocado mixture; lightly fold in the beaten whites until no streaks of white remain. Pour into a greased 8-cup soufflé dish or straight-sided casserole.
6. Bake in moderate oven (350°) 45 minutes, or until puffy and firm. Serve at once with FONDUE SAUCE.

FONDUE SAUCE

Makes about 1¾ cups.

- 2 tablespoons butter or margarine
- 2 tablespoons all purpose flour
- ¼ teaspoon salt
- ¼ teaspoon pepper
- ½ cup milk
- ½ cup white wine
- 1 can (3 or 4 ounces) sliced mushrooms
- 1 cup shredded process Swiss cheese (4 ounces)

Melt butter or margarine in a small heavy saucepan; remove from heat. Blend in flour, salt and pepper; slowly stir in milk, wine, mushrooms and liquid and cheese. Cook over low heat, stirring constantly, until sauce thickens and bubbles 1 minute.

BAKED CRAB-TUNA FONDUE

Perfect for entertaining—you make it hours ahead and bake at mealtime.

Bake at 350° for 1 hour, 15 minutes.
Makes 6 servings.

- 1 can (about 6¼ ounces) crab meat
- 1 can (about 3½ ounces) tuna
- 5 cups cubed French bread
- 1 package (8 ounces) Muenster cheese, cubed
- 2 tablespoons chopped parsley
- 4 eggs
- 3 cups milk
- 3 tablespoons butter or margarine, melted
- 2 teaspoons dry mustard
- 1 teaspoon grated onion

1. Drain crab meat; flake and remove bony tissue, if any. Drain and flake tuna. Combine crab and tuna in a small bowl.
2. Layer one-third each of bread, seafood, cheese and parsley in a buttered 6-cup soufflé or straight-sided casserole. Repeat with remaining bread, seafood, cheese and parsley to make 2 more layers.
3. Beat eggs with milk, melted butter or margarine, mustard and onion until blended in a medium-size bowl; pour mixture over layers; cover with plastic. Chill at least 3 hours, or overnight. Uncover.
4. Bake in moderate oven (350°) 1 hour, 15 minutes, or until puffed and golden. Serve immediately.

FRENCH ONION SCALLOP

Sort of an onion-cheese fondue, it goes very well with a mixed green salad.

Bake at 350° for 30 minutes.
Makes 6 servings.

- 6 large onions, sliced
- ¼ cup (½ stick) butter or margarine
- ¼ cup all purpose flour
- ½ teaspoon salt
- ¼ teaspoon pepper
- 2 cups milk
- 1 teaspoon Worcestershire sauce
- 6 slices process Swiss cheese, cut into pieces (from an 8-ounce package)
- 6 slices slightly dry French bread, buttered and cut into large cubes

1. Cook sliced onions in boiling water to cover in large saucepan for 10 to 12 minutes, or just until tender but still firm; drain well. Arrange in a buttered shallow 6-cup casserole.
2. While onions cook, melt butter or margarine in medium-size saucepan. Blend in flour, salt and pepper; cook, stirring constantly, just until bubbly; slowly stir in milk and Worcestershire sauce until well blended.
3. Cook, stirring constantly, until sauce thickens and bubbles 3 minutes. Stir in cheese; cook over low heat until cheese melts.
4. Pour over onions; stir to mix; arrange bread cubes around edge.
5. Bake in moderate oven (350°) 30 minutes, or until bread is golden.

FRENCH LAMB CHOPS

Vermouth flavors thick lamb chops and lima beans.

Makes 4 servings.

- 4 shoulder lamb chops, ¾-inch thick
- 1 tablespoon vegetable oil
- ¼ pound mushrooms, sliced
- 1 medium-size onion, sliced
- ⅔ cup dry vermouth
- 1 package (10 ounces) frozen lima beans
- ⅔ cup water
- ¾ teaspoon salt
- ½ teaspoon coriander
- ⅛ teaspoon pepper
- 1 tablespoon cornstarch
- ¼ cup chopped parsley

1. Brown chops well on both sides in oil in a large skillet; remove and reserve. Sauté mushrooms and onion in same pan until soft.
2. Return chops to pan; add vermouth, lima beans, water, salt, coriander and pepper; cover.
3. Simmer 30 minutes, or until lamb is tender. Blend ¼ cup water and cornstarch in a cup; stir into pan.
4. Cook, stirring constantly, until sauce thickens and bubbles 3 minutes; stir in parsley.

LEMON MEATBALLS

The Arab influence is still seen in French cuisine.

Makes 6 servings.

- 1½ pounds ground chuck
- 1 small onion, grated
- ½ cup uncooked brown rice
- 1½ teaspoons salt
- ¼ teaspoon pepper
- 3½ cups beef broth
- 2 eggs
- 2 tablespoons all purpose flour
- 2 tablespoons lemon juice
- 1 package (9 ounces) frozen artichoke hearts
- 1 jar (4 ounces) pimiento, drained and diced

1. Mix chuck, onion, rice, salt and pepper in a large bowl. Shape mixture into 36 meatballs.
2. Place meatballs in a large nonstick skillet (see Buyer's Guide). Pour beef broth over.
3. Simmer 40 minutes, or until tender, stirring meatballs occasionally to permit even cooking. Remove meatballs with a slotted spoon and keep warm.
4. Beat eggs with flour and lemon juice in a small bowl. Stir mixture into pan juices. Add artichoke hearts and pimiento. Cook over low heat until sauce thickens; do *not* boil.
5. Return meatballs and simmer 5 minutes. Taste and season with salt and pepper. Sprinkle with chopped mint leaves and serve with pita bread, if you wish.

BEEF RAGOÛT ORLEANS

From this city of good cooking, a recipe that takes a little time, but the final dish could make your reputation as a gourmet cook.

Makes 8 servings.

- ½ pound thickly sliced bacon
- 2 pounds beef chuck, cubed
- 1 large onion, chopped (1 cup)
- 1 cup finely chopped carrot
- 1 cup finely chopped celery
- 2 cloves garlic, minced
- 2 teaspoons salt
- 1 teaspoon leaf thyme, crumbled
- 1 bay leaf
- ¼ teaspoon pepper
- 2 cups dry red wine
- ¼ cup all purpose flour
- 1 pound fresh mushrooms
- 1 bunch leeks
- 1 bunch carrots
- ¼ cup (½ stick) butter or margarine
- 1 envelope or teaspoon instant chicken broth
- ½ cup water

1. Cut bacon into 1-inch pieces; place in a saucepan; cover with water. Bring to boiling; lower heat and simmer 10 minutes. Dry bacon on paper towels. Fry bacon until crisp in a large kettle or Dutch oven. Remove bacon and reserve; pour off all but 2 tablespoons fat into a cup.
2. Brown beef, a few pieces at a time, in kettle; remove and reserve. Sauté onion, carrot, celery and garlic in pan drippings, adding more bacon fat if needed; stir in salt, thyme, bay leaf and pepper; return beef to kettle; add wine, bring slowly to boiling; reduce heat to simmer; cover.
3. Simmer 1½ hours, or until beef is very tender; remove bay leaf; discard. Remove beef from liquid with slotted spoon; keep warm.
4. Pour liquid, half at a time, into an electric blender container; add flour, half at a time; cover container; whirl at high speed 1 minute. (Or press liquid through a sieve with a wooden spoon into a bowl; cool slightly; stir in flour until well blended.) Return liquid to kettle; bring to boiling. Cook, stirring constantly, until sauce thickens and bubbles 3 minutes; return beef to kettle and keep warm.
5. While beef cooks, wipe mushrooms with damp paper towel; cut leeks into 5-inch pieces and halve; wash well to remove all sand; pare and cut carrots into 5-inch pieces.
6. Sauté mushrooms in butter or margarine in a large skillet; remove. Sauté leeks lightly in skillet; remove. Add carrots and sauté 5 minutes; add instant chicken broth and water to skillet; cover and simmer 15 minutes, or until carrots are almost tender, spoon to one side. Return mushrooms and leeks to pan. Cover, simmer 10 minutes, or until vegetables are tender.
7. Spoon vegetables around beef; sprinkle beef with cooked bacon and chopped parsley, if you wish. Pour liquid in skillet over beef and serve with French bread.

OLD-FASHIONED LENTIL SOUP

A ham bone enriches this soup with smoky flavor and tangy bits of meat.

Makes 6 servings.

- 1 ham bone
- 6 cups water
- 1¼ cups dried lentils (from a 1-pound package)
- 4 medium-size carrots, pared and sliced
- 1 large onion, chopped (1 cup)
- 2 teaspoons salt
- 1 teaspoon sugar
- ¼ teaspoon pepper
- 1 bay leaf

1. Combine ham bone, water, lentils, carrots, onion, salt, sugar, pepper and bay leaf in a kettle; cover; bring to boiling; simmer 1 hour, or until lentils are tender.
2. Remove ham bone; strip off bits of meat and add to soup. Remove bay leaf. Ladle soup into heated bowls.

BROCCOLI-CHEESE RING

It's decorative enough for a party.

Makes 6 servings.

- 1 bunch broccoli (about 2 pounds)
- 1 Bermuda onion, chopped (2 cups)
- 2 tablespoons butter or margarine
- 2 tablespoons all purpose flour
- ½ teaspoon salt
- ⅛ teaspoon pepper
- 1½ cups milk
- 2 cups shredded process American cheese (8 ounces)
- ¼ cup mayonnaise or salad dressing
- 12 thin slices French bread, toasted

1. Trim and discard outer leaves and tough ends from broccoli; split large stalks lengthwise. Cook in about 1-inch depth boiling salted water in large saucepan 10 to 15 minutes, or until crisply tender; drain carefully; keep hot.
2. While broccoli cooks, sauté onion in butter or margarine just until soft in a medium-size saucepan. Blend in flour, salt and pepper; cook, stirring constantly, until mixture bubbles; stir in milk. Cook, stirring constantly, until sauce thickens and bubbles 3 minutes; stir in cheese until melted; fold in mayonnaise or salad dressing until well blended.
3. Arrange broccoli with stems toward middle on a heated round platter; stand toast between broccoli stems to form a circle; spoon hot sauce into middle.

SALMON QUICHE

Salmon and Swiss cheese bake in a velvety custard on a delicate crust.

Bake at 450° for 15 minutes, then at 325° for 30 minutes.
Makes 6 servings.

- 1 can (about 8 ounces) salmon
- 2 cups shredded Swiss cheese (8 ounces)
- 2 teaspoons grated onion
- 1 tablespoon all purpose flour
- ¼ teaspoon salt
- 1 unbaked 9-inch pastry shell
- 3 eggs
- 1 cup milk

1. Drain salmon; remove any skin or small bones; flake fish.
2. Combine cheese, onion, flour and salt in medium-size bowl; fill pastry shell with alternate layers of salmon and cheese mixture.
3. Beat eggs and milk in a large measuring cup or a medium-size bowl; pour over layers in shell.
4. Bake in very hot oven (450°) 15 minutes; reduce oven temperature to slow (325°); bake 30 minutes longer, or just until firm in center. Serve with mixed green salad, if you wish.

LIVER RIVIERA

A stove-top meal you make in minutes.

Makes 4 servings.

    1 pound beef or lamb liver, sliced
       All purpose flour
    4 slices bacon
    1 small onion, chopped (¼ cup)
    ¼ cup chili sauce
    1 teaspoon salt
    ⅛ teaspoon leaf thyme, crumbled
    ⅛ teaspoon pepper
    ¾ cup water
    1 can (6 ounces) sliced mushrooms
   16 cherry tomatoes
       OR: 2 tomatoes, cut into wedges
    4 slices white or whole wheat toast,
       halved diagonally

1. Flour liver slices lightly, then cut into thin strips with a sharp knife.
2. Cook bacon until crisp in a medium-size skillet; remove and reserve. Pour out drippings, reserving 4 tablespoons; return 2 tablespoons to pan.
3. Brown liver with onion in bacon drippings. Stir in chili sauce, salt, thyme, pepper and water; cover.
4. Simmer 3 minutes, or just until liver loses its pink color. (Over-cooking toughens this delicate meat, so watch it carefully and remove from heat at once.) Remove from pan; keep warm on a heated serving platter.
5. Sauté mushrooms and cherry tomatoes or tomato wedges in reserved 2 tablespoons drippings 3 minutes, or until tomato skins just start to pop.
6. Surround liver with mushrooms and tomatoes. Garnish with reserved bacon, toast halves and chopped parsley, if you wish.

CIPÂTÉ STEW

Inspired by a French-Canadian dish, a trio of meats is simmered in a savory sauce and topped with flaky biscuits.

Bake at 350° for 1 hour,
then at 400° for 15 minutes.
Makes 8 servings.

    1 broiler-fryer, cut up (2½ pounds)
    ⅓ cup all purpose flour
    2 teaspoons seasoned salt
    ½ teaspoon lemon pepper
    2 tablespoons vegetable oil
    1 pound beef chuck, cubed
    ½ pound cooked ham, cubed
    8 small yellow onions, peeled
    4 cups water
    1 can (3 or 4 ounces) sliced
       mushrooms
    2 tablespoons bottled steak sauce
    1 package (9 ounces) frozen cut
       green beans
       Flaky Biscuits (recipe follows)

1. Shake chicken, a few pieces at a time, in a mixture of flour, salt and pepper in a plastic bag to coat well.
2. Brown chicken in oil in a large skillet and spoon into a 12-cup casserole. Shake beef and ham cubes in seasoned flour. Brown, a few pieces at a time, in pan drippings; add to casserole. Brown onions lightly in pan drippings; add to casserole.
3. Stir any remaining seasoned flour into pan drippings; add water; cook, stirring constantly, until mixture thickens and bubbles; add mushrooms with liquid and bottled steak sauce. Pour over meats; cover.
4. Bake in moderate oven (350°) 1 hour, or until meats are tender; remove cover and stir in green beans. Increase oven temperature to hot (400°); arrange FLAKY BISCUITS in a ring on top of meats.
5. Bake in hot oven (400°) 15 minutes, or until biscuits are golden. Let cool 10 minutes before serving.

FLAKY BISCUITS

Bake at 400° for 15 minutes.
Makes 8 biscuits.

    2 cups all purpose flour
    2 teaspoons baking powder
    1 teaspoon salt
    ¼ cup vegetable shortening
    ¾ cup milk

1. Sift flour, baking powder and salt into a medium-size bowl; cut in shortening with a pastry blender. Stir in milk, just until blended.
2. Turn out onto a lightly floured pastry cloth or board and knead several times. Pat out to a ½-inch thick round. Cut into 8 rounds with a 2½-inch biscuit cutter. Re-roll any trimmings and cut into additional biscuits to be baked on a cookie sheet, along with stew.

BOEUF PIERRE

White wine and kidney beans flavor yesterday's roast beef.

Bake at 375° for 30 minutes.
Makes 4 servings.

    2 cups cubed cooked beef
    2 tablespoons butter or margarine
    ½ teaspoon salt
    ½ teaspoon leaf thyme, crumbled
    ⅛ teaspoon pepper
    1 cup dry white wine
    2 cans (1 pound each) white kidney
       beans, drained
    1 can (1 pound) small boiled onions,
       drained
    ½ cup chopped parsley

1. Brown beef in butter or margarine in a medium-size skillet; stir in salt, thyme, pepper and wine; heat.
2. Spoon into a 6-cup casserole; stir in beans and onions; cover.
3. Bake in moderate oven (375°) 30 minutes, or until bubbly hot. Sprinkle with chopped parsley. Serve with French bread, if you wish.

VEAL MARENGO

Napoleon's chef, Durand, created the original Chicken Marengo, right after the Battle of Marengo. Our simplified version uses quick-cooking veal.

Bake at 400° for 20 minutes.
Makes 6 servings.

    1 package (8 ounces) noodles
    1 tablespoon butter or margarine
    1 tablespoon vegetable oil
    6 frozen breaded veal patties
    1 can (3 or 4 ounces) whole
       mushrooms, drained
    1 can (1 pound) whole boiled onions,
       drained
    1 envelope (1½ ounces) spaghetti
       sauce mix
    1 can (1 pound) tomatoes
    1 can (1 pound) tomato wedges
    ½ cup packaged garlic croutons
    2 tablespoons chopped parsley

1. Cook noodles, following label directions; drain. Spread in an 8-cup casserole.
2. Heat butter or margarine with oil in a large skillet; sauté veal patties about 3 minutes on each side. Overlap browned patties down center of noodles; keep warm.
3. Toss mushrooms and onions in same skillet to brown lightly. Arrange around patties.
4. Add spaghetti sauce mix to same skillet with tomatoes, tomato wedges and juice from the can of tomato wedges. Stir over low heat until sauce bubbles; pour sauce over all. Sprinkle with croutons.
5. Bake in a hot oven (400°) 20 minutes, or until sauce is bubbly. Sprinkle with chopped parsley. Serve with marinated artichoke hearts.

VEAL VITEMENT

The French version of English mixed grill.

Broil for 14 to 16 minutes.
Makes 6 servings.

    1½ pounds veal cutlet, cut into
       ½-inch slices
    ¼ cup bottled blue cheese salad
       dressing
    1 Bermuda onion, peeled and cut
       into 6 slices
    ¼ cup (½ stick) butter or margarine,
       melted
       Salt and pepper
    3 medium-size tomatoes, halved
    6 slices bacon
    1 can (3 or 4 ounces) whole
       mushrooms, drained

1. Place veal on broiler rack; brush top thickly with half of blue cheese salad dressing.
2. Place onion slices on rack with veal; brush with part of melted butter or margarine; sprinkle with salt and pepper.
3. Broil, 4 to 6 inches from heat, 7 to 8 minutes. Turn veal and onion

slices; brush veal with remaining blue cheese dressing.

4. Place tomato halves, bacon slices and mushrooms alongside veal and onion on rack. Brush tomato halves, onion slices and mushrooms with remaining butter or margarine; sprinkle with salt and pepper.

5. Continue to broil, turning bacon once, 7 to 8 minutes longer, or until veal is richly golden, bacon is crisp and tomatoes and mushrooms are heated through.

6. Arrange meats and vegetables on heated serving platter. Serve with lemon wedges, if you wish.

ALGERIAN COUSCOUS

A North African everyday dish that's both economical and exotic. Semolina-grain couscous is to the Arabs what pasta is to the Italians and potatoes are to the Irish.

Makes 8 servings.

- 2 large onions, chopped (2 cups)
- 2 tablespoons vegetable or olive oil
- 1 broiler-fryer, cut up (about 2½ pounds)
- 1 pound lean lamb, cut into 1½-inch cubes
- 3 cups water
- 4 carrots, pared and cut into 1-inch pieces
- 1 tablespoon salt
- ¼ teaspoon pepper
- ¼ teaspoon ground ginger
- 1 three-inch piece stick cinnamon
- 1 teaspoon salt
- 1 cup water
- 1 package (about 1 pound) couscous (see Cook's Tip)
- 4 small zucchini, washed and cut into ½-inch slices
- 2 medium-size tomatoes, chopped
- 1 can (1 pound, 4 ounces) chick peas, drained
- 1 cup seedless raisins
- ⅓ cup butter or margarine, melted

1. Sauté onion until golden in oil in a large skillet, about 5 minutes. Transfer to a stockpot or similar deep, narrow kettle. Brown chicken and lamb in same skillet; transfer to pot as they brown.

2. Add the 3 cups water to skillet; bring to boiling, scraping up brown bits; pour over meat. Stir in carrots, the 1 tablespoon salt, pepper, ginger and cinnamon. Bring to boiling.

3. Dissolve the 1 teaspoon salt in 1 cup water; sprinkle about ½ cup over couscous in a large bowl to moisten; place in a large, fine-mesh sieve. Hang sieve on edge of stockpot over, but not touching, stew. Cover tightly with foil to keep steam in. Simmer 40 minutes.

4. Remove sieve; stir zucchini, tomatoes, chick peas and raisins into stew. Sprinkle remaining salted water over couscous; mix or stir with a fork. Set sieve over stew again to steam,

covering tightly with foil. Simmer 30 minutes longer, or until meats and vegetables are tender. Thicken stew with a little flour mixed with water, if you wish. Turn couscous into a large bowl; drizzle melted butter or margarine over and toss to mix well.

5. To serve, spoon stew into center of a deep platter. Arrange steamed and buttered couscous around edge. Serve with tall glasses of iced tea flavored with lime and cloves.

COOK'S TIP: Couscous is sold in the gourmet shops of many large metropolitan department stores, and also in specialty food shops and some supermarkets. If you are unable to obtain it in your area, substitute brown or white rice or kasha, and cook, following label directions.

MOUSSAKA À LA TURQUE

The famous Middle Eastern dish with a French flair.

Bake at 375° for 30 minutes,
then at 375° for 1 hour, 30 minutes.
Makes 6 servings.

- 2 large eggplants (about 1¼ pounds each)
- 2 large onions, chopped (2 cups)
- 1 clove garlic, minced
- ¼ cup olive or vegetable oil
- ½ pound mushrooms, chopped
- 2 cups ground cooked lamb
- 1 tablespoon salt
- ¼ teaspoon pepper
- 1 teaspoon leaf oregano, crumbled
- 3 eggs
- 2 cups soft white bread crumbs (4 slices)
  Vegetables Provençale (recipe follows)

1. Halve eggplants lengthwise; place, cut-side down, in a 15x10x1-inch baking pan. Place baking pan on rack in oven; pour boiling water in pan to a depth of ½ inch.

2. Bake in moderate oven (375°) 30 minutes, or till eggplant is soft when pressed with fingertip. Remove eggplant from baking pan; drain on paper towels.

3. Scoop out inside of eggplant, being careful not to break the skin. (A grapefruit knife works well.) Chop eggplant into small pieces.

4. Sauté onion and garlic in oil until soft in a large skillet; add mushrooms; sauté 3 minutes. Add eggplant and sauté until liquid in pan has evaporated. (Both mushrooms and eggplant give off liquid when cooked.) Stir in cooked lamb, salt, pepper and oregano; cook 3 minutes; remove mixture from heat.

5. Beat eggs in a large bowl; stir in bread crumbs, then eggplant mixture, until well blended.

6. Line an 8-cup charlotte mold or a straight-sided mold or bowl with egg-

plant shells, skin-side out; spoon eggplant mixture into skins; fold skins over mixture. Cover mold with a double thickness of foil.

7. Place mold on a rack in a kettle or steamer; pour in boiling water to half the depth of the mold.

8. Bake in moderate oven (375°) 1 hour, 30 minutes; remove mold from water and remove foil cover; allow to stand on wire rack 10 minutes.

9. Unmold onto heated serving platter; remove any excess moisture from platter. Spoon VEGETABLES PROVENÇALE around the mold. Serve with baked caramel custard for dessert.

VEGETABLES PROVENÇALE

Makes 4 cups.

- 1 large onion, chopped (1 cup)
- 1 clove garlic, minced
- 3 tablespoons olive or vegetable oil
- 1 large yellow squash
- 1 large zucchini
- 2 large tomatoes, peeled and chopped
- 2 teaspoons salt
- 1 teaspoon leaf thyme, crumbled
- 1 teaspoon leaf basil, crumbled
- ¼ teaspoon pepper

1. Sauté onion and garlic in oil until soft in large skillet. Trim, halve and slice yellow squash and zucchini. Add to skillet and sauté 3 minutes. Stir in tomatoes, salt, thyme, basil and pepper until well blended. Cover skillet; lower heat.

2. Simmer, stirring occasionally, 30 minutes, or until vegetables are tender and liquid is absorbed.

RATATOUILLE PROVENÇALE

Stir-fry cooking isn't just Oriental. Here, classic French ingredients quick-cook for a savory dish in minutes.

Makes 6 servings.

- 1 pound sweet Italian sausages, sliced
- 1 large onion, sliced
- 1 large green pepper, halved, seeded and coarsely chopped
- 1 clove garlic, chopped
- 1 small eggplant, diced
- 3 medium-size zucchini, diced
- 3 ripe tomatoes, cored and diced
- 1 teaspoon salt
- ½ teaspoon leaf oregano, crumbled
- ¼ teaspoon freshly ground pepper

1. Cook sausages in a large nonstick skillet (see Buyer's Guide); remove with slotted spoon; reserve.

2. Sauté onion, green pepper and garlic until golden in pan drippings. Stir in eggplant, zucchini and tomatoes. Add salt, oregano and pepper. Return sausages to pan.

3. Simmer, stirring occasionally, 15 minutes, or until vegetables are tender and sausages are heated through.

MARROW BEAN CASSEROLE

Dry vermouth gives the classic French touch to this bean and lamb casserole.

Bake at 325° for 3 hours.
Makes 8 servings.

- 1 package (1 pound) dried marrow or Great Northern beans
- 8 cups water
- 2 large onions, chopped (2 cups)
- 1 tablespoon salt
- 1 pound lamb shoulder, cubed
- 2 tablespoons olive or vegetable oil
- 2 cloves garlic, minced
- 1 cup dry vermouth or white wine
- 2 envelopes or teaspoons instant beef broth
- 1 teaspoon leaf thyme, crumbled
- ½ teaspoon pepper
- 1 bay leaf

1. Pick over beans and rinse under running water. Combine beans and water in a large kettle. Bring to boiling; cover kettle. Boil 2 minutes; remove from heat; let stand 1 hour. Return kettle to heat; bring to boiling; add onions and salt; lower heat and simmer 1 hour, or until beans are firm but tender.
2. Brown lamb cubes in vegetable oil in a 12-cup flame proof casserole or a large skillet; push to one side; add garlic and sauté 3 minutes; stir in vermouth or white wine, instant beef broth, thyme, pepper and bay leaf; bring to boiling.
3. Drain beans, reserving liquid. Combine beans with lamb mixture in casserole; add enough reserved liquid to cover beans and lamb; cover casserole.
4. Bake in slow oven (325°) 2 hours, 30 minutes, adding more reserved liquid, if needed, to prevent beans from drying out. Remove cover; bake 30 minutes longer, or until beans are very tender.

LAMB CASSOULET

From southwestern France, a slow-simmering classic, laden with beans and meat.

Bake at 325° for 3 hours.
Makes 8 servings.

- 2 pounds stewing lamb
- 2 teaspoons salt
- 1 pound (2 cups) dried marrow beans
- 1 cup grated raw carrots
- ¼ pound salami, cut into ½-inch cubes
- 8 slices bacon, diced
- 1 large onion, chopped (1 cup)
- 1 clove garlic, minced
- 1 can (1 pound) tomatoes
- 1 bay leaf
- ½ teaspoon leaf savory, crumbled
- ½ teaspoon salt

1. Combine lamb and the 2 teaspoons salt with cold water to cover in a large kettle or Dutch oven. Cover; heat to boiling, then simmer 1 hour, or until lamb is tender.
2. Remove meat from broth and let cool until easy to handle. Strain broth into a 4-cup measure; let stand until fat rises to top; skim off fat. Add water to broth, if needed, to make 4 cups.
3. Pick over meat, discarding fat and bones; dice meat; cover; chill.
4. Combine beans and reserved broth in large kettle; cover; heat to boiling; cook 2 minutes. Remove from heat; let stand 1 hour. (All this can be done ahead, if you like.)
5. When ready to finish dish, reheat beans to boiling; stir in carrots and salami; cover. Cook 1 hour, or until skins of beans burst when you blow on a few in a spoon.
6. Sauté bacon until crisp in a large skillet; remove and drain on paper towels. Pour drippings into cup; return 2 tablespoons to pan. Add onion and garlic; sauté just until soft.
7. Stir in tomatoes, bay leaf, leaf savory, salt, lamb and bacon; heat to boiling; stir into beans in kettle. Pour into a 16-cup casserole; cover.
8. Bake in slow oven (325°) 2 hours; uncover; if mixture seems dry, add a little water. Bake 1 hour longer, or until beans are tender; remove bay leaf before serving.

BLANQUETTE DE VEAU

Breast of veal is a bargain meat, and it makes a delicious stew.

Makes 8 servings.

- 1 boned breast of veal (about 3 pounds)
- 1 stalk celery with leaves
- 3 sprigs parsley
- ½ teaspoon leaf thyme, crumbled
- 1 bay leaf
- 3 cups water
- 2 teaspoons salt
  Dash ground nutmeg
- 1 pound small white onions, peeled
- ½ pound mushrooms
- 5 tablespoons butter or margarine
- 5 tablespoons all purpose flour
- 1 cup milk
- 2 egg yolks
  Parsley

1. Trim fat from breast of veal; cut meat into 1-inch cubes. Remove celery leaves from stalk; slice stalk; reserve. Tie celery leaves, parsley, thyme and bay leaf in cheesecloth.
2. Place meat and herbs in kettle or Dutch oven; add water, salt and nutmeg. Heat to boiling; lower heat; cover. Simmer 45 minutes; add sliced celery and onions. Simmer 40 minutes longer, or until meat and vegetables are tender.
3. Remove and discard cheesecloth. Transfer meat and vegetables to a shallow heated serving dish; cover and keep warm. Reduce broth to 2 cups by boiling rapidly, uncovered, 10 minutes.
4. Meanwhile, remove and set aside stems from mushrooms. Sauté caps in 2 tablespoons of the butter or margarine in a large saucepan until nicely browned, about 5 minutes; remove; reserve.
5. Chop stems finely; sauté in remaining butter or margarine in saucepan, 5 minutes. Stir in flour; cook until bubbly. Gradually add reduced broth and milk. Cook, stirring constantly, until sauce thickens and bubbles 3 minutes. Remove from heat.
6. Beat egg yolks slightly in a small bowl; slowly stir in 1 cup hot sauce. Stir back into sauce in pan. Pour sauce over meat and vegetables. Garnish with reserved mushroom caps and chopped parsley.

PROVENÇALE LAMB PIE

Stretch a little bit of lamb with sausage and garden vegetables in a ratatouille-like pie.

Bake at 375° for 40 minutes.
Makes 8 servings.

- 2 hot Italian sausages
- 3 small onions, quartered
- 1 small green pepper, halved, seeded and diced
- 2½ cups cooked cubed lamb
- 2 tablespoons vegetable oil
- 1 small eggplant, pared and cubed
- 3 tablespoons all purpose flour
- 1 can (1 pound) tomatoes
- 2 cups water
- 1 envelope or teaspoon instant beef broth
- 1 teaspoon salt
- ½ teaspoon leaf basil, crumbled
- ½ teaspoon leaf rosemary, crumbled
- 2 zucchini, washed, trimmed and sliced
- 1 package (8 ounces) refrigerator buttermilk biscuits

1. Slice sausages into 1-inch pieces; brown in large skillet. Add onions and pepper; sauté until soft in drippings from sausage. Remove sausage and vegetables from skillet with slotted spoon; place in a 12-cup casserole.
2. Brown lamb in same skillet. Remove to casserole. Add oil and eggplant to skillet; sauté 5 minutes; sprinkle with flour. Stir in tomatoes, water, instant beef broth, salt, basil and rosemary. Bring to boiling, stirring constantly. Boil 1 minute. Pour over meat in casserole; add zucchini. Mix well.
3. Pat buttermilk biscuits with your hands on a lightly floured pastry cloth or board into pencil-thin strips. Arrange on top of stew in a lattice pattern.
4. Bake in moderate oven (375°) 40 minutes, or until pastry is golden brown and pie is bubbly hot.

SAUSAGE CASSOULET

A quick and economical version of the French classic.

Bake at 350° for 60 minutes.
Makes 6 servings.

- **2 cans (1 pound each) cooked dried lima beans, drained**
- **1 jar (1 pound) diced carrots, drained**
- **1 cup thinly sliced celery**
- **2 tablespoons instant minced onion**
- **1 teaspoon mixed salad herbs, crumbled**
- **2 packages (8 ounces each) brown-and-serve sausage patties, quartered**
- **1 can (about 1 pound) stewed tomatoes**
- **2 tablespoons chopped parsley**

1. Combine lima beans, carrots, celery, onion and salad herbs in a 10-cup casserole.
2. Brown sausage patties, half at a time, in a medium-size skillet; remove with a slotted spoon and place over vegetables in casserole. Pour out all drippings from pan.
3. Add tomatoes to pan; heat to boiling, scraping brown bits from bottom of pan; pour into casserole.
4. Bake in moderate oven (350°) 30 minutes; stir lightly. Bake another 30 minutes, or until slightly thickened. Sprinkle parsley over top.

SPRING LAMB RAGOÛT

Classically called Navarin Printanier, this is lamb stew with a French flavor.

Makes 8 servings.

- **3 pounds lean boneless lamb, cut into 1½- to 2-inch cubes**
- **3 tablespoons olive or vegetable oil**
- **3 tablespoons all purpose flour**
- **3 tablespoons finely chopped shallots**
  OR: 1 small onion, chopped (¼ cup)
- **1 clove garlic, crushed**
- **1 can condensed beef broth**
- **1 can (1 pound) tomatoes**
- **1½ teaspoons salt**
- **1 teaspoon leaf thyme, crumbled**
- **2 tablespoons butter or margarine**
- **12 small white onions, peeled**
- **4 small white turnips, pared and quartered**
- **4 carrots, pared and cut into 2-inch lengths**
- **12 small new potatoes, peeled**
- **1 package (10 ounces) frozen peas**
- **2 tablespoons chopped parsley**

1. Brown lamb, a few pieces at a time, in oil in a Dutch oven. Sprinkle flour over meat; cook over moderate heat, stirring and tossing meat with wooden spoon until evenly coated, about 5 minutes. (This browns flour slightly.) Remove and reserve.
2. Add shallots or onion and garlic

to Dutch oven; sauté, stirring often, 5 minutes, or until golden brown. Stir in beef broth and tomatoes; bring to boiling, stirring constantly to loosen browned bits in pan. Return browned lamb. Stir in salt and thyme. Bring to boiling; reduce heat; cover. Simmer 1 hour. Skim off fat, if any.
3. While lamb simmers, heat butter or margarine in a large skillet; add onions, turnips and carrots. Sauté, stirring often, 10 minutes, or until vegetables are browned and glazed.
4. Add glazed vegetables and potatoes to lamb, pushing them down under liquid; cover; simmer 45 minutes longer, or until lamb and vegetables are tender. Stir in peas and parsley; cover; simmer 5 minutes longer. Sprinkle with additional parsley, if you wish.

RAGOÛT JARDINIÈRE

An inviting meatball dish with five different vegetables. So quick to make, too.

Makes 8 servings.

- **1 pound bulk sausage**
- **1 pound ground veal**
- **2 eggs**
- **1 cup soft bread crumbs (2 slices)**
- **¼ cup chopped parsley**
- **½ teaspoon salt**
- **1 large onion, chopped (1 cup)**
- **1 large cabbage (about 3 pounds)**
- **1 cup sliced carrots**
- **1 cup mixed vegetable juice**
- **1 teaspoon salt**
- **½ teaspoon leaf basil, crumbled**
- **¼ teaspoon pepper**
- **1 package (10 ounces) frozen lima beans**
- **1 package (10 ounces) frozen peas**

1. Mix sausage, veal, eggs, bread crumbs, parsley and the ½ teaspoon salt in a medium-size bowl. Shape lightly into 48 small balls.
2. Brown slowly, turning several times, in a large skillet or an electric frypan.
3. Remove meatballs; reserve. Drain all but 3 tablespoons fat from pan. Stir in onion and sauté just until soft. (This much cooking can be done ahead, if you wish.)
4. Cut cabbage in half; slice one half into 8 wedges, then shred other half finely, to make about 6 cups. Stir shredded cabbage into onion in pan; cook 2 minutes, or just until wilted.
5. Stir in carrots, mixed vegetable juice, the 1 teaspoon salt, basil and pepper. Arrange cabbage wedges on top; cover. Bring to boiling; simmer 15 minutes.
6. Separate frozen limas and peas by tapping packages on counter; stir into vegetables in skillet; top with meatballs. Cover; cook 15 minutes longer, or until limas are tender and meatballs are heated through.

VEGETABLES MORNAY

A meatless entrée that's delicious with tomato-basil salad.

Bake at 350° for 30 minutes.
Makes 6 servings.

- **¼ cup (½ stick) butter or margarine**
- **2 Bermuda onions, chopped (4 cups)**
- **2 cloves garlic, minced**
- **1 can condensed cream of celery soup**
- **1 cup milk**
- **¼ teaspoon seasoned pepper**
- **1 can (1 pound) cut green beans, drained**
- **2 packages (8 ounces each) sliced process Swiss cheese**
- **12 thick slices French bread**

1. Melt butter or margarine in a large skillet; stir in onions and garlic; cover. Cook 15 minutes; stir in soup, milk and pepper; heat, stirring several times, until bubbly.
2. Make two layers each of beans, cheese slices and sauce in a buttered 8-cup casserole; arrange bread slices, overlapping, on top.
3. Bake in moderate oven (350°) 30 minutes, or until bubbly hot.

MEATLOAF AU GRATIN

There's cheese baked in it and on it.

Bake at 350° for 1 hour, 30 minutes.
Makes 8 servings.

- **2 pounds ground beef**
- **1 cup grated Cheddar cheese (4 ounces)**
- **1 egg**
- **2 cups soft bread crumbs (4 slices)**
- **1 small onion, grated**
- **1 tablespoon Worcestershire sauce**
- **1 tablespoon prepared mustard**
- **1 teaspoon salt**
- **¼ cup (½ stick) butter or margarine, melted**
- **1 teaspoon dillweed**
- **1 teaspoon sugar**
- **½ teaspoon salt**
- **¼ teaspoon pepper**
- **1 pound carrots, pared and cut into 4-inch lengths**
- **1 can (8 ounces) tomato sauce**

1. Mix ground beef lightly with ¾ cup of the cheese, egg, bread crumbs, onion, Worcestershire sauce, mustard and the 1 teaspoon salt until well blended. Shape into a loaf in a shallow baking pan.
2. Mix melted butter or margarine, dillweed, sugar, salt and pepper. Place carrots around loaf in pan; brush with butter mixture.
3. Bake in moderate oven (350°) 1 hour, turning carrots once after 30 minutes. Pour off drippings.
4. Pour tomato sauce over loaf; sprinkle with remaining ¼ cup cheese. Baste carrots with butter mixture. Bake 30 minutes longer.

(Continued from page 96.)

ASPARAGUS CHICKEN

When asparagus comes to market early in the spring, try this elegant recipe.

Makes 6 servings.

- ½ pound asparagus
- 3 chicken breasts (about 12 ounces each), skinned and boned
- 6 tablespoons vegetable oil
- 1 bunch green onions, trimmed and sliced thin (¾ cup)
- 1 can (3 or 4 ounces) sliced mushrooms
- 1 can condensed chicken broth
- 1½ teaspoons ground ginger
- 1 teaspoon salt
- 1 teaspoon sugar
- ¼ teaspoon garlic powder
- 2 tablespoons cornstarch
- ⅓ cup dry Sherry
- 3 tablespoons soy sauce
- 4 cups cooked rice

1. Break tough, woody ends from asparagus; wash the stalks in cold water; drain well. Split each stalk lengthwise, then cut into 1½-inch lengths.
2. Slice the chicken into thin strips about 1½ inches long.
3. Heat 4 tablespoons of the vegetable oil in a large skillet. Stir in the chicken, sauté, stirring several times, 4 minutes, or until chicken turns white. Remove from skillet to a bowl; keep warm.
4. Heat the remaining 2 tablespoons vegetable oil in same skillet. Stir in the asparagus and green onions; sauté 2 minutes. Stir in the chicken, mushrooms and liquid, chicken broth, ginger, salt, sugar and garlic powder; cover. Simmer 3 minutes.
5. Mix cornstarch, Sherry and soy sauce until smooth in a cup; stir into mixture in skillet. Cook, stirring constantly, until mixture thickens and bubbles 3 minutes. Serve over rice.

STEAK TERIYAKI

Teriyaki has been an appetizer favorite for some time. Now it takes its place among main-dish favorites.

Broil for 4 minutes.
Makes 6 servings.

- 1 boneless sirloin steak, 1½ inches thick and weighing about 2 pounds
- 18 small white onions, peeled and boiled 5 minutes
- 2 large green peppers, halved, seeded and cubed
- ¾ cup soy sauce
- ½ cup dry Sherry
- ½ cup chopped green onions
- 1 clove garlic, crushed
- 1 tablespoon sugar
- 1 teaspoon ground ginger

1. Trim any excess fat from steak; cut into ⅛-inch thick diagonal slices. (You should get about 40 slices.) Place beef strips in a large shallow glass dish. Add onions and peppers.
2. Combine soy sauce, Sherry, green onions, garlic, sugar and ground ginger in a 2-cup measure; pour over beef and vegetables; cover dish.
3. Marinate meat and vegetables in refrigerator overnight, or at least 2 hours.
4. Remove meat and vegetables from marinade; pat dry on paper towels and thread, accordion-style, on eighteen 5-inch bamboo skewers. Arrange skewers on broiler pan.
5. Broil, 3 inches from heat, 2 minutes; turn; brush with marinade; broil 2 minutes longer, or until done.

SENEGALESE SOUFFLÉ

A delicate chicken-curry soufflé that puts leftover chicken to extra good use. Flaked coconut is the nut-like topper.

Bake at 350° for 1 hour.
Makes 6 servings.

- 6 eggs
- ½ cup finely diced celery
- 1 small onion, finely chopped (¼ cup)
- 2 tablespoons butter or margarine
- 2 tablespoons all purpose flour
- ¾ teaspoon curry powder
- ⅛ teaspoon pepper
- 1½ cups milk
- 1 envelope (2 to a package) chicken noodle soup mix
- 1 cup diced cooked chicken OR: 1 can (5 ounces) boned chicken, diced
- 3 tablespoons flaked coconut

1. Separate the eggs, putting whites into medium-size bowl, yolks into large bowl.
2. Sauté celery and onion lightly in butter or margarine in medium-size saucepan; stir in flour, curry powder and pepper; cook, stirring constantly, until bubbly; add milk and dry soup mix, stirring to blend.
3. Cook, stirring constantly, until mixture thickens and bubbles 1 minute; let cool while beating eggs.
4. Beat egg whites just until they form soft peaks in a medium-size bowl.
5. Beat the egg yolks until creamy-thick in a large bowl; slowly stir in the curry sauce and diced chicken; lightly fold in beaten egg whites with wire whip until no streaks of sauce or egg white remain.
6. Pour into an 8-cup soufflé dish or straight-sided baking dish; sprinkle coconut in ring over top; set in baking pan on oven rack; fill pan with boiling water to depth of 1 inch.
7. Bake in moderate oven (350°) 1 hour, or until top is puffy-firm and golden; serve immediately.

SUKIYAKI

Pronounced "skee-yak-kee," this beef dish came to Japan from Europe with the Portuguese explorers in the 16th century.

Makes 6 servings.

- 1 sirloin steak fillet (about 1½ pounds)
- ¼ cup peanut or vegetable oil
- ½ pound green beans, tipped and cut into 1-inch pieces
- 1 small green pepper, halved, seeded and cut into thin strips
- 1 small red pepper, halved, seeded and cut into thin strips
- 1 cup thinly sliced celery
- ½ cup soy sauce
- 1 cup water
- 1 small head Chinese cabbage, shredded
- 1 bunch green onions, trimmed and cut into 2-inch pieces
- 4 large mushrooms, trimmed and sliced

1. Trim all fat from steak; cut meat into very thin strips. (For easier cutting of raw beef, partially freeze steak 30 minutes to firm meat.)
2. Heat oil in a large skillet or wok with a cover. Add steak strips and sauté, stirring occasionally, 2 to 3 minutes, or until brown; remove with a slotted spoon and keep warm.
3. Add green beans, green and red pepper and celery to pan; sauté 2 to 3 minutes, or until vegetables soften.
4. Combine soy sauce and water in a cup; pour over vegetables; cover. Simmer 5 minutes. Stir in shredded cabbage, green onions and mushrooms; cover. Cook 5 minutes longer, or until cabbage wilts and vegetables are crisply tender.
5. Return cooked steak strips to pan and heat until piping hot. Serve over hot cooked rice with additional soy sauce, if you wish.

CHINATOWN FRIED RICE

Chill cooked rice overnight so grains are fluffy dry before sautéing.

Makes 6 servings.

- 2 cups water
- 1 envelope instant vegetable broth OR: 1 vegetable bouillon cube
- ¼ teaspoon ground cumin
- 1 cup regular rice
- 1 medium-size onion, chopped (½ cup)
- ½ clove garlic, minced
- 2 cups diced cooked ham, pork or chicken
- 3 tablespoons vegetable oil
- ½ teaspoon salt
- ¼ teaspoon chili powder
- ⅛ teaspoon ground mace

1. Bring water with vegetable broth or bouillon cube and cumin to boiling in a medium-size saucepan; crush cube, if used, with a spoon; stir in rice;

cover. Cook 15 minutes, or just until rice is tender and liquid is absorbed. Spoon into a bowl; chill.

2. When ready to finish dish, sauté onion and garlic in 1 tablespoon of the oil until soft in a large skillet; push to one side; sauté meat 3 minutes; remove and set aside.

3. Turn rice out onto paper towels; fluff with a fork to separate grains. Sauté lightly in same pan, adding remaining 2 tablespoons oil.

4. Stir in onion mixture, salt, chili power and ground mace; cover; heat slowly just until hot. Spoon into a heated serving bowl. Garnish with parsley and serve with toasted slivered almonds, chopped radishes and sliced green onions, if you wish.

STIR-FRIED SCALLOPS

A Chinese style skillet dish, full of color and crunch, low in calories.

Makes 4 servings.

- 1 pound scallops
- 2 tablespoons vegetable oil
- 1 teaspoon salt
- 1 clove garlic
- 1 cup thinly sliced carrots
- 1 cup thinly sliced celery
- 1 large onion, chopped (1 cup)
- 1 can (5 ounces) sliced bamboo shoots, well drained
- ¾ cup water
- 1 tablespoon soy sauce
- 1 tablespoon dry Sherry
- 1 envelope or teaspoon instant chicken broth
- ½ teaspoon sugar
- 1 tablespoon cornstarch
- 1 package (10 ounces) fresh spinach, washed and trimmed

1. Slice the scallops into very thin circles with a sharp, thin-blade knife.

2. Heat a wok or large, heavy skillet until it sizzles when sprinkled with a few drops of water; add 1 tablespoon of the oil; heat; stir in salt. Spear garlic with fork; brown on all sides in oil in pan; remove and discard.

3. Add scallops to the skillet; cook, stirring very rapidly, 30 seconds; push to one side. Add remaining 1 tablespoon oil and heat. Add the carrots, celery, onions and bamboo shoots, cooking and stirring very rapidly for 2 minutes after each addition, then pushing to one side of skillet.

4. Make well in center of pan and add the water, soy sauce, Sherry, instant chicken broth and sugar; stir to mix. Cover and simmer for 3 minutes.

5. Combine cornstarch and 2 tablespoons cold water in a cup; stir until smooth.

6. Add spinach; cover; cook for 3 minutes longer, or until the spinach wilts. Stir in the cornstarch mixture; cook until mixture thickens, clears and bubbles 3 minutes.

CHICKEN CHOW MEIN

Be your own Chinese chef—make the Chow Mein and the crispy noodles.

Makes 4 servings.

- 1 cup thinly sliced celery
- 1 cup shredded Chinese cabbage
- 2 tablespoons peanut or vegetable oil
- ¼ cup soy sauce
- 2 teaspoons sugar
- ½ teaspoon salt
- 2 envelopes or teaspoons instant chicken broth
- 1 cup water
- 2 tablespoons cornstarch
- ¼ cup water
- 1 can (1 pound) bean sprouts, drained
- 2 cups cooked chicken, cut into thin strips
  Fried Noodles (recipe follows)

1. Sauté celery and cabbage in oil in a large wok or skillet 2 minutes; add soy sauce, sugar, salt, instant broth and water; bring to boiling, stirring constantly.

2. Mix cornstarch with ¼ cup water in a cup. Add bean sprouts and chicken to skillet. Stir in cornstarch mixture; bring to boiling, stirring constantly. Cook 1 minute longer, or until mixture thickens. Serve with FRIED NOODLES and fluffy hot rice.

FRIED NOODLES

Makes 4 cups.
- 1 package (8 ounces) thin spaghetti
  Vegetable oil for frying

1. Cook spaghetti in boiling water 3 minutes; put in a colander and place over simmering water 20 minutes.

2. Fill a large heavy saucepan or electric skillet ½ full with vegetable oil; heat to 370° on a deep-fat thermometer.

3. Drop spaghetti, a handful at a time, into hot fat; fry 3 minutes, or until golden. Continue with remaining spaghetti. Drain on paper towels.

STIR-FRIED CHICKEN BOWL

Add hot red pepper to the garlic, if you want a zippier dish.

Makes 6 servings.

- ¼ cup peanut or vegetable oil
- 3 whole chicken breasts, skinned, boned and cut into ½-inch strips
- 1 clove garlic, crushed
- 1 bunch green onions, trimmed and cut into 1-inch lengths
- 1 can (8 ounces) water chestnuts, drained and sliced
- 1 bunch broccoli, trimmed and cut into ¼-inch thick diagonal slices
- 1 cup chicken broth
- 2 tablespoons cornstarch

¼ cup soy sauce

1. Heat oil and sauté chicken, garlic and green onions for 2 minutes over medium-high heat in a large nonstick skillet or wok. Add water chestnuts and broccoli and stir-fry 5 minutes, or until vegetables are crisply tender.

2. Stir chicken broth into cornstarch in a 2-cup measure; mix well. Add soy sauce. Stir mixture into skillet.

3. Simmer 2 to 3 minutes, or until sauce thickens and bubbles 3 minutes. Garnish with finely chopped ripe tomato, if you wish.

PORK AND SHRIMP LO MEIN

A mild stir-fried noodle dish with a character all its own.

Makes 6 servings.

- 1 package (8 ounces) vermicelli
- ½ pound fresh or frozen small shrimp, shelled and deveined
- 1 teaspoon salt
- 2 teaspoons cornstarch
- ¼ cup peanut or vegetable oil
- 6 Chinese mushrooms, soaked 30 minutes in hot water
  OR: 6 large fresh or canned mushrooms, drained
- ½ pound lean pork, cut into ¼-inch strips
- 4 cups shredded Chinese cabbage
- 2 tablespoons water
- 2 tablespoons dry Sherry
- 1 tablespoon soy sauce
- 2 teaspoons salt
- ¼ teaspoon monosodium glutamate (optional)
- 1½ cups fresh spinach leaves, well-washed
- 2 cups shredded iceberg lettuce

1. Parboil vermicelli 4 minutes; drain; rinse in cold water; drain.

2. Sprinkle the 1 teaspoon salt over shrimp; let stand 10 minutes; rinse in cold water; drain. Place in a bowl; mix with cornstarch to coat evenly.

3. Heat oil in a wok or large skillet; add shrimp and stir-fry 1 minute, or until pink and firm; remove with a slotted spoon and keep hot.

4. Drain Chinese mushrooms, if used; slice very thinly.

5. Add pork to oil in wok; stir-fry ½ minute, just until pork turns gray; stir in mushrooms and cabbage; stir-fry 1 to 2 minutes until cabbage is wilted but still crisp. Add water, Sherry, soy sauce, the 2 teaspoons salt, msg, if used, and vermicelli; stir just until mixed. Stir in spinach; cook, stirring constantly, 1 minute. Stir in lettuce. Arrange on a heated serving platter; sprinkle shrimp on top. Serve immediately with a salad of mandarin orange segments and leaf lettuce with an oil and vinegar dressing.

COOK'S TIP: If you wish, mix equal amounts of cider vinegar and soy sauce to serve with the LO MEIN.

(Continued from page 120.)

GERMAN TWO-TONE RYE

Light and dark rye are twisted together in one loaf, yet you start from the same basic dough. Shown on page 19.

Bake at 350° for 45 minutes.
Makes 2 loaves.

- 4 cups all purpose flour
- 4 cups whole rye flour
- 2 envelopes active dry yeast
- 2½ cups very warm water
- ¼ cup (½ stick) butter or margarine, melted
- ⅓ cup dark molasses
- 1 tablespoon salt
- 2 teaspoons caraway seeds, crushed
- 1 cup whole-bran cereal
- ¼ cup dry cocoa (not a mix)
- 2 teaspoons instant coffee
- 1 teaspoon cornstarch
- ½ cup cold water

1. Combine 3 cups all purpose flour with rye flour in a medium-size bowl until well blended; reserve.
2. Sprinkle yeast with 1 teaspoon sugar into very warm water in a large bowl. ("Very warm water" should feel comfortably warm when dropped on wrist.) Stir until well blended and allow to stand 10 minutes, or until mixture starts to bubble.
3 Stir in butter or margarine, molasses, salt and caraway seeds; pour half of mixture into a second large bowl.
4. To half of yeast mixture, add bran, cocoa and coffee, stirring to mix well. Stir in enough rye-flour mixture to make a soft dough (about 3 cups). Turn dough out onto a lightly floured pastry cloth or board. Knead until smooth and elastic, about 5 minutes, using only as much additional all purpose flour as needed to keep dough from sticking.
5. Place dough in a greased medium-size bowl; turn to cover with shortening; cover with a clean towel. Let rise in a warm place, away from draft, 45 minutes, or until double in bulk.
6. Stir enough rye flour mixture, part at a time, into remaining half of yeast mixture to make a soft dough (about 3 ½ cups). Turn dough out onto a lightly floured pastry cloth or board. Knead until smooth and elastic, about 5 minutes, adding only as much remaining all purpose flour as needed to keep dough from sticking. Let rise, following directions in Step 5. Grease two large cookie sheets; sprinkle with cornmeal.
7. When both doughs have doubled, punch down; knead a few times; divide in half. Roll each of the four pieces on cloth or board with hands to form a thick rope 18 inches long. For each loaf: Twist a light and dark rope together; pinch together at ends. Place loaf on cookie sheet; repeat with remaining 2 ropes.
8. Let rise again in a warm place, away from draft, 45 minutes, or until double in bulk.
9. Bake in moderate oven (350°) 45 minutes, or until loaves give a hollow sound when tapped.
10. While loaves are baking, combine cornstarch with cold water in a small saucepan; stir until smooth. Cook, stirring constantly, until mixture thickens and bubbles 1 minute. Brush over baked loaves; return to oven; bake 3 minutes longer. Remove to wire racks; cool completely.

FRENCH WHOLE WHEAT BREAD

Whole grain wheat gives French bread a nutty flavor. Shown on page 19.

Bake at 400° for 35 minutes.
Makes 2 loaves.

- 2 envelopes active dry yeast
- 3¼ cups very warm water
- 2 tablespoons sugar
- 1 tablespoon salt
- 2½ cups whole wheat flour
- 4½ cups all purpose flour
  Cornmeal
- 1 egg, lightly beaten

1. Sprinkle yeast with 1 teaspoon sugar into very warm water in a large bowl. ("Very warm" water should feel comfortably warm when dropped on wrist.) Stir until well blended and allow to stand 10 minutes, or until mixture begins to bubble.
2. Stir in sugar, salt, whole wheat flour and 2 cups all purpose flour; beat until smooth; gradually beat in 2 more cups all purpose flour to make a soft dough.
3. Turn dough out onto a lightly floured pastry cloth or board. Knead until smooth and elastic, about 5 minutes, using only as much additional flour as needed to keep dough from sticking.
4. Place in a greased large bowl; turn to cover with shortening; cover with a clean towel. Let rise in a warm place, away from draft, 45 minutes, or until double in bulk.
5. Punch dough down; turn out onto cloth or pastry board; knead 1 minute. Divide dough in half; roll out, half at a time, to a 15x10-inch rectangle. Roll up tightly from long side, jelly-roll fashion; pinch long seam tightly to seal. Roll loaf gently back and forth with hands to taper ends.
6. Grease a double French bread form (see page 20), or 2 large cookie sheets; sprinkle with cornmeal. Place loaf in bread form or diagonally on cookie sheet. Repeat shaping with second half of dough.
7. Let rise 30 minutes, or until double in bulk. Brush with slightly beaten egg. Make several evenly spaced diagonal cuts, about ¼-inch deep, in loaves, using very sharp knife.
8. Bake in hot oven (400°) 25 minutes; quickly brush with cold water. Bake 10 minutes longer, or until breads give a hollow sound when tapped. Remove from bread forms or cookie sheets to wire racks; cool completely or serve warm.

ENGLISH CHEESE BREAD

New round bread bakers give an exciting shape to Cheddar cheese bread. Shown on page 18, wrapped in a British paper.

Bake at 350° for 30 minutes.
Makes 2 round loaves.

- 1 envelope active dry yeast
- 1 cup very warm water
- ¼ cup dry milk powder
- 1 tablespoon sugar
- 1 teaspoon salt
- 3 tablespoons vegetable oil
- 3 cups all purpose flour
- 1 cup shredded Cheddar cheese (4 ounces)
  Seasoning for tossed salads (see Cook's Guide)

1. Sprinkle yeast with 1 teaspoon sugar into very warm water in a large bowl. ("Very warm" water should feel comfortably warm when dropped on wrist.) Stir until well blended and allow to stand 10 minutes, or until mixture begins to bubble.
2. Stir in dry milk powder, sugar, salt and oil until well blended; beat in 2 cups flour until smooth; stir in cheese; beat in remaining flour to make a soft dough.
3. Turn dough out onto a lightly floured pastry cloth or board; knead 5 minutes, until smooth and elastic, using only as much flour as needed to keep dough from sticking.
4. Place dough in a greased large bowl; turn to cover with shortening; cover with a clean towel. Let rise, away from draft, 30 minutes, or until double in bulk; punch dough down.
5. Grease two Bake-a-Round® tubes (see page 20), following manufacturer's directions, or one 9x5x3-inch loaf pan; sprinkle generously with seasoning for salads.
6. For round loaves: Divide dough in half; roll each half to a 12x4-inch rectangle; roll up tightly from long side, jelly-roll fashion; pinch seam tightly to seal. Fold a 20-inch piece of wax paper in thirds, lengthwise; place loaf at one end of wax paper; pull other end of paper through tube until dough is centered in tube; roll tube, allowing dough to fall off wax paper; remove paper; seal tube ends with aluminum foil. Repeat with second half of dough.
7. For 9x5x3-inch loaf: Roll out dough to an 18x9-inch rectangle. Roll

up from short side, jelly-roll fashion. Press each end to seal; fold under loaf; place in prepared 9x5x3-inch loaf pan.

8. Let rise 45 minutes, or until double in bulk. Remove foil from tubes and place in rack, if used, following package directions.

9. Bake in moderate oven (350°) 30 minutes for tubes and 45 minutes for loaf pan, or until bread is golden. Remove from tubes or pan and cool completely on wire racks.

ITALIAN SOURDOUGH BREAD

San Fransican bakers combine the tangy taste of sourdough and crunchy texture of Italian bread in this special treat. Photograph is on page 18.

Bake at 400° for 40 minutes.
Makes 2 loaves.

- 1 envelope active dry yeast
- 1 cup very warm water
- 1½ cups Sourdough Starter (recipe follows)
- 2 tablespoons sugar
- 2 teaspoons salt
- 5½ cups all purpose flour
  Cornmeal
- 1 egg white
- 2 tablespoons cold water

1. Sprinkle yeast with 1 teaspoon sugar into very warm water in a large bowl. ("Very warm water" should feel comfortably warm when dropped on wrist.) Stir until well blended and allow to stand 10 minutes, or until mixture begins to bubble. Stir in SOURDOUGH STARTER, sugar and salt.

2. Beat in 2 cups flour until smooth. Beat in enough remaining flour to make a soft dough.

3. Turn dough out onto a lightly floured pastry cloth or board. Knead until smooth and elastic, about 10 minutes, using only as much additional flour as needed to keep dough from sticking.

4. Place dough in a greased large bowl; turn to cover with shortening; cover with a clean towel. Let rise in a warm place, away from draft, 1 hour, or until double in bulk.

5. Punch dough down; turn out onto board; invert bowl over dough; let rest 20 minutes.

6. Grease a double French bread form (see page 20) or two large cookie sheets; sprinkle with cornmeal.

7. Divide dough in half and knead each half a few times. Roll each half into a 15x10-inch rectangle. Roll up tightly from long side, jelly-roll fashion; pinch long seam tightly to seal. Roll loaf gently back and forth with hands to taper ends. Place loaf in bread form or place loaf diagonally on prepared cookie sheet. Repeat shaping with second half of dough.

8. Let rise again in a warm place, away from draft, 45 minutes, or until double in bulk.

9. Make slits 2 inches apart on top of loaves with a very sharp knife or razor blade. Beat egg white and cold water together in a small cup; brush over loaves.

10. Bake in hot oven (400°) 40 minutes, or until loaves are golden and give a hollow sound when tapped. Remove bread loaves to wire racks and cool completely.

SOURDOUGH STARTER

Makes 4 cups.
- 2 cups milk
- 2 cups all purpose flour

Pour milk into a glass or ceramic bowl and cover bowl with cheesecloth. (Do not cover cheesecloth with plastic wrap.) Let stand in the outdoors for 1 day. Stir in flour and re-cover bowl with cheesecloth. Place outside for 2 days. Place bowl in a sunny spot indoors and allow to stand until mixture bubbles and starts to sour, about 2 days. Spoon into a quart jar with a screw cap and store in refrigerator at least 1 day before using. (If top of starter should start to dry out at any time during this process, stir in a little lukewarm water.) This method takes about 7 days to make. Once you have your starter, measure the required amount for each recipe and replace with an equal amount of flour and milk. For example, when you remove 1½ cups of sourdough starter, simply combine ¾ cup milk and ¾ cup flour and stir into jar. Cover jar with cheesecloth and place in sunny spot for 1 day. Remove cheesecloth; cover jar and return to refrigerator. In the past, people had more time to make bread, so they only used sourdough starter to make the dough rise. To quicken the process, we add commercial yeast, but you still get the special flavor.

cook's guide

Page 11: White toaster bread—Pepperidge Farm® Toasting White.
Page 25: Frozen gravy with sliced beef in a cooking bag—Banquet® cookin' bag; frozen mixed vegetables with onion sauce—Birds Eye®.
Page 26: Ham—Hormel® Tender Chunk Ham; luncheon meat—Spam®; chicken-flavored rice and vermicelli mix—Rice a Roni®; precooked rice—Minute® Rice; frozen green beans, broccoli, onions and mushrooms — Seabrook Farms® frozen Italian combination.
Page 27: Italian-style vegetables with seasonings—Birds Eye® International Recipes; Hawaiian-style vegetables with seasonings—Birds Eye® International recipes; instant cream of chicken soup—Lipton® Cup-a-Soup or Nestlé® Souptime®; red cooking wine—Holland House®; frozen peas with cream sauce—Birds Eye®; French fried potato sticks—O&C® potato sticks; whole wheat flakes—Wheaties®.
Page 28: Frozen chicken chow mein in a cooking bag—Banquet® cookin' bag; beef-flavored rice and vermicelli mix—Rice a Roni®.
Page 31: Mixed vegetable juice—V-8 Cocktail Vegetable Juice.
Page 43: Mixed vegetable juice—V-8 Cocktail Vegetable Juice.
Page 71: Frozen Italian vegetables in sauce—Birds Eye® International Recipes.
Page 96: Frozen Chinese-style vegetables—Birds Eye® International Recipes.
Page 104: Macaroni—Creamettes® macaroni.
Page 113: Chicken-flavor rice and vermicelli mix—Rice a Roni; frozen Spanish-style zucchini, carrots and pearl onions in sauce—Birds Eye® International Recipes.
Page 124: Seasoning for tossed salads—McCormick's® Salad Supreme.

buyer's guide

Cover: Soup tureen, cream cup and saucer are Alt Amsterdam by Villeroy & Boch, 225 Fifth Avenue, New York, N.Y. 10010.
Page 1: Left photo—dinner plate, Clerissy, by Villeroy & Boch, 225 Fifth Avenue, New York, N.Y. 10010; right photo—rectangular deep dish porcelain ovenware, Ceylon, from Mayhew, 509 Park Avenue, New York, N.Y. 10021.
Page 2: Oval platter, Sahara, by Villeroy & Boch, 225 Fifth Avenue, New York, N.Y. 10010.
Page 4: Sizzle platter (with hardwood holder, not shown) by Nordic Ware®, Northland Aluminum Products, Inc., Minneapolis, Minn. 55416.
Page 9: Jug, platter and salad set, Sahara, by Villeroy & Boch, 225 Fifth Avenue, New York, N.Y. 10010.
Page 10: 2-qt. oblong baking dish is Pyrex® Ware Clear Ovenware by Corning Glass Works, Corning, N.Y. 14830.
Page 14: Soup tureen, cream cup and saucer, Alt Amsterdam, by Villeroy & Boch, 225 Fifth Avenue, New York, N.Y. 10010.
Page 20: Double French Bread Pan by Stone Hearth, Chichester, N.Y. 12416; Bake-A-Round Duo Baker

with Rack is from the Culinaria Collection, Corning Glass Works, Corning, N.Y. 14830.

Pages 22 & 23: Appliances (from left)—Presto® Cast Aluminum Pressure Cooker with polished aluminum finish, model #PCC6 by National Presto Industries, Inc., Eau Claire, Wis. 54701; Toast 'N Broil Toast-R-Oven® Toaster, model #T23/3123 by General Electric, Housewares Division, Bridgeport, Conn. 06602; Electric Wok by The West Bend® Company, West Bend, Wis. 53095; 4-qt. Crock-Pot®, model #3154 by Rival® Manufacturing Company, Kansas City, Mo. 64129; Stainless Steel Multi-Cooker® Buffet Style Frypan, model #7-30 by Sunbeam Appliance Company, a division of Sunbeam Corporation, 5450 W. Roosevelt Road, Chicago, Ill. 60650; Amana®, Radarange® microwave oven, Amana Refrigeration, Inc., Amana, Iowa 52204. Serving pieces (from left)—rectangular deep dish porcelain ovenware, Ceylon, from Mayhew, 509 Park Avenue, New York, N.Y. 10021; dinner plate, Clerissy, by Villeroy & Boch, 225 Fifth Avenue, New York, N.Y. 10010; oval platter, Sahara, by Villeroy & Boch; 14″ platter, Marseilles, from Mayhew; quiche pan from Mayhew.

Page 37: To order the cookbook, *Ladies Choices' II*, send a check for $5.25 to: Ladies of Charity, Carney Hospital Auxiliary, 2100 Dorchester Avenue, Dorchester, Mass. 02124, Attention: Mary P. Lizio. To order the cookbook, *Company's Coming*, send a check for $3.95 to: WICI Cookbook, 3425 Woodland, Ames, Iowa 50010.

Page 52: 2-qt. covered (cover not shown) casserole, Brown Gourmet Fireproof Porcelain by Villeroy & Boch, 225 Fifth Avenue, New York, N.Y. 10010.

Page 56: 9½″ skillet with lid, Botanica enamelled steel holloware by Villeroy & Boch, 225 Fifth Avenue, New York, N.Y. 10010.

Page 61: Nonstick Dutch oven is by T-Fal® or Dupont® Teflon.

Page 65: Pair of Galician Silver Candlesticks inscribed "To the daughter of the Rabbi on the occasion of her marriage from the community," circa 1830, from Atikoth, Inc., 415 East 53rd Street, New York, N.Y. 10022.

Page 66: Mocha-colored tiles from Country Floors Inc., 300 East 61st Street, New York, N.Y. 10021.

Page 68: Funchal Table from Country Floors Inc., 300 East 61st Street, New York, N.Y. 10021.

Page 77: The Soufflé Plus is by Corning® Creative Glass; mixing bowl is from a 3-piece set by Pyrex® Ware Clear Ovenware, both from Corning Glass Works, Corning, N.Y. 14830. Door panel is from Howard Kaplan Country French Antiques, 35 East 10th Street, New York, N.Y. 10003.

Page 80: 10½″ skillet is Revere Ware® Limited Edition Collection by Revere Copper and Brass Inc., Clinton, Ill. 61727.

Page 89: 1.8-qt. saucepan with lid, Botanica enamelled steel holloware by Villeroy & Boch, 225 Fifth Avenue, New York, N.Y. 10010.

Page 117: Large nonstick skillet is by T-Fal® or Dupont® Teflon.

Page 119: Large nonstick skillet is by T-Fal® or Dupont® Teflon.

acknowledgements

The editors gratefully acknowledge the help of the American Egg Board; the American Lamb Council; Angostura Aromatic Bitters; the Banana Bunch; California Fresh Nectarines; the California Frozen Vegetable Association; Florida Fresh Vegetables; Florida Oranges; Fresh California Bartlett Pears; Frozen Food Facts; the Idaho Potato Commission; the International Natural Sausage Casing Association; Lea & Perrins® Worcestershire Sauce; the National Peanut Council; the North Atlantic Seafood Association; the Shrimp Association of the Americas; South African Rock Lobster; Sunkist® California—Arizona Citrus Fruits; Tabasco®; T-Fal® Cooking Pans; the Tuna Association; Western Iceberg Lettuce; the Wheat Flour Institute.

credits

Photography credits—René Velez: page 20. **Casserole Chart illustration** (page 26 & 27): Blake Hampton.

index

INDEX